Beyond Reforms

Beyond Reforms
Structural Dynamics and Macroeconomic Vulnerability

Editor

José Antonio Ocampo

A COPUBLICATION OF STANFORD ECONOMICS AND FINANCE,
AN IMPRINT OF STANFORD UNIVERSITY PRESS, AND THE WORLD BANK

Library of Congress Cataloging-in-Publication Data has been applied for.

ISBN 0-8213-5819-7   (World Rights except North America)
ISBN 0-8047-5272-9 (Hardcover)   (North America)
ISBN 0-8047-5273-7 (Softcover)   (North America)
e-ISBN 0-8213-5820-0
DOI: 10.1596/978-0-8213-5819-7

Latin American Development Forum Series

This series was created in 2003 to promote, debate, and disseminate information and analysis, and convey the excitement and complexity of the most topical issues in economic and social development in Latin America and the Caribbean. It is sponsored by the Inter-American Development Bank, the United Nations Economic Commission for Latin America and the Caribbean, and the World Bank. The manuscripts chosen for publication represent the highest quality in each institution's research and activity output, and have been selected for their relevance to the academic community, policy makers, researchers, and interested readers.

Advisory Committee Members

Contents

centenary of the birth of Raúl Prebisch, the intellectual father of the institution.

The book is organized in two parts. The first part looks at issues of long-term growth and development patterns, and the second part focuses on issues of macroeconomic vulnerability and its social effects. The eight chapters offer theoretical and methodological contributions from different schools of economic thought but share a common focus: how to improve upon the frustratingly poor economic performance observed in Latin America, as well as in some other parts of the developing world, during the recent phase of economic liberalization. The title of the book, *Beyond Reforms*, captures the major theme of the essays: the importance of going beyond the debate regarding the need for a "first" and a "second" generation of reforms in order to understand other forces that have been generally overlooked in the debate on market reforms. Taking such forces into account is thus crucial in order to overcome the disappointing economic performance that has characterized many countries in the context of economic liberalization.

The theme of the first chapter is the determinants of "dynamic efficiency" in developing countries, which is seen as the result of two basic processes. The first process is the ability of a given system to innovate, which, in the broad Schumpeterian sense, is defined as the capacity to generate new economic activities or new ways of doing previous activities; under this definition, the major form of "innovation" in developing countries is the transfer of production sectors previously developed in the industrial world. The second process is the capacity of the innovation to generate complementarities, linkages, or networks resulting in an integrated production fabric. These two forces are closely interlinked with a third, which is the capacity to reduce the dualism or structural heterogeneity that characterizes production structures in developing countries—that is, the coexistence of high-productivity and low-productivity economic activities. A simple macroeconomic model shows how these forces interact with the macroeconomic balance, generating a dual link between gross domestic product (GDP) growth and productivity growth. The main policy implication of the chapter is the need to concentrate on a strategy for the transformation of production structures that involves three major sets of policy interventions: inducing innovation (in the broad sense of the term), promoting linkages, and reducing structural heterogeneity. The absence of such a strategy, together with the weak domestic linkages that characterize the new production activities generated during the liberalization process, can be seen, in this light, as essential explanations for weak growth in Latin America during the reform period.

The second chapter, by Mario Cimoli and Nelson Correa, looks at the same issue from a slightly different angle: the combined effect of the technological gap relative to developed countries and the propensity to import, which jointly determine the trade multiplier in an open economy—that is, the capacity of a given rate of export expansion to generate a pattern of overall economic (GDP) growth. This relationship is the result of long-run balance of payments equilibrium conditions. Using this framework, the authors claim that Latin America has slowly narrowed the productivity gap, but that this has been insufficient to offset the extraordinary increase in the elasticity of demand for imports generated by trade liberalization. The result has been a decline of the trade multiplier between the pre- and postreform periods, thus generating a "low-growth trap." Cimoli and Correa argue that the major reason for this has been the existence of a dual economic structure in which productivity improves in very small enclaves that have few linkages with the rest of the system, thereby leading to an increasing dualism between high- and low-productivity sectors within countries. The major policy implication is the need to narrow the productivity gap, which, given the links between the pattern of specialization and the process of endogenous knowledge generation and diffusion, is necessarily tied to changes in the pattern of specialization.

Chapter 3, by Gabriel Palma, takes as its starting point the inverted-U pattern followed by the share of manufacturing in total employment as a result of the process of structural change generated by increases in per capita income. The author finds that, worldwide, this relationship has become more adverse in recent decades, thereby generating a widespread process of "de-industrialization"; he also contends that it is more adverse, at any given level of per capita income, for countries that generate a trade surplus in primary commodities or services than it is for those with a trade surplus in manufacturing. However, Palma argues that a country's position within these patterns is not independent of economic policy. Thus, several Scandinavian and Southeast Asian countries rich in natural resources have been able to swim against the de-industrialization tide, indicating that there is no inevitable "curse of natural resources." During the import-substitution era, Latin America was also able to generate levels of industrialization typical of countries with a trade surplus in manufacturing. Trade liberalization has induced diverging patterns in the region. At one extreme, Brazil and the Southern Cone countries underwent a change of reference group as they shifted toward a pattern typical of primary exporters and, in the process, generated a strong de-industrialization. The additional de-industrialization generated by changes in the reference group is, according to the author, the best definition of *Dutch disease*— although, in these Latin American countries, this effect was generated by liberalization policies rather than by a discovery of new natural resources. In the opposite pattern, manufacturing exporters in Central America and, to a lesser extent, Mexico have been able to maintain higher levels of industrialization but, relative to the Asian countries, have been characterized by very low export-income multipliers.

The theme of the fourth chapter, by Rob Vos, is the social effects of structural reforms. The author tries to explain why, contrary to the initial assumptions of reformers, labor inequality has tended to increase in Latin America during the 1990s, thus weakening the links between economic growth and poverty reduction. In this regard, the author explores the effects of trade liberalization, as well as the real exchange rate and the demand effects of capital account liberalization. The major conclusion is that, although there is evidence of skill biases in several countries, rising labor inequality was associated much more closely with the exchange rate appreciation generated by capital inflows. The latter led to the incapacity of tradable sectors to absorb labor, as many firms in these sectors were forced to downsize in order to cope with international competition. Labor was then absorbed into low-productivity agriculture and informal urban services. Rising productivity and income dualism between high-productivity and low-productivity sectors are thus seen as more important determinants of rising income inequality than are the skill bias of technical change and liberalization. This conclusion ties in nicely with the analyses presented in the first two chapters of the book, which give a central role to such dualism. It also means that structural reforms have interacted poorly with short-term macroeconomic adjustment mechanisms associated with capital account liberalization, leading, in Vos' words, to "export-led growth on a slippery path."

The emphasis on macroeconomic effects in chapter 4 serves as a bridge to the second part of the book, in which issues of macroeconomic vulnerability are analyzed. Chapter 5, by Lance Taylor, looks at the determinants of business cycles. Business cycles may be thought of as the result of two opposite forces: one that tends to generate a potential instability, and a stabilizing force that counteracts it, with the net effect being a stable or unstable cycle, depending on which force prevails. In the first of the three models presented in the chapter, this potential instability is generated by real exchange rate dynamics that, in the short term, generate contractionary demand effects, whereas the lagged response of exports to real exchange rate competitiveness provides the stabilizing force. In the second model, of a developing-country debt cycle, the destabilizing factor is the dynamics of the country risk premium, which feeds back into itself, thereby generating waves of optimism and pessimism. The ways the economy adjusts to changes in the availability of finance through variations in the trade balance provide the stabilizing force. In the third model, the potential destabilizing forces are self-reinforcing waves of investor optimism or pessimism, coupled with the tendency of corporate debt to follow investors' "animal spirits," whereas the financial prudence of corporations provides the stabilizing force. As Taylor argues, the first two cycles have been clearly present in the dynamics of developing countries, whereas the third cycle, which is more typical of the developed world, has also become relevant to some developing countries.

An interesting case of destabilization is explored by Manuel Marfán in chapter 6: that of "successful" developing countries in which the private sector experiences a wave of exuberant behavior. The author develops a very conventional model in which prices are determined by cost-push (exchange rate) and demand pressures, and sustainable growth is determined by both domestic capacity and sustainable balance of payments conditions. In this context, faced with exuberant private sector behavior, the central bank can always meet its inflation target, but only through a real exchange rate appreciation and an unsustainable increase in the current account deficit. This means, in turn, that the inflation rate is not a suitable indicator of economic overheating in an open economy. Whereas monetary policy is ineffective in achieving the real targets—in this case, a sustainable current account—fiscal policy can fill the gap by generating a fiscal surplus to compensate for overheating that originates in the private sector. However, Marfán argues correctly that it is not the public sector's institutional role to compensate for excess private spending, a fact that imposes a policy dilemma with no conventional solution. The author then suggests two unconventional solutions: a flexible countercyclical sales tax, and a tax on financial flows, which has the nice political-economy advantage of taxing the true source of the problem.

The seventh chapter, by Roberto Frenkel, analyzes debt sustainability issues. The author considers, in particular, under what conditions adverse financial shocks affecting a country's risk premium lead to destabilizing debt dynamics. Such adverse shocks lead directly to an increase in the debt service and the demand for external funding, but also to higher domestic interest rates that adversely affect domestic economic activity. Both are reflected, in the short run, in a rising debt-GDP ratio, which will be mitigated by the improvement in the trade balance generated by the contraction of economic activity. A sustainable debt trajectory is then defined as one in which the debt-GDP ratio peaks some time after the initial shock and then falls. The major conclusion is that vulnerability to external shocks basically depends on the initial debt-export ratio: the lower this ratio is, the larger the rise in the risk premium that a country will be able to withstand without its debt-GDP ratio entering into an explosive trajectory. If sustainability is guaranteed, then faster export growth will accelerate the transition to lower debt ratios. More restrictive conditions are found when political conditions require that debt servicing be consistent with a positive growth rate or when political constraints set a limit on the maximum proportion of GDP that may be transferred abroad. When the risk premium is endogenously determined, the possibility of multiple equilibria arises, which paves the way for self-fulfilling prophesies.

The last chapter, by Jaime Ros, deals with divergence and growth collapses, and serves to tie together the issues analyzed in both parts of the book. The author argues, first of all, that classical development theory provides the only consistent framework for understanding the major patterns of economic growth observed in the world since the 1950s—that is, the coincidence of poverty traps at low income levels and accelerations of growth at middle income levels, a result, in the latter case, of increasing returns to capital in the context of the reallocation of labor from low-productivity to high-productivity activities. Whereas the first case induces divergence in per capita income, the second case tends to generate convergence. At the same time, however, the classical approach does not explain another stylized fact: the tendency of accelerations of growth to be accompanied by growth slowdowns or even negative growth at intermediate levels of per capita income. Basing his findings on empirical evidence, Ros contends that vulnerability to growth collapses is associated with income inequality and with the pattern of specialization, as determined by the abundance of natural resources and economic size. In relation to the latter, a mineral/oil specialization seems to generate a higher probability of collapse relative to an agricultural specialization because of a mix of low linkages, high capital intensity, and concentration of ownership, whereas small economies are much more vulnerable because of their high levels of specialization.

Viewed as a whole, this collection presents a more precise view of the difficult risks and challenges that characterize the new economic era, and advances a set of alternative economic policies to manage the open developing-country economies of the early 21st century. Ideas that have been absent from the reform agenda over the past two decades, particularly interventions that affect the pattern of specialization and capital account regulations that mediate between capital flows and domestic macroeconomic performance, are seen as being critical in bringing about the improved economic and social performance that liberalization has so far failed to produce.

We think that this collection sheds new light on issues that were largely overlooked during the reform period and that must be faced squarely in order to overcome the shortcomings that have affected Latin America and many other parts of the developing world during their recent phase of liberalization.

José Antonio Ocampo
Under-Secretary-General of the United Nations for Economic and Social Affairs, former Executive Secretary of ECLAC

I

Growth and the Dynamics of Productive Structure

1

The Quest for Dynamic Efficiency: Structural Dynamics and Economic Growth in Developing Countries

José Antonio Ocampo

DEBATES ON ECONOMIC GROWTH SINCE THE mid-1980s have left a legacy of analytical innovations and rich empirical contributions. The explicit recognition of the role of scale economies in economic growth (as well as in international and regional analysis), the related revival of ideas expounded by classical development economics, and the contribution of neo-Schumpeterian and evolutionary theories, as well as of institutional economics, are among the most important analytical innovations.[1] On the empirical side, extensive analyses have been made of the relative weight of institutional, policy, and geographical factors in explaining the divergence in income levels and growth experiences in the world economy.[2]

The richness and diversity of analytical paradigms contrast with trends in policy design, where the triumph of liberal economics is the dominant rule. After an era marked by strong State intervention and

The author is United Nations Under-Secretary-General for Economic and Social Affairs. This chapter draws from previous works by the author, particularly from Ocampo and Taylor (1998) and from (Ocampo 2002). I am grateful to Oscar Altimir, Alice Amsden, Alicia Bárcena, Ricardo Bielschowsky, Mario Cimoli, Jõao Carlos Ferraz, Valpy Fitzgerald, Jorge Katz, Juan Carlos Moreno-Brid, María Angela Parra, Codrina Rada, Dani Rodrik, Jaime Ros, Lance Taylor, Daniel Titelman, Andras Uthoff, and Rob Vos for very useful comments on previous drafts of this chapter.

protectionism, it was expected that less interventionist, open economies would provide the basis for rapid growth in the developing world. These expectations have been largely frustrated so far. Latin America represents, in this regard, an outstanding example of a region where the record of economic liberalization has not only been disappointing, but indeed has been considerably poorer than that of State-led (or import-substitution) industrialization.[3]

Recent controversies shed light on the frustrations that trends in policy making have generated. Nonetheless, this involves going beyond the aggregate dynamics that has been the focus of the recent literature and delving into the analysis of the dynamics of heterogeneous production structures. In this regard, recent contributions should be complemented by old ideas that have received little attention in contemporary debates, including the growth-productivity connections associated, in particular, with the Kaldorian tradition (Kaldor 1978) and the linkages among firms and sectors emphasized by Hirschman (1958).

This chapter argues that economic growth in developing countries is intrinsically tied to the dynamics of production structures and to the specific policies and institutions created to support it. These policies and institutions include, in particular, those that facilitate the diffusion of innovations generated in the industrialized world (including new technologies and the development of new production sectors), encourage the creation of linkages among domestic firms and sectors, and seek to reduce the dualism or structural heterogeneity that characterizes production-sector structures in developing countries—that is, the coexistence of a high-productivity (modern) and a low-productivity (informal) sector. Avoiding macroeconomic instability is also essential, if instability is understood in a broad sense that includes not only high inflation and unsustainable fiscal imbalances, but also sharp business cycles, volatile relative prices, unsustainable current account disequilibria, and risky private sector balance sheets. However, macroeconomic stability is not a sufficient condition for growth. The broader institutional context and the adequate provision of education and infrastructure are essential "framework conditions," but generally do not play a direct role in bringing about changes in the momentum of economic growth.

The chapter makes extensive use of concepts elaborated by the old and the new development and growth literature. The elements on which the analysis is built are well known. The particular emphasis and the way the elements are put together have a number of novel aspects. The chapter is divided into four sections. The first section takes a look at some methodological issues and growth regularities. The second section focuses on the dynamics of production structures. The third provides a very simple model of the linkages between productive and macroeconomic dynamics. The last section draws policy implications.

Some Methodological Issues and "Stylized Facts"

Time series and cross-section analyses have identified some regularities that characterize growth processes. The role of institutions, productivity growth, physical and human capital accumulation, economic policies, and geography, as well as the changes in gross domestic product (GDP) and employment structures that go along with economic growth, are among the variables that have been extensively researched.

The analysis of the causal linkages among these variables raises two methodological issues. The first relates to the need to differentiate between factors that play a direct role in generating *changes in the momentum of economic growth* versus those that are essential for growth to take place but that do not play a direct role in determining such variations. This differentiation has been subject to different terminological approaches. Maddison (1991, ch. 1) referred to them as a difference between "proximate" and "ultimate" causality, whereas Rodrik (2003) differentiated between factors that "ignite" and those that "sustain" growth.

Institutions are the best case in point. Everybody would probably agree today that a certain measure of stability in the basic social contract that guarantees smooth business-labor-government relationships (including the particular ideologies that serve this purpose), a nondiscretionary legal system and patterns of business behavior that guarantee the security of contracts, and an impartial (and, ideally, efficient) State bureaucracy are crucial to facilitate modern, capitalist growth. Nonetheless, although in some cases they may become proximate causes of growth (or of the lack of it), as in the successful reconstruction (or breakdown) of sociopolitical regimes, they generally play the role of "framework conditions" for economic growth rather than that of direct causes of changes in the momentum of economic growth. Indeed, an important empirical observation is that some country characteristics, particularly institutional development, are fairly constant over decades, whereas growth is not.[4] This emphasizes the importance of proximate causality or factors that ignite growth. We will thus focus on these factors in this chapter.

A second methodological issue relates to the fact that a regular feature of economic growth is the simultaneous movement of a series of economic variables: improved technology, human capital accumulation, investment, savings, and systematic changes in production structures.[5] Yet these variables are, to a large extent, *results* of economic growth.

Thus, protection has been a source of growth in some periods in specific countries, but has blocked it in others. The same thing can be said
of freer trade. Mixed strategies have worked well under many circumstances. The degree of openness in the world economy has, obviously,
been a decisive factor in this regard.[16] The fact, mentioned earlier, that
successful experiences of manufacturing export growth in the developing world were generally preceded by periods of import-substitution
industrialization indicates that simplistic generalizations are not very
useful. Bairoch (1993, part I) came to a similar conclusion regarding
protection and economic growth in "late industrializers" among what
are now developed countries during the pre-WWI period. He also
reached the paradoxical conclusion that the fastest periods of growth in
world trade prior to WWI were not those characterized by the most liberal trade regimes.

The Dynamics of Production Structures

The central theme of this chapter is that the dynamics of production
structures are the root cause of changes in the momentum of economic
growth. These dynamics interact with macroeconomic balances, generating a positive feedback that results in "virtuous" circles of rapid economic
growth, or, alternatively, growth traps. Some measure of macroeconomic
stability, broadly defined, is a necessary condition and, obviously, enters
into the corresponding macroeconomic balances. A facilitating institutional environment, and an adequate supply of human capital and infrastructure, are framework conditions, but are not active determinants of
the growth momentum.

The ability to constantly generate new dynamic activities is, in this
view, the essence of successful development. In this sense, growth is
essentially a *meso*economic process, determined by the dynamics of production structures, a concept that summarizes the evolution of the sectoral
composition of production, intra- and intersectoral linkages, market
structures, the functioning of factor markets, and the institutions that
support all of them. Dynamic microeconomic changes are the building
blocks, but the *systemwide* processes matter most. Moreover, the characteristics of the structural transformation largely determine macroeconomic dynamics, particularly through its effects on investment and trade
balances.

The dynamics of production structures may be visualized as the interaction between two basic, though multidimensional, forces, namely
(1) *innovations,* broadly understood as new activities and new ways of
doing previous activities, and the *learning processes* that characterize
both the full realization of their potentialities and their diffusion

through the economic system; and (2) the *complementarities, linkages, or networks* among firms and production activities, and the *institutions* required for the full development of such complementarities, whose maturation is also subject to learning. *Elastic factor supplies* are, on the other hand, essential to guarantee that these dynamic processes can deploy their full potentialities. The combination of these three factors determines what we can characterize as the *dynamic efficiency* of a given production system.

These different mechanisms perform complementary functions: Innovations are the basic engine of change; their diffusion and the creation of production linkages are the mechanisms that determine their capacity to transform and generate integrated production systems; the learning that accompanies these processes and the development of complementarities generate dynamic economies of scale and specialization, which are essential to rising productivity; and elastic factor supplies are necessary in order for innovative activities to operate as the driving force of economic growth.

Innovations and Associated Learning and Diffusion Processes

The best definition of innovations, in the broad sense in which this concept is used here, was provided by Schumpeter (1961, ch. II) almost a century ago ("new combinations," in his terminology): (1) the introduction of new goods and services or of new qualities of goods and services; (2) the development of new production methods or new marketing strategies; (3) the opening up of new markets; (4) the discovery of new sources of raw materials or the exploitation of previously known resources; and (5) the establishment of new industrial structures in a given sector. Thus, this broad concept includes both the more common use of the concept of innovations in the economic literature (technological innovations), and what Hausmann and Rodrik (2003) have recently called "discovery" (of what one is good at producing), as well as other forms that are usually disregarded today. Innovations, in this broad sense, may arise in established firms and sectors (in a constantly changing world, firms that do not innovate will tend to disappear), but they involve many times the creation of new companies and the development of new sectors of production.

Innovation includes the "creation" of firms, production activities, and sectors, but also the "destruction" of others. The particular mix between creation and destruction—or, alternatively, between the substitution and complementary effects of innovations[17]—is critical. The term *creative destruction,* coined by Schumpeter (1962), indicates that there tends to be net creation. This is, of course, essential in order for innovations to lead weight of innovative activities (and, obviously, on their capital intensity). High investment is thus associated with a high rate of innovation and structural change.

On the other hand, innovations involve learning. Technical know-how must go through a learning and maturing process that is closely linked to the production experience. More generally, to reduce the technology gaps that characterize the international economic hierarchy—to *leapfrog* in the precise sense of the term[19]—an encompassing research and development strategy, and an accompanying educational strategy, are necessary. Essential insights into learning dynamics have been provided by the "evolutionary" theories of technical change.[20] These theories emphasize the fact that technology is to a large extent tacit in nature—that is, that detailed "blueprints" cannot be plotted out. This has three major implications.

The first is that technology is incompletely available and imperfectly tradable. This is associated with the fact that technology is, to a large extent, composed of intangible human and organizational capital. This implies that, in order to benefit from technical knowledge, even firms that purchase or imitate it must invest in mastering the acquired or imitated technology. Because this is the general case in developing countries, it implies that, although technology is largely transferred from industrial countries, there is still an active absorption process that must take place. This process involves adaptation and may call for redesigns and other secondary innovations, which will further build up human and organizational capital. The efficiency with which this absorption process takes place will determine, in turn, the productivity of the relevant firms. This explains why firms with similar access to "knowledge" will generally have quite different productivities. Different organizational and marketing strategies will generate further firm-specific features, which are the essential factors behind the selection process that takes place in any sector through time. Existing firms or new entrants could challenge any equilibrium in the resulting industrial structure. According to our definition, major breakups in existing industrial structures are themselves innovations. The entry of developing countries into mature activities also belongs to this category.

The second implication of "tacitness" is that technology proficiency cannot be detached from production experience, that is, it has a strong "learning by doing" component.[21] Daily production and engineering activities have, in this sense, a "research and development" component. This link is the specific microeconomic basis of dynamic economies of scale.

A third feature of technical change, unrelated to tacitness, indicates that competition will produce pressures that guarantee the generation and diffusion of innovations. As a result of the latter, innovative firms only imperfectly appropriate the benefits from investments in innovations. Intellectual property rights provide a mechanism for appropriating those benefits more fully in the case of technical innovations or new products and designs, but such a mechanism is not present in other forms of innovations (such as the development of new activities or a new marketing strategy). Innovations have thus mixed private/public-good attributes. The rate of innovation depends, then, on the particular balance between costs, risks, benefits, and their appropriability (including their legal protection, in cases where this is possible).

It must be emphasized that these three attributes of technical change—imperfect tradability, close association with production experience, and private/public attributes—are equally characteristic of other forms of knowledge, particularly organizational and commercial know-how (and, as we will see below, institutional development). Because of its "social capital" attributes, imperfect tradability and imperfect appropriability are paramount in the case of organizational knowledge. Commercial know-how plays a crucial role that tends to be overlooked in most analyses, and it certainly plays a pivotal role in international trade (Keesing and Lall 1992). Indeed, one of the most important determinants of the expansion of firms relates to their ability to develop appropriate channels of information and marketing and to build a commercial reputation (goodwill) and a known trademark. Moreover, familiarity with the market enables producers to modify their products and their marketing channels and helps buyers to learn about suppliers, generating clientele relationships that are important to guarantee the stable growth of firms. The crucial role that these factors play is reflected in the fact that marketing departments in larger firms are usually staffed by high-quality personnel. The corresponding capital is organizational in nature and cannot be detached from commercial experience. The dynamic economies of scale are reflected here in reductions in transaction costs, which are associated with the firms' accumulated reputation and trademark recognition. On the other hand, although the reputation of a particular firm can hardly be copied, its discovery of market opportunities will certainly be imitated. The public-good attributes are thus important and play a vital role in determining the patterns of specialization. As regional economics has recognized for a long time, the agglomeration of producers of certain goods and services in particular locations is largely determined by this factor.

Complementarities and the Associated Institutional Development

Complementarities are associated with the development of networks of suppliers of goods and specialized services, marketing channels, and organizations and institutions that disseminate information and provide coordination among agents. This concept summarizes not only the role that backward and forward linkages play in economic growth (Hirschman 1958), but also the role of (private, public, or mixed) institutions that are created to reduce information costs (for example, on technology and markets) and to solve the coordination failures that characterize interdependent investment decisions (Chang 1994). Together they determine how integrated a production system is.

The development of complementarities has demand as well as supply effects. The demand effects are part of the Keynesian multiplier mechanism; their absence implies, in turn, that Keynesian leakages may be large, as reflected, for example, in high propensities to import from abroad (for example, in assembly activities). Thus, the strength or weakness of the complementarities is a structural determinant of macroeconomic multipliers. This, together with the association between the rate of investment and innovations, which has already been explored in the previous section, are two of the essential linkages between economic structures and macroeconomic performance.

The supply effects of complementarities are associated with the positive externalities that different economic agents generate among themselves through cost reductions made possible by economies of scale in production or lower transport and transaction costs (economies of agglomeration), through the induced provision of more specialized inputs or services (economies of specialization), or through the externalities generated by the sharing of knowledge and the development of human capital that can move among firms (technological or, more broadly, knowledge spillovers). These "strategic complementarities" are the basis of the dynamic economies of scale of a mesoeconomic character that determine the competitiveness—or lack of competitiveness—of production sectors in a given region or country. Under these conditions, competitiveness involves more than microeconomic efficiency: It is essentially a sectoral or even a systemwide feature (ECLAC 1990; Fajnzylber 1990).

In an open economy, demand linkages may be induced by protection. This may facilitate positive supply (agglomeration) effects, but may also generate costs for other production sectors if it involves the protection of intermediate and capital goods. On the other hand, because they cannot be imported, the efficient provision of *nontradable* inputs and specialized services always plays an essential role in guaranteeing systemwide competitiveness.[22] Three nontradable activities are particularly relevant in this regard. The first category is made up of sectors that produce specialized inputs and services, including knowledge, logistic, and marketing services, for which closeness to producers who use the inputs or services is a critical factor. The second is the development of specialized financial services, particularly those that are important in facilitating the innovation process—the supply of long-term and venture capital. Indeed, because of the asymmetric information that characterizes financial markets, financial services (particularly for small and medium-sized firms) are largely nontradable. The third is the provision of adequate infrastructure.

Institution-building shares the first two features of technological development—imperfect tradability and close association with experience— and, by its very nature, has dominant public-good attributes. As already indicated, the two crucial services that institutions provide are the reduction of information costs and the solution of the coordination failures that characterize interdependent investment decisions. Many of the relevant institutions may be created directly by the private sector: producer organizations that share information that has public-good attributes, develop joint labor training facilities, and create strategic alliances to penetrate new markets or promotional agencies to encourage complementary investments. However, given their strong public-good attribute, their services tend to be provided in suboptimal quantities. The competitive pressure among firms is quite commonly a major obstacle to the creation and consolidation of such institutions, or a source of competing organizations of suboptimal size.

Elastic Factor Supplies

The capacity of innovations and complementarities to generate strong growth effects depends critically on how elastic the supply of factors of production for innovative sectors is. The crucial role played by the ability of innovative activities to attract capital and labor, and to gain access to the natural resources they need to expand, was mentioned in the first section of this chapter as a relevant stylized fact. The crucial role played by venture capital and the availability of long-term finance for innovative activities, and the fact that these services have a large nontradable component, have also been noted.

Schumpeter (1961) emphasized the elastic supply of capital as essential to facilitate the effects of innovations on economic growth. More broadly, elastic factor supplies play a crucial role in Keynesian and Kaleckian models in which investment—and, thus, aggregate demand— drives not only short-term economic activity, but also long-term growth (Kaldor 1978; Robinson 1962; Taylor 1991). As these models make clear, elastic factor supplies can be guaranteed in several ways: (1) by the existence of unemployed or, more typically, underemployed resources (an issue that was also emphasized in the first section); (2) by the endogenous financing of capital accumulation through a redistribution of income toward profits; (3) by interregional and international factor mobility; (4) by social reorganization that allows greater participation in opportunities and, through this mechanism, drives aggregate demand. The availability of finance plays a crucial role in facilitating this process. Third, if domestic savings or external financing are not fully endogenous, savings or balance of payments gaps will become effective constraints on aggregate demand and will thus determine the shape of the curve.[31] Finally, technical change enhances international competitiveness, affecting the trade balance and, thus, aggregate demand; if the economy is foreign-exchange-constrained, the reduction in the trade balance relaxes this constraint and thus also has aggregate supply effects.

It must be emphasized that TT is not an aggregate production function in the traditional neoclassical sense. Rather, its positive slope implies that there is some underutilization of resources at any point in time, and thus growth induces a better allocation of resources (and the lack of growth, a misallocation, particularly through the underemployment of labor). Thus, through the virtuous-circle effects that it generates, growth has aggregate *supply* effects: the induced productivity improvements that are expressed in the TT curve. The aggregate demand effects typical of Keynesian growth models are captured, on the other hand, in the GG function. Similarly, it should be underlined that complementarities have supply (economies of agglomeration and specialization and knowledge spillovers) as well as demand (variations in the Keynesian multiplier generated by changes in the propensity to import) effects. Whereas the former are captured in the TT function, the latter affect the GG curve. If the economy is foreign-exchange-constrained, the corresponding changes in import dependence will also have aggregate supply effects that, in this case, will affect the GG function.

Because both curves have positive slopes, the effects that they capture reinforce each other, generating alternating positive feedbacks but also possible negative feedbacks. A stable equilibrium exists when TT is flatter than GG, as shown in figure 1.1a. In Keynesian and foreign-exchange gap models—the two macroeconomic closures we will consider here—the slope of GG will depend on the elasticity of investment, exports, and imports to productivity; if they are relatively inelastic, the corresponding schedule will be steep; if elasticities are high, it will be flatter. Given the determinants of the technical progress function, TT will be flatter if the following conditions prevail: (1) both micro- and mesoeconomic dynamic economies of scale are not too strong; (2) labor underemployment is moderate; and (3) fixed factors are not very important in the long run.

However, under significant initial (unskilled and/or skilled) labor underemployment or significant underutilization of infrastructure (that is, when these factors operate as fixed factors), the slope of TT may be high. Figure 1.1b thus presents a case in which the slope of TT is initially steep

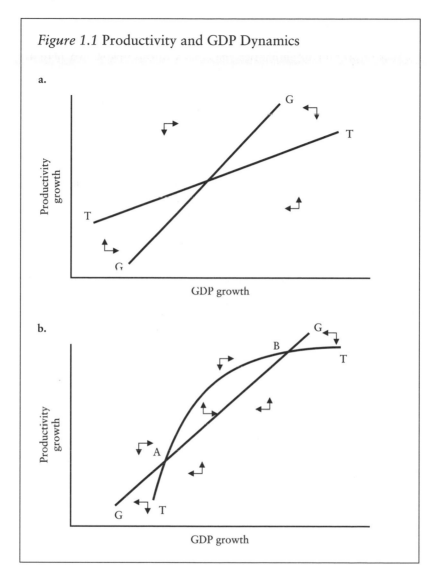

Figure 1.1 Productivity and GDP Dynamics

but falls at higher rates of economic growth. In this case, there will be a stable equilibrium at B, similar to that shown in figure 1.1a, and an unstable equilibrium at A. Any displacement from saddle point A will lead the economy to a new, higher stable equilibrium at B or, alternatively, to a low-growth trap. Obviously, depending on the position of the curves, other possibilities may exist that can generate explosive virtuous or vicious circles. Also, nothing guarantees that equilibrium will always arise at a positive rate of growth.

It is important to emphasize that the relationships shown here are taken to be medium- or long-term in character.[32] However, because many of the processes we are analyzing are time-bound, the steady-state properties of the model are actually uninteresting. Indeed, innovations may be seen as "spurts" that shift the technical progress function, but tend to weaken through time as innovations spread. Thus, a new wave of innovation shifts the TT function upward and turns it steeper, to T'T' in figure 1.2, accelerating both productivity and income growth. However, as this particular wave of innovations come to be fully exploited and their structural effects fully transmitted, the function will shift down and become flatter, to TT in figure 1.2. Productivity and GDP growth will then slow down.[33] If the GG function also shifts leftward (because of weakened "animal spirits"), the slowdown will become even sharper.

A favorable macroeconomic shock—improved access to external financing in a foreign-exchange-constrained economy and improved long-term expectations or long-term investment financing that have a positive effect on investment in a Keynesian model—will shift the GG function rightward to G'G'. The micro/meso/macroeconomic links summarized in the technical progress function now amplify the favorable

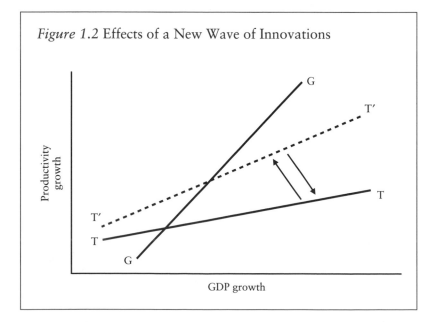

Figure 1.2 Effects of a New Wave of Innovations

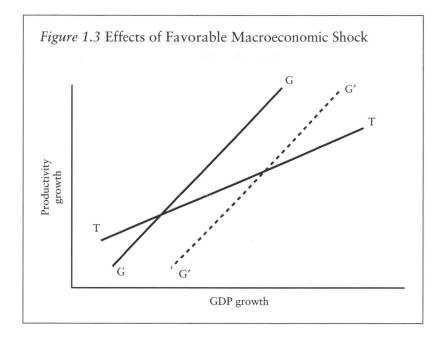

Figure 1.3 Effects of Favorable Macroeconomic Shock

macro effects. A negative macroeconomic shock will have the opposite effect. This could include any factor that increases macroeconomic instability. In line with the considerations discussed in the first section of this chapter, *any* form of instability matters, including instability in the price level or in major relative prices, an increase in the intensity of the business cycle, or any factor that adversely affects public or private sector debt sustainability, among others. A particularly severe case would be present if a leftward shift in GG in figure 1.3 were to leave no equilibrium point, leading to a downward spiral of GDP and productivity growth.

This simple framework may be used to analyze the effects of trade reforms—and, more broadly, of economic liberalization processes—on growth. For that purpose, we have to assume a specific relationship between competition and the rate of innovation. In this regard, a tradition of economic thought, which can be traced to Schumpeter, has emphasized the ability of large firms to internalize the benefits from innovation, a fact that may generate positive links between market concentration and innovations. Contrary to that tradition, the neoclassical defense of liberalization views the lack of competitive pressure as a factor that has adverse effects on productivity. This view highlights the fact that managers of large firms may be inclined to appropriate part of the monopoly power they hold in the form of "leisure" (reduced efforts to minimize costs). Increased competition has, in this case, positive effects on productivity. It should be emphasized, however, that this assumption implies that firms were *not* initially profit-maximizers (Rodrik 1992).

Another link between reforms and productivity that was mentioned earlier has to do with the fact that the uncertainties that characterize structural shocks may lead firms to adopt defensive attitudes. Thus, the initial response to a shock may be rationalization rather than a new wave of innovation and investment. The latter may only come with a lag, when uncertainties are reduced. If this is so, the TT curve may not be affected, or indeed may be adversely affected, and the effects of increased competition on productivity will be only transitional.

If the neoclassical assumption about the links between competition and innovation is correct, then opening the economy to competition displaces the TT function upward. Liberalization unleashes, in this case, a degree of innovativeness that the more protected and State-interventionist environments of the past repressed. Domestic firms will also have better access to imported inputs and capital goods. However, this is not all that matters. The destruction of domestic linkages and previous technological capabilities would have the opposite effect. Specialization in activities with weaker dynamic economies of scale would tend to make the TT function flatter. If firms shrink, their capacity to cover the fixed costs associated with innovative activities will also decline. One way to express these opposite effects is to say that, although the microeconomic effects of competition on productivity growth may be positive, specialization may have negative microeconomic effects and the mesoeconomic (structural) factors, in particular, may be adverse. The net effects of reforms on TT are thus unclear. On the other hand, through either Keynesian mechanisms or the supply effects characteristic of a foreign-exchange-constrained economy, the increase in the propensity to import generated by trade reform will lead to a leftward shift in the GG function.

Figure 1.4 provides three possible outcomes (there may be others). In case A, the neoclassical effects on TT are strong and prevail over weaker adverse movements of the GG function. Both GDP and productivity growth speed up. In case B, neoclassical effects on TT continue to prevail but are weaker, whereas GG effects are strong. Productivity growth speeds up but overall economic growth slows down. An implication of this is that labor under- and unemployment increase. In case C, adverse structural effects on TT prevail over the positive effects of competition, generating a reduction in both GDP and productivity growth. Under- and unemployment increase sharply. This implies that there is no general presumption that liberalization will accelerate growth, and that the microeconomic links emphasized by defenders of

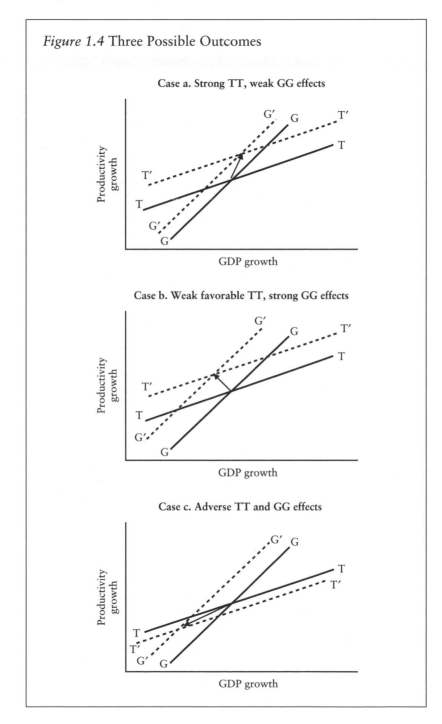

Figure 1.4 Three Possible Outcomes

Case a. Strong TT, weak GG effects

Case b. Weak favorable TT, strong GG effects

Case c. Adverse TT and GG effects

liberalization may be swamped by adverse structural and macroeconomic effects.

Policy Implications

The previous analysis indicates that institutions that guarantee stability in the basic social contract, the protection of business contracts, and an efficient State bureaucracy, as well as the formation of human capital and the development of infrastructure, are certainly important to economic growth, but play the role of framework conditions that, by themselves, are unlikely to affect the growth momentum.

The key to rapid growth in the developing world is thus a combination of *strategies aimed at the dynamic transformation of production structures* with appropriate *macroeconomic conditions and stability,* in the broad sense of the latter term; to improve the distributive effects of growth, such a strategy should be supplemented with policies aimed at *reducing the structural heterogeneity of production structures.*[34] Because, according to the views presented here, innovations and investment are deeply tied, this view coincides with Rodrik's (1999, 2003) call for a domestic capital accumulation strategy to kick-start growth, in conjunction with an appropriate macroeconomic environment. This may be seen as the combination that explains the rapid growth of the Asian economies. The vigorous growth that took place in Latin America during the period of State-led industrialization was also the product of a structural change strategy that was initially based on import substitution, but then began to rely increasingly on "mixed" models combining import substitution with export promotion (Cárdenas, Ocampo, and Thorp 2000b, ch. 1). Unlike what happened in the Asian countries, the lack of suitable macroeconomic conditions in the region bred the debt crisis of the 1980s that led to a sharp break in the growth pattern.

The focus on structural dynamics helps to identify the specific policy areas authorities should target to accelerate economic growth. Accordingly, efforts should be made to (1) *encourage innovation,* in the broad sense of the term, and the associated learning processes in the areas of technologies, productive organization, and marketing; to the extent that innovations in developing countries are largely associated with the transfer of sectors of production from the industrialized world, a strategy of *diversification of the production structure* is the key to increased innovations; (2) *encourage the development of complementarities* that generate positive demand and, above all, supply effects that result in the development of sectoral and systemwide competitiveness; in the latter case, *nontradable* inputs and specialized services should be a special focus of attention, particularly in terms of the development of sectors that produce specialized inputs and services (knowledge, logistics, and marketing services), a strong and deep domestic financial system, and adequate infrastructure; and (3) *encourage the development of small firms* through training, technological diffusion, appropriate financing channels, and the promotion of different forms of associations among small entrepreneurs and of productive technological and commercial links between large and small firms.

Under current conditions, we can identify five essential characteristics of the strategies that should serve as the framework for these policies. In the first place, the emphasis should be on integrating the developing countries into the world economy. Second, there must be a proper balance between individual entrepreneurial initiative, which is decisive for a dynamic process of innovation, and the establishment of institutions aimed at increasing information and coordination among agents. Among the latter, different mixes of public and private institutions should be considered, according to the tradition of each country. Moreover, different mixes of supranational (for example, within the framework of integration processes), national, and local (decentralized) institutions should also be designed. Third, there should be a mix of horizontal and selective policies. Indeed, insofar as policies are intended to strengthen competitiveness, a degree of selectivity aimed at reinforcing successful patterns of specialization and helping to breed new sectors (creating comparative advantages) is essential. Furthermore, under budget constraints, any horizontal policy must be detailed and, hence, necessarily becomes selective. Clear cases of these sorts are the allocation of resources from funds for technological development and export promotion. Recognizing that there is an implicit selectivity in horizontal policies will lead to a better allocation of scarce resources than the alternative neutral stance. Fourth, all incentives should be granted on the basis of performance, generating *reciprocal control mechanisms,* to borrow Amsden's (2001) term (see also Hausmann and Rodrik 2003). Indeed, the institutional structure itself should be subject to periodic evaluation, within its own learning path. Finally, special attention should be given to the opportunities that small firms provide both for growth and for improving the social outcomes of structural transformations.

A complex issue relates to the framework of international rules, especially those of the World Trade Organization. In this regard, although priority should certainly be given to taking advantage of the maneuvering room provided under existing agreements, there is a strong sense that a larger *policy space* (to borrow the term extensively used at the 11th session of the United Nations Conference on Trade and Development that took place in São Paulo in 2004) should be made available to the authorities of developing countries, who were restricted too narrowly in the Uruguay Round of trade negotiations. In particular, according to the analysis presented in this chapter, they should be allowed to apply selective policies and performance criteria to encourage innovation and create the complementarities that are essential to development.

The assumption that dynamic productive development, and the particular institutions that support it, are automatic results of market mechanisms has been demonstrated by the facts to be wrong. In Latin America, the weakening of the public and private sector institutions that had been established to support productive and technological development during the period of State-led industrialization was a central feature of the "lost decade" of the 1980s. In the 1990s they were further weakened as a result of explicit policy decisions. Some institutions have since been developed around production clusters, free trade zones, the promotion of small and medium-sized enterprises, or the development of demand subsidies to allocate technology funds. The suboptimal development of institutions related to the production sector has thus become a direct institutional deficiency affecting economic growth, which is generally ignored in the call to strengthen institutional development. This institutional deficiency is probably not very important if growth is to remain at current levels. It is crucial, however, if the region is seeking to achieve the rapid rates of structural change (including penetration into dynamic technology-intensive sectors) that are essential to gradually bridge the gap separating it from the industrialized world.

In the past, development banks played a crucial role in the developing world in guaranteeing the availability of capital for new activities, and in many areas they continue to do so. It is unclear whether privatized financial sectors will provide an adequate substitute for them. Private investment banking and venture capital are the best alternatives, but past and recent experience indicates that their expansion in developing countries on an optimal scale is not automatic; indeed, these activities are highly concentrated in a few industrial countries. Access to international services of this sort may thus be of paramount importance in order to guarantee finance for innovative activities, but this may generate a strong bias in favor of multinational and large national firms and against small and medium-sized enterprises. It should be mentioned, in this regard, that some of the most important innovations in financial development in the developing world in recent decades—the pension fund revolution in Latin America, for example—have an explicit bias against risk taking.

Finally, I would like to emphasize two implications of the previous analysis. The first is that structural transformation is not a "once and for all" process, a belief that is implicit in current views of structural reforms. It is rather an ongoing task, as the structural transformation process is continuous and may face obstacles at any stage that may block development. To the extent that, in developing countries, innovative activities are largely the result of the spread of new sectors and technologies previously created in the industrial center, these activities may, at any given point in time, be considered as the new set of "infant sectors" to be promoted (more as infant *export* than as import-substitution activities, today). Thus, the essential counterpart of intellectual property right protection, the essential tools for fostering innovations in the developed countries, are instruments to promote the transfer of these sectors to the developing world through the design of trade rules that facilitate and even encourage such transfers, together with appropriate incentives and institutions to further the growth of these infant sectors in developing countries. The instruments developed to promote innovative activities in earlier stages may serve this purpose, but they may have to be readapted or new institutions may have to be created to solve the specific issues involved in guaranteeing the successful development of new sectors in a more interdependent world economy. If leapfrogging is the desired objective of economic policy, then the corresponding strategy will certainly be broader in scope.

The final implication is that the process of transformation is not by any means smooth. Destruction is a constant companion of creation, and structural heterogeneity is a persistent feature that can increase at different phases of the development process. Distributive tensions are presumably associated with both factors. There is, in this regard, no unique Kuznets trajectory, because there may be periods of increased structural heterogeneity in the middle stages of the development process as a result of structural transformations or macroeconomic imbalances. Facilitating the transfer of resources from less dynamic to more dynamic activities, avoiding transformation processes that increase structural heterogeneity, and working to upgrade low-productivity activities and generate positive linkages with high-productivity activities would, in this context, be critical elements in achieving a more equitable development process.

Endnotes

1. The recent literature is extensive. Among the most useful contributions are Aghion and Howitt (1992 and 1998), Barro and Sala-i-Martin (1995), Lucas (1988), Nelson (1996), Rodrik (1999, 2003), Romer (1986), Ros (2000), and Taylor (1991).

2. See, for example, Easterly (2001) and Rodrik, Subramanian, and Trebbi (2002).

3. On Latin America's recent growth frustrations, see Cimoli and Correa (ch. 2, this volume), ECLAC (2003a), Ocampo (2004b), and Stallings and Peres (2000). On the record of State-led industrialization, see Cárdenas, Ocampo, and Thorp (2000b).

4. See, for example, Easterly et al. (1993), Kenny and Williams (2001), and Pritchett (2000).

5. Nonetheless, it has also been argued that there is much less association between some of these variables and economic growth than was traditionally assumed. This has been claimed, in particular, in relation to physical and human capital. See Easterly (2001, part II).

6. There may also be intermediate alternatives: Some factors may not "cause" growth in the sense of accelerating the growth momentum, but can block it. Indeed, this is the case of macroeconomic stability, as has already been pointed out.

7. The divergence of experience is brought about in a novel and forceful way in Pritchett (2000).

8. For example, some of the important differences in per capita income within Latin America were established in the early 20th century and have been remarkably stable since then (Cárdenas, Ocampo, and Thorp 2000a, ch. 1).

9. This chapter will concentrate on asymmetries associated with the productive sector, and only peripherally with macroeconomic and financial asymmetries. For a more extensive analysis of these, see Ocampo (2003b).

10. The contrast made here has some elements in common with the contrast between "yeast" and "mushrooms" views of economic growth (Harberger 1998).

11. Relative to the economic history of Latin America, see Cárdenas, Ocampo, and Thorp (2000a, ch. 1).

12. We will refer below to the phenomenon of increased specialization at the firm level (economies of scope) as "economies of specialization," because it will be assumed (following, indeed, the line of inquiry pursued by Adam Smith) that the opportunities for such specialization are determined by the size of the market and are thus part of the mesoeconomic effects to which we will refer below as "complementarities."

13. See, for example, the empirical evidence provided by Loayza, Fajnzylber, and Calderón (2002).

14. See the survey on the literature of the 1980s by Edwards (1993) and the critical survey of the literature of the 1990s by Rodríguez and Rodrik (2001). My own contributions to this debate were included in UNCTAD (1992, part III, ch. 1).

15. Evidence on this matter has come in different forms. Empirical research has provided evidence that policy regimes (as well as geographical factors) have no significant effect on growth when institutional factors are taken into account (Easterly and Levine 2002; Rodrik, Subramanian, and Trebbi 2002). It has also shown that there is little evidence that market reforms are associated with accelerations of economic growth, though they may play a limited role in sustaining them (Hausmann, Pritchett, and Rodrik 2004).

16. This is generally forgotten when the period of State-led industrialization in Latin America is analyzed. Import substitution obviously made more sense in the closed world economy of the 1930s to 1950s (and in the midst of the protectionist wave that characterized the industrial world in the late 19th and early 20th centuries) than in the period of gradual but incomplete opening of the industrial world to the exports of developing countries that started in the mid-1960s (Cárdenas, Ocampo, and Thorp 2000b, ch. 1).

17. This is the way Easterly (2001, ch. 9) posed the issue.

18. Outsourcing of technology and some features of information and communications technology may have reduced the need for technological followers to invest in learning and adapting technology. However, they have not eliminated the general link between the development of new activities and the investments associated with them.

19. *Leapfrogging* is generally used to refer to the adoption of the latest (for example, modern information and telecommunications) technologies, even when previous technologies were not used in a given location. However, this is just a necessary condition for the successful development of a specific activity at a particular moment in time. It does not necessarily involve rising up through the international economic hierarchy, which is the appropriate sense in which the term *leapfrogging* should be used.

20. See, in particular, Dosi et al. (1988), Nelson (1996), Nelson and Winter (1982), and, with respect to developing countries, Katz (1987), Katz and Kosacoff (2000), and Lall (1990, 2003). Similar concepts have been developed in some versions of the new growth theory in which "knowledge capital" is a form of "human capital" having three specific attributes: It is "embodied" in particular persons, it is capable of generating significant externalities, and it is costly to acquire (Lucas 1988). However, these theories do not capture a basic corollary of these attributes: firm specificity and the corresponding coexistence of heterogeneous producers in any given sector of production. This fact turns the concept of "representative producer" into an abstraction that eliminates elements that play an essential role in determining the nature of competition and the divergence in the growth of firms, regions, and nations through time.

21. This may also apply to technology creation. In this sense, the probability of major innovations, even when they are the result of explicit research and development efforts, depends on the accumulated technological knowledge and production experience of firms.

22. This also applies to the provision of foodstuffs, particularly perishables, if they affect nominal wages and thus production costs. Indeed, in the early stages of development of modern activities in the developing world, guaranteeing the availability of an elastic supply of foodstuffs was essential and, as such, became an important determinant of the development of new export activities.

23. As we have pointed out, this factor has not been entirely absent in the industrial world either, even as late as the post-World War II "golden age" (see Cripps and Tarling 1973).

24. Obviously, mobility is not perfect or costless, particularly when it involves different skills.

25. This does not mean that the skilled workers who migrate will necessarily be absorbed in high-productivity activities in the receiving countries. There may be, in effect, a net loss of human capital.

26. A particular case of a shallow innovation is the takeover of domestic firms by multinationals, if it weakens domestic demand linkages (by the change in the network of suppliers) and concentrates research and development abroad. Maquila exports may have a similar character, although they can reduce underemployment and may serve as a mechanism for transmitting some organizational and marketing innovations. They may also deepen through time and gradually create domestic linkages, thus becoming a labor-absorbing innovation.

27. This is a central conclusion of the ECLAC project on structural reforms in Latin America, which developed a typology of phases of response to structural reforms. According to this typology, an "offensive" attitude only comes with a lag, particularly when the new institutional environment settles down. See Katz (2000), Moguillansky and Bielschowsky (2000), and Stallings and Peres (2000).

28. These issues hark back to the traditional controversies on the terms of trade, including the fallacy of composition effects. For recent reviews of these controversies, see Ocampo and Parra (2003) and Sapsford and Singer (1998).

29. For prior versions of this model, see Ocampo (2002) and Ocampo and Taylor (1998). A recent mathematical formulation is provided by Rada and Taylor (2004).

30. To the extent that new technology is embodied in new equipment, a higher rate of investment induced by faster growth will also increase productivity growth, and should thus be added to the list.

31. For a full analysis of gaps in macroeconomic adjustment, see Taylor (1994). As is well known, saving adjusts through variations in economic activity (the Keynesian mechanism), income redistribution between sectors with high and low propensities to save, particularly between capital owners and workers (the Kaleckian mechanism), and variations in the trade balance (external savings). Depending on the source of the rigidity of the mechanism, inflationary gaps, distributive struggles, or external gaps may arise. For a full treatment of these issues, see Taylor (1991).

32. There are also short-run relationships between productivity and economic growth associated with short-term changes in capacity utilization. However, those effects must be seen as deviations from GG.

33. Of course, there is no presumption that TT will return to its original position. This is the case that, for the sake of simplicity, is shown in figure 1.2.

34. In this regard, see also the agenda laid out in ECLAC (2004).

Bibliography

Aghion, Philippe, and Peter Howitt. 1998. *Endogenous Growth Theory.* Cambridge, MA: MIT Press.

———. 1992. "A Model of Growth Through Creative Destruction." *Econometrica* 60 (2): 323–51.

Amsden, Alice. 2001. *The Rise of the Rest: Non-Western Economies' Ascent in World Markets.* Oxford: Oxford University Press.

Arthur, W. Brian. 1994. *Increasing Returns and Path Dependence in the Economy.* Ann Arbor: University of Michigan Press.

Bairoch, Paul. 1993. *Economics and World History: Myths and Paradoxes.* Chicago: University of Chicago Press.

Balassa, Bela. 1989. *Comparative Advantage Trade Policy and Economic Development.* New York: New York University Press.

Barro, Robert J. 1997. *Determinants of Economic Growth: A Cross-Country Empirical Study.* Cambridge, MA: MIT Press.

Barro, Robert J., and Xavier Sala-i-Martin. 1995. *Economic Growth.* New York: McGraw-Hill.

Cárdenas, Enrique, José Antonio Ocampo, and Rosemary Thorp (eds.). 2000a. *The Export Age: The Latin American Economies in the Late Nineteenth and Early Twentieth Centuries.* Vol. 1 of *An Economic History of Twentieth Century Latin America.* Oxford: Palgrave-Macmillan/St. Antony's College.

———. 2000b. *Industrialisation and the State in Latin America: The Post War Years.* Vol. 3 of *An Economic History of Twentieth Century Latin America.* Oxford: Palgrave-Macmillan/St. Antony's College.

Chang, Ha-Joon. 1994. *The Political Economy of Industrial Policy.* London: Macmillan.

Chenery, Hollis, Sherman Robinson, and Moshe Syrquin. 1986. *Industrialization and Growth: A Comparative Study.* Washington, DC: World Bank.

Cripps, T. F., and R. J. Tarling. 1973. "Growth in Advanced Capitalist Economies 1950–1970." Occasional Paper 40, Department of Applied Economics, University of Cambridge, Cambridge, UK.

Dosi, Giovanni, Christopher Freeman, Richard Nelson, Gerald Silverberg, and Luc Soete (eds.). 1988. *Technical Change and Economic Theory*. London: Pinter Publishers.

Easterly, William. 2001. *The Elusive Quest for Growth: Economists' Adventures and Misadventures in the Tropics*. Cambridge, MA: MIT Press.

Easterly, William, and Ross Levine. 2002. "Tropics, Germs and Crops: How Endowments Influence Economic Development." Working Paper 15, Center for Global Development, Washington, DC.

Easterly, William, Michael Kremer, Lant Pritchett, and Lawrence Summers. 1993. "Good Policy or Good Luck? Country Growth Performance and Temporary Shocks." *Journal of Monetary Economics* 32 (3): 459–83.

ECLAC (Economic Commission for Latin America and the Caribbean). 2004. *Productive Development in Open Economies*. Santiago, Chile: ECLAC.

———. 2003a. *A Decade of Light and Shadow: Latin America and the Caribbean in the 90s*. Santiago, Chile: ECLAC.

———. 2003b. *Globalization and Development: A Latin American Perspective*. Palo Alto: Stanford University Press.

———. 2002. "Growth with Stability: Financing for Development in the New International Context." Santiago, Chile: ECLAC.

———. 2000. *Equity, Development and Citizenship*. Santiago, Chile: ECLAC.

———. 1990. *Changing Production Patterns with Social Equity*. Santiago, Chile: ECLAC.

Edwards, Sebastián. 1993. "Openness, Trade Liberalization, and Growth in Developing Countries." *Journal of Economic Literature* 31 (3): 31–57.

Fajnzylber, Fernando. 1990. "Industrialization in Latin America: From the 'Black Box' to the 'Empty Box.'" *Cuadernos de la CEPAL* 60. Santiago, Chile: ECLAC.

Fujita, Masahisa, Paul Krugman, and Anthony J. Venables. 1999. *The Spatial Economy: Cities, Regions and International Trade*. Cambridge, MA: MIT Press.

Freeman, Chris, and Luc Soete. 1997. *The Economics of Industrial Innovation*. 3rd ed. Cambridge, MA: MIT Press.

Furtado, Celso. 1961. *Desarrollo y subdesarrollo*. Buenos Aires: Editorial Universitaria.

Gerschenkron, A. 1962. *Economic Backwardness in Historical Perspective*. Cambridge, MA: Harvard University Press.

Grossman, Gene M., and Elhanan Helpman. 1991. *Innovation and Growth in the Global Economy*. Cambridge, MA: MIT Press.

Harberger, Arnold C. 1998. "A Vision of the Growth Process." *American Economic Review* 88 (1): 1–31.

Hausmann, Ricardo, and Dani Rodrik. 2003. "Economic Development As Self-Discovery." *Journal of Development Economics* 72 (2): 603–33.

Hausmann, Ricardo, Lant Pritchett, and Dani Rodrik. 2004. "Growth Accelerations." Working Paper 10566, NBER, Cambridge, MA.

Helleiner, Gerald K. (ed.). 1994. *Trade Policy and Industrialization in Turbulent Times*. New York: Routledge.

———— (ed.). 1992. *Trade Policy, Industrialization, and Development: New Perspectives.* New York: Oxford University Press.

Heymann, Daniel. 2000. "Major Macroeconomic Upsets, Expectations and Policy Responses." *CEPAL Review* 70: LC/G. 2095-P.

Hirschman, Albert O. 1958. *The Strategy of Economic Development.* New Haven, CT: Yale University Press.

Kaldor, Nicholas. 1978. *Further Essays on Economic Theory.* London: Duckworth.

Katz, Jorge. 2000. *Reformas estructurales, productividad y conducta tecnológica.* Santiago, Chile: ECLAC.

————. 1987. "Domestic Technology Generation in LDCs: A Review of Research Findings." In *Technology Generation in Latin American Manufacturing Industries,* ed. Jorge Katz, 13–55. London: Macmillan.

Katz, Jorge, and Bernardo Kosacoff. 2000. "Technological Learning, Institution Building, and the Microeconomics of Import Substitution." In *Industrialisation and the State in Latin America: The Post War Years.* Vol. 3 of *An Economic History of Twentieth Century Latin America,* eds. Enrique Cárdenas, José Antonio Ocampo, and Rosemary Thorp, 36–57. Oxford: Palgrave-Macmillan/St. Antony's College.

Keesing, Donald B., and Sanjaya Lall. 1992. "Marketing Manufactured Exports from Developing Countries: Learning Sequences and Public Support." In *Trade Policy, Industrialization, and Development: New Perspectives,* ed. Gerald K. Helleiner, 176–93. New York: Oxford University Press.

Kenny, Charles, and David Williams. 2001. "What Do We Know About Economic Growth? Or, Why Don't We Know Very Much?" *World Development* 29 (1): 1–22.

Krugman, Paul. 1995. *Development, Geography and Economic Trade.* Cambridge, MA: MIT Press.

————. 1990. *Rethinking International Trade.* Cambridge, MA: MIT Press.

Lall, Sanjaya. 1990. *Building Industrial Competitiveness in Developing Countries.* Paris: OECD.

————. 2003. "Technology and Industrial Development in an Era of Globalization." In *Rethinking Development Economics,* ed. Ha-Joon Chang, 377–403. London: Anthem Press.

Lewis, W. Arthur. 1969. *Aspects of Tropical Trade, 1883–1965.* Stockholm: Almqvist & Wiksell.

————. 1954. "Economic Development with Unlimited Supplies of Labour." *Manchester School of Economic and Social Studies* 22: 139–91.

Loayza, Norman, Pablo Fajnzylber, and César Calderón. 2002. "Economic Growth in Latin America and the Caribbean: Stylized Facts, Explanations, and Forecasts." Photocopy, World Bank, Washington, DC.

Lucas, Robert E., Jr. 1988. "On the Mechanics of Economic Development." *Journal of Monetary Economics* 22 (1): 3–42.

Maddison, Angus. 2001. *The World Economy—A Millennial Perspective.* Paris: OECD.

————. 1991. *Dynamic Forces in Capitalist Development: A Long-Run Comparative View.* New York: Oxford University Press.

Moguillansky, Graciela, and Ricardo Bielschowsky. 2000. *La inversión en un proceso de cambio estructural: América Latina en los noventa.* Santiago, Chile: ECLAC.

Moreno-Brid, Juan Carlos. 1999. "Mexico's Economic Growth and the Balance of Payments Constraint: A Cointegration Analysis." *International Review of Applied Economics* 13 (2): 149–59.

Myint, H. 1971. *Economic Theory and the Underdeveloped Countries.* New York: Oxford University Press.

Nelson, Richard R. 1996. *The Sources of Economic Growth.* Cambridge, MA: Harvard University Press.

Nelson, Richard R., and Sidney G. Winter. 1982. *An Evolutionary Theory of Economic Change.* Cambridge, MA: Harvard University Press.

Ocampo, José Antonio. 2004a. "A Broad View of Macroeconomic Stability." Paper presented at the Universal Forum for Cultures, "From the Washington Consensus Towards a New Global Governance," Barcelona, September 17–18.

———. 2004b. "Lights and Shadows in Latin American Structural Reforms." In *Economic Reforms, Growth and Inequality in Latin America. Essays in Honor of Albert Berry,* ed. Gustavo Indart, 31–62. Aldershot, UK: Ashgate.

———. 2003a. "Developing Countries' Anti-Cyclical Policies in a Globalized World." In *Development Economics and Structuralist Macroeconomics: Essays in Honour of Lance Taylor,* eds. Amitava Dutt and Jaime Ros, 374–405. Aldershot, UK: Edward Elgar.

———. 2003b. "International Asymmetries and the Design of the International Financial System." In *Critical Issues in International Financial Reform,* eds. Albert Berry and Gustavo Indart, 45–73. New Brunswick, NJ: Transaction Publishers.

———. 2002. "Structural Dynamics and Economic Development." In *Social Institutions and Economic Development: A Tribute to Kurt Martin,* ed. Valpy FitzGerald, 55–85. Dordrecht, The Netherlands: Kluwer.

———. 1986. "New Developments in Trade Theory and LDCs." *Journal of Development Economics* 22 (1): 129–70.

Ocampo, José Antonio, and María Angela Parra. 2003. "The Terms of Trade for Commodities in the Twentieth Century." *CEPAL Review* 79: 7–35.

Ocampo, José Antonio, and Lance Taylor. 1998. "Trade Liberalisation in Developing Economies: Modest Benefits But Problems with Productivity Growth, Macro Prices, and Income Distribution." *Economic Journal* 108 (450): 1523–46.

Ohlin, B. 1933. *Interregional and International Trade.* Cambridge, MA: Harvard University Press.

Pérez, Carlota. 2002. *Technological Revolutions and Financial Capital. The Dynamics of Bubbles and Golden Ages.* Cheltenham, UK: Edward Elgar.

———. 2001. "Technological Change and Opportunities for Development As a Moving Target." *CEPAL Review* 75: 109–30.

Pérez, Esteban, and Juan Carlos Moreno-Brid. 1999. "Terms of Trade, Exports and Economic Growth in Central America: A Long-Term View." *Banca Nazionale del Lavoro Quarterly Review* 52 (211): 431–49.

Pinto, Aníbal. 1970. "Naturaleza e implicaciones de la 'heterogeneidad estructural' de la América Latina." *El Trimestre Económico* 145 (January–March): 83–100.

Prebisch, Raúl. 1964. *Nueva política comercial para el desarrollo.* Mexico City: Fondo de Cultura Económica.

———. 1951. "Theoretical and Practical Problems of Economic Growth." Mexico City: Economic Commission for Latin America.

Pritchett, Lant. 2000. "Understanding Patterns of Economic Growth: Searching for Hills Among Plateaus, Mountains and Plains." *World Bank Economic Review* 14 (2): 221–50.

———. 1997. "Divergence, Big Time." *Journal of Economic Perspectives* 11 (3): 3–17.

Rada, Codrina, and Lance Taylor. 2004. "Empty Sources of Growth Accounting, and Empirical Replacements à la Kaldor with Some Beef." Working Paper 2004–5, Bernard Schwartz Center for Economic Policy Analysis, New School University, New York.

Robinson, Joan. 1962. *Essays in the Theory of Economic Growth.* London: Macmillan.

Rodríguez, Francisco, and Dani Rodrik. 2001. "Trade Policy and Economic Growth: A Skeptic's Guide to the Cross-National Evidence." In *NBER Macroeconomics Annual 2000,* Vol. 15, eds. Ben S. Bernanke and Kenneth Rogoff, 261–325. Cambridge, MA: MIT Press.

Rodrik, Dani. 2003. "Growth Strategies." Cambridge, MA: Kennedy School of Government, Harvard University.

———. 2001. "Development Strategies for the Next Century." Paper prepared for the ECLAC conference, "Development Theory at the Threshold of the Twenty-first Century." Santiago, Chile, August 28–29.

———. 1999. *The New Global Economy and Developing Countries: Making Openness Work.* Washington, DC: Overseas Development Council.

———. 1992. "Closing the Productivity Gap: Does Trade Liberalization Really Help?" In *Trade Policy, Industrialization, and Development: New Perspectives,* ed. Gerald Helleiner, 155–75. New York: Oxford University Press.

Rodrik, Dani, Arvind Subramanian, and Francesco Trebbi. 2002. "Institutions Rule: The Primacy of Institutions over Geography and Integration in Economic Development." Photocopy, Harvard University, Cambridge, MA.

Romer, P. M. 1986. "Increasing Returns and Long-Run Growth." *Journal of Political Economy* 94 (5): 1002–37.

Ros, Jaime. 2000. *Development Theory and the Economics of Growth.* Ann Arbor: University of Michigan Press.

Rosenstein-Rodan, P. N. 1943. "Problems of Industrialization of Eastern and South-Eastern Europe." *Economic Journal* 53: 202–11.

Sapsford, David, and Hans W. Singer. 1998. "The IMF, the World Bank and Commodity Prices: A Case of Shifting Sands?" *World Development* 26 (9): 1653–60.

Schumpeter, Joseph. 1962. *Capitalism, Socialism and Democracy.* 3rd ed. New York: Harper Torchbooks.

———. 1961. *The Theory of Economic Development.* New York: Oxford University Press.

Solow, Robert M. 2000. *Growth Theory: An Exposition.* 2nd ed. New York: Oxford University Press.

———. 1956. "A Contribution to the Theory of Economic Growth." *Quarterly Journal of Economics* 70 (5): 65–94.

Stallings, Barbara, and Wilson Peres. 2000. *Growth, Employment and Equity: The Impact of the Economic Reforms in Latin America and the Caribbean.* Santiago, Chile: ECLAC.

Taylor, Lance. 1994. "Gap Models." *Journal of Development Economics* 45: 17–34.

———. 1991. *Income Distribution, Inflation, and Growth. Lectures on Structuralist Macroeconomic Theory.* Cambridge, MA: MIT Press.

UNCTAD (United Nations Conference on Trade and Development). 1999. *Trade and Development Report, 1999.* Geneva: UNCTAD.

———. 1992. *Trade and Development Report, 1992.* Geneva: UNCTAD.

van Wijnbergen, Sweder. 1984. "The Dutch Disease: A Disease After All?" *Economic Journal* 94: 41–55.

Nurkse, and Kuznets anticipated this outcome. They asserted that trade liberalization would not necessarily sustain faster rates of growth and that trade could not be a sustainable engine of growth unless the domestic market were sufficiently developed. Moreover, they stated that heavy dependence on demand from developed economies could be a trap for less developed countries if they were unable to develop their endogenous technological capabilities or to capture the benefits of technological change domestically (Kuznets 1980; Nurkse 1953; Prebisch 1950).

International obstacles to growth are also identified in orthodox views regarding gains from trade. For example, the theory of comparative advantage states that nations with differing endowments of capital, labor, and natural resources will gain by specializing in those areas where their relative costs of production are low and by importing in those areas where their relative costs are high. Furthermore, the greater the differences in endowments among countries (and the differences between rich and poor countries are indeed great), the bigger the gains from trade are likely to be. However, in order to specialize in products with high value added rather than simply to serve as a source of low-wage labor and production for economically advanced nations, a country must have the capacity to absorb and retain talent, to produce new knowledge, and, finally, to reduce the gap separating it from the technological frontier (Dosi, Pavitt, and Soete 1990), thereby increasing its participation in international trade in a "virtuous" manner.

Latin America's poor growth performance in the wake of its liberalization strategies encapsulates a complex set of issues related to the role played by the trade balance, the specialization pattern, and the process of accumulating technology. Latin America's balance of payments can act as a serious constraint on the attainment of faster growth. The acceleration of growth to rates closer to those of other countries has caused imports to grow more rapidly than exports and has weakened the mechanisms that link exports to domestic growth. Thus, as the region becomes more dependent on exogenous demand for its exports, bottlenecks have emerged, because the aggregate level of imports continues to exceed the capacity to export. At a more micro level, this situation raises major questions concerning the accumulation of domestic technological capacity in Latin America and the gap that these countries exhibit with respect to the international productivity frontier (Cimoli and Katz 2001; ECLAC 2004). New patterns of production specialization and trade have arisen, with knowledge-intensive industries losing ground in terms of their share of gross domestic product (GDP) while nontradable activities, natural-resource processing industries, and maquila-type assembly operations (catering mostly to U.S. markets) increase their share. The sources of technological change and productivity growth have shifted significantly, with a rapidly increasing share of external sources emerging at the expense of domestic ones. Thus, the development of new ways of linking sectors and firms with foreign sources of know-how—and with the rapid diffusion of information technologies—has affected the pattern of accumulation of technological capacity in terms of structure and performance. As a result of these factors, the gap in technology relative to the world's "best practice" frontiers has become narrower only in selected enclaves.

Building on these ideas, this chapter presents an analysis of growth patterns in Latin America. The analysis characterizes long-term growth as being determined by the joint effect of two types of factors: balance of payments conditions and the characteristics of international specialization on the one hand, and differences in technology and in the capacity to capture the benefits of technical change on the other. Differences in technology will be introduced as one of the main variables that determine growth potential through the effect of what will be referred to here as the *technology gap* (Cimoli, Dosi, and Soete 1986; Dosi, Pavitt, and Soete 1990). In line with this approach, the analysis will also demonstrate that the incentives created by trade liberalization do not necessarily lead to a virtuous path and that the growth rate must be reduced if trade equilibrium is to be preserved. Higher growth rates are possible only if there is an increasing trade deficit. The analysis will also show that a virtuous link between exports and growth requires an increasingly robust capacity to reduce the technology gap in relation to more advanced economies.

The first section presents a simple model that incorporates the technology gap into a traditional framework in which the Harrod multiplier plays the central role in the determination of the *long-run growth potential*. The second introduces evidence on the functioning of liberalization strategies and their effect on growth performance. The third section discusses the dependency between exports and domestic growth and identifies the difficulty of reducing the technology gap as the main reason why the region finds itself in a low-growth trap today. The fourth section of the chapter presents, at a more micro level, a description of the variables that explain the current gap in technological capacity, and offers an overview of how the region has increasingly come to specialize in knowledge-poor activities. The final section summarizes the findings and presents conclusions.

Openness, Technology, and Growth: A Simple Model

The model presented here is a long-run model of growth in which trade patterns, domestic technological capabilities, and production specialization patterns operate as the main determinants of output growth; as a result, long-term income and productivity effects overshadow the impact of relative prices. The model is based on Cimoli, Dosi, and Soete (1986) and Cimoli (1988, 1994). Its main characteristics can be viewed not only in terms of modeling methodologies, but also in terms of how some properties of trading patterns and the asymmetries between them are considered. The first characteristic relates to national consumption patterns and trade specialization, which are approximated by the income elasticity of imports. The second stresses the importance of technology gaps, which are approximated by differences in productivity growth. The third characteristic is the balance of trade, which determines the growth rate differential between trading economies, as indicated by the Harrod trade multiplier and the well-known Kaldorian export-based models. From this perspective, in the short run a developing economy can receive foreign capital inflows and temporarily increase or maintain its rate of growth, but this situation is unsustainable in the long run unless the economy's production specialization is restructured so as to increase its participation in international markets or lead to competitive import substitution[1] (Dutt 2001; Harrod 1933; Kaldor 1966, 1975; Lawson, Palma, and Sender 1989; McCombie and Thirlwall 1994; Thirlwall 1979, 1997).

Recalling the original expression of the Harrod trade multiplier and including in it the technology gap (see annex A), our trade multiplier may be expressed as

$$\dot{y} = \frac{\Psi}{\varepsilon} \dot{x} \qquad\qquad (2.1)$$

$$\Psi = \dot{\pi}/\dot{\pi}^*, \text{ and } \varepsilon = \dot{m}/\dot{y},$$

where $\dot{y}$ is the income growth rate, Ψ is the technological gap, $\dot{\pi}$ is the growth rate of labor productivity in the home country, $\dot{\pi}^*$ is the y growth rate of labor productivity at the technological frontier, ε is the income elasticity of imports, $\dot{m}$ is the import growth rate, Ψ/ε is the trade multiplier, and $\dot{x}$ is the export growth rate attributable to the growth of world demand and the income elasticity of demand for exports.

The above equation tells us that the rate of growth of domestic income that will ensure the balance of trade in an open economy is a function of exports and the parameters reflecting the technology gap and import elasticity. In this sense, this equation can be taken as a formalization of Harrod's foreign trade multiplier, as reformulated by Kaldor and by Thirlwall. Our approach differs from the one taken by the latter authors, however, because it includes a proxy for the technology gap. That is, changes in domestic income are not only a function of foreign income and demand for imports, but are also dependent on the productivity gap and on the domestic capacity to upgrade technology and diffuse it massively throughout the production system. When $\Psi = 1$, the productivity growth rate is the same in the domestic and foreign economies. Thus, if $\Psi > 1$, the domestic economy is reducing the gap with respect to the foreign one. Conversely, when $\Psi < 1$, the gap between the domestic and foreign economies is increasing.[2]

This idea concerning the technology gap reflects contributions made in the 1960s in the field of technology and trade (Freeman 1963; Hirsch 1965; Hufbauer 1966; Posner 1961; Vernon 1966). This approach has stressed international *asymmetries in technology* as the main determinant of trade flows and patterns of specialization. Technology is characterized as a good that is not free and that gives an important advantage to the first innovator country. Moreover, in a dynamic context, asymmetries in levels of technology and innovation capacity largely account for the evolution of each country's pattern of specialization and growth capacity. In Posner (1961), the pattern of trade is explained by countries' initially asymmetric access to technological knowledge in a world characterized by similar demand patterns. In this context, trade between countries will continue if differences in their respective abilities to innovate and imitate persist. After a certain interval, most countries will be able to imitate the new commodity and restore technological parity, thereby eliminating the basis for trade. Freeman (1963) and Hufbauer (1966) have stressed the differences between the factors that determine specialization before and after imitation takes place. Thus, during the innovation process, the effects of patents, commercial secrecy, and static and dynamic economies of scale are the main determinants. However, once imitation occurs, the traditional process of adjustment in production cost and competitiveness will determine the specialization. In Hirsch (1965) and Vernon (1966), technological asymmetries are associated with distinct phases in a technology's evolution and a specific international distribution of innovation capacity in the production of new commodities. In the initial phase, innovative advantage is the main factor driving the production of new commodities in the advanced countries. Over time, the technology evolves into a mature phase characterized by the standardization of products and processes. In this latter phase, international competition is based on the technology being transferred, productivity improvements, and production-cost advantages.

Many of these studies have undoubtedly scored points with policy makers, who have increasingly come to recognize the significance of technology for international competitiveness. The recent "structuralist-evolutionary" approach devotes increasing attention to uneven international technological change as an engine of growth, with emphasis on the dynamics of specialization, as in Amable (1992, 1993), Metcalfe

(1989), and Soete and Verspagen (1992), and on the dynamics of catching up, as analyzed in Verspagen (1990, 1991) and Dosi and Freeman (1992).

Equation (2.1) highlights the multiplier effects of the differences in technology between the two countries and the income elasticity of imports. Domestic growth is weighted by the technology gap, which accounts for the distance between the two countries' productivity growth rates. The extent to which exports can generate sustainable growth rates is thus limited when the existing technology gap is widening. Conversely, when the technology gap narrows, the domestic growth rate will be very sensitive to changes in exports. This rate is also inversely related to import elasticity, which measures the proportional change in demand for imports with respect to a proportional change in domestic income. The growth rate is affected by an increase in imports as measured by ε, the income elasticity of demand for imports. The higher the value of ε, the lower the growth rate consistent with equilibrium on the current account. In sum, the potential for domestic growth is based on the growth rate's sensitivity to both the technology gap multiplier and the income elasticity of imports. Thus, a *virtuous growth path* can emerge when the reduction of the technology gap more than offsets the increase in import elasticity. Conversely, a *vicious growth path* emerges when the increase in import elasticity is greater than the reduction of the technology gap.

This analysis also implicitly points to the influence of international specialization on each economy's potential growth rate. The simple analysis that follows describes the role played by the specialization pattern in determining the trade multiplier Ψ/ε. The ΨM curves in the top left quadrant of figure 2.1 indicate the various combinations of the technology gap multiplier and the elasticity of imports that guarantee equilibrium on the trade balance. The $M\varepsilon$ curves in the lower left quadrant depict the home country's specialization pattern; their positive slant reflects the positive association between an increase in demand for imports and an increase in the income elasticity of goods consumed domestically (commonly known as Engel's law). A movement from $M\varepsilon_1$ to $M\varepsilon_2$ indicates that the home country has improved its specialization and reduced the income elasticity of imports. That is, the home country has improved its capacity to narrow the gap separating it from countries that produce goods with higher knowledge content and higher income elasticity. The top right quadrant shows the trade multiplier (Ψ/ε).

For a given Ψ and a specialization pattern indicated by $M\varepsilon_1$ (which implicitly define a domestic market that demands imports with high income elasticity), the multiplier obtained will be less than 1. In this case, an increase in exports will result in a worsening of the multiplier. That is, when the ΨM curve moves left toward ΨM_2 and imports move from

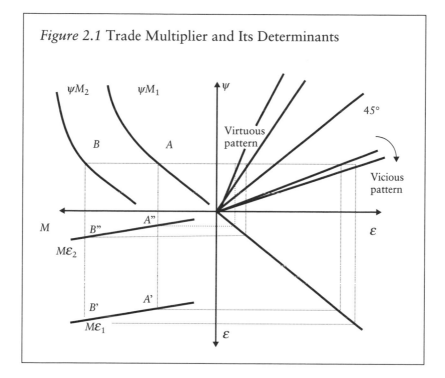

Figure 2.1 Trade Multiplier and Its Determinants

A' to B' along the $M\varepsilon_1$ curve, the multiplier schedule in the top right quadrant will turn clockwise. Conversely, for a given Ψ, the multiplier will improve only when the specialization improves. This is the case when the $M\varepsilon$ curve moves to $M\varepsilon_2$, the combination between M and ε moves to point B'', and the multiplier moves to an angle above 45 degrees. To sum up, the trade multiplier Ψ/ε improves and starts to move along a virtuous path when the productivity gap narrows and/or the specialization pattern improves. On the other hand, if the productivity gap does not change and the specialization pattern is stable, an increase in exports will not produce an improvement in the multiplier.[3]

The assumption of equilibrium on the trade balance does not rule out the possibility that the actual growth rate may be higher or lower than the balance of payments–constrained growth rate. If it is lower, a trade surplus will emerge; conversely, if the actual growth rate is higher than the constrained one, then the trade balance will deteriorate. From a monetary standpoint, the current account deficit may create financing problems and exchange rate volatility, and it must be financed by either long-term or short-term capital inflows. As is well known, given its high

Table 2.2 Theoretical Abacus of the Trade Multiplier

Growth Pattern	Trade Multiplier	Structural Determinants
Virtuous	$\dfrac{\Psi}{\varepsilon} > 1$	The domestic capacity to reduce the technology gap is greater than the increase in the income elasticity of imports; hence, increased participation in international trade fosters output growth.
Stable	$\dfrac{\Psi}{\varepsilon} = 1$	The domestic capacity to reduce the technology gap offsets the country's import requirements, thus limiting the multiplier effect of trade participation on income growth.
Vicious	$\dfrac{\Psi}{\varepsilon} < 1$	The limited capacity to reduce the technology gap and the fast growth in import requirements hamper the beneficial effect of increased participation in international trade.

results are reflected in the trade balance situation in the postreform period. As table 2.4 shows, most countries had built up surpluses at the beginning of the period, but those surpluses have now been reduced and/or transformed into deficits. Moreover, deficits have increased at an accelerated rate.

This situation is rooted in the characteristics of the specialization pattern and, particularly, in the limited nature of the progress made in reducing the technology gap. Although Latin America has narrowed the productivity gap, the decrease has not been as large as the increase in import elasticity.[7] In particular, when a country starts out with a wide technology gap, it is the reduction of this gap that will result in the clearest improvement in the relative domestic growth rate (that is, an increase in Ψ). However, if the demand for imports increases at a higher rate, the positive effect of shrinking the technology gap is neutralized and/or eliminated. This is the case in Latin America, where the reduction of the technology gap was not enough to offset the striking increase in import elasticity. As in the Prebisch-Singer case, the negative impact on domestic income is represented as a combination of adverse structural conditions: a fast increase in income elasticity and a slow reduction in the technology gap.

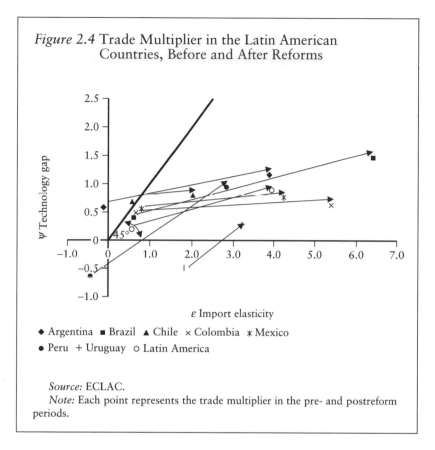

Figure 2.4 Trade Multiplier in the Latin American
Countries, Before and After Reforms

◆ Argentina ■ Brazil ▲ Chile × Colombia ✳ Mexico
● Peru + Uruguay ○ Latin America

Source: ECLAC.
Note: Each point represents the trade multiplier in the pre- and postreform periods.

Another finding concerns the link between exports and growth when exports are driven exogenously by growth in developed countries. Thus, if the trade multiplier decreases over time, the same rate of growth in domestic income can be achieved only if exports increase at a higher rate. Moreover, a slowdown in the growth of world demand for a country's exports and a reduction of the multiplier will amplify the negative impact on income growth.

At the aggregate level, the dynamics of productivity growth are the result of overlapping phenomena. Productivity growth has not been fast enough, nor has the restructuring of the pattern of production specialization involved enough high-value-added activities, to enable the region's countries to attain a significant improvement in international competitiveness. The technology gap has been reduced only in tightly circumscribed production enclaves, and a new dualism has become more visible in the production system. At the same time, Latin America has

Table 2.3 Structural Change in Latin America, Before and After Reform

			Before Reform		After Reform	
Before Reform	After Reform	Country	Import Elasticity (ε)	Technology Gap (Ψ)	Import Elasticity (ε)	Technology Gap (Ψ)
1970–90	1991–9	Argentina	–0.07	0.61	3.97	1.19
1970–89	1990–9	Brazil	0.59	0.39	6.42	1.48
1970–84	1985–98	Chile	0.65	0.71	1.98	0.79
1970–89	1990–9	Colombia	0.68	0.46	5.47	0.68
1970–85	1986–99	Mexico	0.82	0.53	4.28	0.78
1970–89	1990–6	Peru	–0.42	–0.61	2.92	0.98
1970–7	1978–99	Uruguay	1.53	–0.48	2.98	0.31

Source: ECLAC.
Note: Apparent import elasticity and labor productivity (hence the technology gap) are standardized at constant 1985 prices.

Table 2.4 Growth Rate and Trade Balance Applied to the Model, After Reform

After Reform	Country	Actual Growth Rate	Balance of Payments Equilibrium Growth Rate	Trade Balance (% GDP)		
				First Year	Last Year	Difference
1991–9	Argentina	3.95	2.69	1.47	−3.82	−5.30
1990–9	Brazil	2.42	1.28	3.16	−2.36	−5.52
1985–98	Chile	6.75	4.21	7.45	3.39	−4.07
1990–9	Colombia	2.50	0.78	3.78	−3.52	−7.30
1986–99	Mexico	3.16	2.06	3.62	2.48	−1.14
1990–6	Peru	5.08	2.81	0.81	−4.33	−5.14
1978–99	Uruguay	2.06	0.45	1.96	−4.43	−6.38

Source: ECLAC.

Note: The trade balance and income growth for each period are calculated using weighted averages based on country size.

radically modified the pattern of technology accumulation and knowledge diffusion across firms and sectors. Such changes are giving rise to a complex process of "destruction" of deeply rooted forms of production organization and of institutions, thereby gradually (and painfully) forcing the countries to establish an outward-oriented and deregulated incentive regime together with a production system specializing in activities having a low knowledge content (ECLAC 2004).

Understanding the Microeconomic Sources of Technology Gaps

According to the analysis carried out in the previous section, the characteristics of domestic production and of trade patterns appear to be the structural determinants of growth patterns. In effect, the taxonomy presented in table 2.2 allows us to identify domestic capacity for reducing the technology gap as a factor that helps to ensure that export growth will drive the economy toward a virtuous pattern of growth; by the same token, this taxonomy also enables us to identify an increasing income elasticity of imports as a factor that hampers this process. At this point, because the trend of the income elasticity of imports depends on the domestic specialization pattern, and considering that technological intensity is a key element in analyzing production structure dynamics, an examination of the microfoundations of knowledge accumulation patterns is necessary in order to understand the reasons behind one of the main determinants of the region's vicious growth pattern, that is, the very limited reduction of the technology gap experienced by Latin American countries during the last decade (for empirical evidence and an analytical formalization, see Cimoli and Katz [2001] and ECLAC [2000, 2004]).

First of all, the weak link between exports and growth reflects a new dualism in the production system and in the pattern of technology accumulation. The benefits of modernization have been very unevenly distributed. Many production activities have been seriously disrupted by trade liberalization and the massive inflow of imports, particularly in technology-intensive fields, which have rapidly begun to de-verticalize their production organization technologies, replacing domestically produced intermediate inputs with cheaper (and sometimes better) imported ones and reorganizing themselves as more of an assembly-type operation based on a much higher import content. The heterogeneity of responses has been quite dramatic, not only across production sectors, but also across individual firms within narrowly defined industries. Thus, failure and success tend to occur side by side, even within the same production activity. The share of GDP accounted for by "large" firms—either local subsidiaries of transnational corporations or domestically owned conglomerates increased significantly during the adjustment process, whereas countless small and medium-sized enterprises were forced to exit the market altogether.

Only a very small group of modernized export firms are actually becoming global in terms of their production orientation and their capacity to acquire foreign technology in international networks. The majority are much less efficient, and this tends to break down local networking activities and hold back knowledge diffusion. The modernized firms are, in fact, characterized by fewer linkages with domestic institutions of higher education and with local research centers and laboratories. Although universities have sought to improve and create linkages with the production system, they are hindered by two factors: their own bureaucratic organization and these firms' demand for knowledge from institutions and research centers located abroad. This is also true of the maquila industry in Mexico and Central America, because the "maquila innovation system" mainly supports and stimulates networking activities with firms and institutions located abroad, thus reinforcing the knowledge and technology advantages of the developed economies.

In the second place, it is worth noticing that, following the trade reforms, the largest economies increased their share of production in sectors such as natural-resource processing industries that produce industrial commodities (such as pulp and paper, iron and steel, vegetable oil, and so forth), maquila industries (electronics, television sets and video equipment, and so forth), nontradable services (telecommunications and energy), and in the somewhat special case of the automotive industry, which has enjoyed special protection from the wave of liberalization. Other industries, such as footwear, garments, and furniture, and industries that produce engineering- and knowledge-intensive products (capital goods, agricultural machinery, machine tools, pharmaceuticals) have seen their share decline throughout the continent.

Most Latin American economies have thus specialized on the basis of their abundant factor endowments: natural resources and labor. Another relevant issue is the role played by large domestic firms and subsidiaries of multinational enterprises (MNEs) that have followed the international pattern in terms of product specialization and technology absorbed from foreign economies. Subsidiaries of MNEs, whose production is mainly concentrated in standardized products (particularly motor vehicles, other consumer durables, and traditional manufactures), have adopted the technologies developed by their parent companies in industrialized countries. The performance of large domestic firms cannot be understood without taking into account their learning efforts during the import-substitution phase. It was during that period that these firms developed economies of scale to enable them to compete in the international market after the economy was opened up. This involved the adoption of plans, blueprints, and designs for the domestic market, as well as efforts to improve organization and increase production capacity. Examples of such firms include large groups in the chemicals, brewing, and glass-container industries, which not only increased their production capacity but also carried out research and development (R&D) activities to support the firms' knowledge base during the import-substitution phase.

The long-term accumulation of local technological capacity has been hampered by the replacement of engineers with machines in the course of the reorganization of production. Obviously, some of the engineering activities carried out on the plant floor during the import-substitution period, either to extend the life cycle of old machines or to perform technical tasks, are now "embodied" in the new pieces of equipment and have been rendered unnecessary, so that frequently the engineers and technicians involved in such activities can be dropped from the payroll. Similarly, entire R&D and project engineering departments can be eliminated when firms become part of worldwide integrated production systems and R&D and engineering efforts are transferred to headquarters. The same phenomenon is observed in the case of public firms providing telecommunications, electricity, and transport services, which, after privatization, discontinued their domestic R&D and engineering departments and have since relied instead on their respective central offices for technology and engineering services. These changes in the organization of production involve the "destruction" of human capital and domestic technological capabilities and their replacement with capital embodied in new technology and with foreign-supplied R&D and engineering services. Some of the skills and technological capabilities rendered redundant by the new production organization arrangements can and have been successfully transferred to other areas of the economy—to a newly emerging and rapidly expanding software industry, for example—but there are clear differences across nations, regions, and industries in terms of the extent to which such redeployment has actually taken place.[8]

Conclusions

The region has slowly narrowed the productivity gap. However, the reduction of this gap has not been enough to offset the extraordinary increase in the elasticity of demand for imports; as a result, the trade multiplier (Ψ/ε) has declined between the pre- and postreform periods. The mechanism that links export growth and income growth has led most countries of the region into a low-growth trap, resulting in a vicious pattern of international specialization. A virtuous pattern can be obtained if the specialization pattern moves toward products with higher technological content and if the regional productivity gap is reduced. Only under such circumstances will the increase in exports lead to sustainable long-term income growth.

The main reason why it has proven to be so difficult to capture the benefits of increased participation in international trade lies in the structure of the production system and in the existing modes of producing and diffusing technical change. A dual structure has arisen in which productivity improves in very small enclaves, and few linkages are generated with the rest of the system. This pattern does not permit a higher increase in, or better diffusion of, knowledge and technical change. Moreover, the poor diffusion of R&D activities and the replacement of local sources of knowledge are radically reducing opportunities for narrowing the technology gap.

Economic reforms have thus led to a pattern of specialization based on allocative efficiency and static comparative advantages in most Latin American countries. In contrast, dynamic advantages require the development and diffusion of technical and organizational innovations and depend increasingly on access to advanced linkages between firms and knowledge flows. As a result, openness to trade has produced a disjointed structure that is unable to diffuse technological capabilities locally to produce an overall improvement across firms and sectors. This pattern adversely affects endogenous knowledge generation and hampers the creation of domestic capacity for closing the technology gap, thereby limiting the potential multiplier effect of export growth on income growth and acting as one of the main barriers to the countries' efforts to capture the benefits of increased participation in international trade.

Annex A

The trade multiplier can be obtained on the basis of the concept developed by Harrod (1933), Kaldor (1966, 1975), and Thirlwall (1979); that is, $\hat{y} = (1/\varepsilon)\hat{x}$. In Cimoli (1994) and Cimoli, Dosi, and Soete (1986), this expression has been further developed with the incorporation of a proxy for the technology gap (Ψ); thus, the trade multiplier may be expressed by $\hat{y} = (\Psi/\varepsilon)\hat{x}$.

This last expression is based on the following assumptions. To obtain an expression of the balance of trade equilibrium condition, we must now specify total domestic imports and exports. These are expressed by M and E, where M is the total demand for imports in the home country and E is the home country's exports (that is, the demand for imports in the foreign country). The trade equilibrium condition, as measured in one currency, is then $M = E$; or, when this initial condition is given, the balance of payments equilibrium on current account can be expressed by $\dot{m} = \dot{e}$ in terms of growth rates. To obtain an expression of the trade multiplier, we must now specify imports and exports. Using standard demand theory, imports may thus be specified as a multiplicative function of domestic income. Thus, $M = y^{\varepsilon}$, where ε is the income elasticity of demand for imports and y is domestic income. Export demand may also be expressed as a multiplicative function in which the arguments are world income (y^*) and the technological gap (Ψ). Exports may be expressed by $E = y^{*\beta\Psi}$. In accordance with the structuralist view (Bacha 1978; McCombie and Thirlwall 1994; Prebisch 1950), we can argue that to maintain an income level equal to that of developed economies, Latin America must reduce the income elasticity of its demand for imports or narrow the technology gap; that is, $y^{\varepsilon} = y^{*\beta\Psi}$. Differentiating it, a dynamic version of the multiplier is obtained: $\varepsilon(\partial y/y) = \Psi\beta(\partial y^*/y^*)$. Substituting $\dot{x} = \beta\dot{y}^*$ in the last equation, we obtain $\hat{y} = (\Psi/\varepsilon)\hat{x}$. Note that $\dot{x}$ is the total export growth attributable to the growth of world income ($\hat{y}^*$) and the income elasticity of demand for exports (β).

Annex B

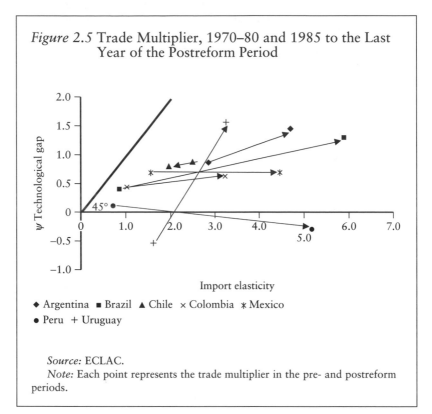

Figure 2.5 Trade Multiplier, 1970–80 and 1985 to the Last Year of the Postreform Period

◆ Argentina ■ Brazil ▲ Chile × Colombia ∗ Mexico
● Peru + Uruguay

Source: ECLAC.
Note: Each point represents the trade multiplier in the pre- and postreform periods.

Table 2.5 Structural Change in Latin America, 1970–80, 1985–99

	1970–1980		1985–circa 1999	
Country	Import Elasticity (ε)	Technology Gap (Ψ)	Import Elasticity (ε)	Technology Gap (Ψ)
Argentina	2.81	0.85	4.72	1.40
Brazil	0.91	0.41	5.95	1.28
Chile	2.37	0.85	1.98	0.79
Colombia	1.03	0.43	3.24	0.64
Mexico	1.57	0.70	4.46	0.69
Peru	0.74	0.10	5.19	−0.28
Uruguay	1.56	−0.52	3.32	1.56

Source: Prepared by author.

Table 2.6 Growth Rate and Trade Balance Applied to the Model, 1985–99

Period	Country	Actual Growth Rate	Balance of Payments Equilibrium Growth Rate	Trade Balance (% GDP)		
				First Year	Last Year	Difference
1985–99	Argentina	2.99	1.97	3.55	–3.82	–7.37
1985–99	Brazil	2.22	1.01	3.85	–2.36	–6.22
1985–98	Chile	6.75	4.21	7.45	3.39	–4.07
1985–99	Colombia	3.32	1.67	0.67	–3.52	–4.20
1985–99	Mexico	2.69	1.66	2.47	2.48	0.01
1985–96	Peru	1.90	–0.08	6.35	–4.33	–10.68
1985–99	Uruguay	3.53	2.34	7.85	–4.43	–12.28

Source: Prepared by author.

Endnotes

1. The long-run character of the model allows us to disregard short-run changes in relative prices, including movements of the real exchange rate. This, in turn, reflects the fact that, in the long term, real exchange rates are relatively stable (Krugman 1989; McCombie and Roberts 2002).

2. In the literature on technology and trade, Ψ has been called the "technological gap multiplier" (Cimoli 1994; Cimoli, Dosi, and Soete 1986).

3. Another way of looking at this model is from both the supply and the demand sides. The supply side is reflected by the technology gap multiplier and differences in the dynamism of production structures (for example, learning processes, sectoral networks, and so forth). The demand side is associated with the dynamism of world demand and the particular features of the specialization pattern.

4. As Anne Krueger has argued, "Insofar as developing countries are relatively abundantly endowed with unskilled labor and relatively short of capital, trade with other [less-developed countries] is likely to increase the imbalance in factor availability, whereas trade with the developed countries may serve as a means of exchanging abundant factors for scarce ones" (Krueger 1978, pp. 270–72). In this respect, trade liberalization would strengthen the region's comparative advantages by allocating resources for these production activities and would thus boost demand for unskilled labor, narrow the wage gap, and reduce the anti-export bias of the import-substitution era, during which the labor factor had been underused. Anne Krueger has also stated, "What is already clear is that the findings of the country studies support the view that altering trade strategies toward greater export orientation will certainly be consistent with the objective of finding more employment opportunities: scepticism based on the Leontief Paradox or factor-market distortion considerations does not seem to be warranted" (Krueger 1978, pp. 270–72).

5. Ψ is calculated with respect to the United States, which in this case is the technological frontier. However, this result does not change if we consider more direct competitors, such as the Republic of Korea (see note 6).

6. The trade multiplier for the Republic of Korea rose from 1.01 to 1.42 between 1970–80 and 1981–99. In this case, it is interesting to note that both the technology gap and the elasticity of demand for imports decreased. Thus, a virtuous pattern was established. These contrasts between Latin America and Korea should be seen in terms of the latter's status as an economy that has consolidated the upgrading of its technological capabilities in the past few decades. One fact that explains the differences between Latin America and Korea is related to the concept of selective intervention, derived from the experiences of developmentalist approaches. For example, one of the keys to the success of this approach has been the ability to program the level and composition of noncompetitive intermediate and capital goods, as in Korea, where quotas, directed credit, and targeting were used to select those industries that were to provide foreign exchange through exports. The industries whose exports were promoted were those in which the country possessed a static comparative advantage, whereas the industries that enjoyed a protective policy were subject to the requirement that they should develop a dynamic comparative advantage. Thus, at the aggregate level, it was also possible to obtain a balanced portfolio in terms of sources and uses of foreign exchange. Among the industries that have received support in order to help them develop dynamic comparative advantages, it seems that the major actors in technological learning have been large business groups—the chaebols—which, at a very early stage of development, were able to internalize skills for the selection of technologies acquired from abroad, their efficient use, and their adaptation and, not much later, were able to grow impressive engineering capabilities (Kim 1993). This process has been further supported by a set of institutions and networks for improving and upgrading human resources (Amsden 1989).

7. The increase in import elasticity is observed over the long term. It is not a transitory phenomenon resulting from income changes, but instead mainly an effect of the specialization pattern.

8. In general, because companies transfer only some of their R&D activities to Latin America, the present concentration of corporate R&D can be expected to lead, by and large, to even sharper international disparities in the pattern of technology accumulation. The internationalization of R&D is carried out within developed economies and regions with already proven technological advantages. This view is supported by the results obtained in empirical studies on the organization of research activities in multinational firms, which clearly show that even multinational companies perform most of their innovative activities in their home country (Cimoli and Katz 2001).

Bibliography

Amable, B. 1993. "National Effects of Learning, International Specialization and Growth Paths." In *Technology and the Wealth of Nations*, eds. Dominique Foray and Christopher Freeman, 5–31. London: Pinter Publishers.

———. 1992. "Effects d'apprentissage, compétitivité hors-prix et croissance cumulative." *Économie Appliquée* 45(3): 5–31.

Amsden, Alice. 1989. *Asia's Next Giant: South Korea and the Last Industrialization*. New York: Oxford University Press.

Bacha, Enmer L. 1978. "An Interpretation of Unequal Exchange from Prebisch-Singer to Emanuel." *Journal of Development Economics* 5 (4): 319–30.

Cimoli, Mario. 1994. "Look-in and Specialisation (Dis)Advantages in a Structuralist Model with Endogenous Growth." In *The Dynamics of Technology,*

Trade and Growth, eds. Jan Fagerberg, Nick von Tunzelman, and Bart Verspagen. London: Edgar Elgar.

———. 1988. "Technological Gaps and Institutional Asymmetries in a North-South Model with a Continuum of Goods." *Metroeconomica* 39 (3): 245–74.

Cimoli, Mario, Giovanni Dosi, and Luc Soete. 1986. "Innovation Diffusion, Institutional Differences and Patterns of Trade: A North-South Model." DRC Paper 36, Science and Technology Policy Research, University of Sussex, Brighton, UK.

Cimoli, Mario, and Jorge Katz. 2001. "Structural Reforms, Technological Gaps and Economic Development: A Latin American Perspective." Paper presented at the DRUID-Nelson and Winter Conference, Aalborg, Denmark, June 12–15. http://www.business.auc.dk/druid/conferences/nw/.

Dosi, Giovanni, and Christopher Freeman. 1992. "The Diversity of Development Patterns: On the Processes of Catching-up, Forging Ahead and Falling Behind." Paper presented at the Conference on Economic Growth and the Structure of Long-Term Development, Varenna, Italy, October 1–3.

Dosi, Giovanni, Keith Pavitt, and Luc Soete. 1990. *The Economics of Technical Change and International Trade*. New York: New York University Press.

Dutt, Amitava. 2001. "Income Elasticities of Imports, North-South Trade and Uneven Development." Unpublished paper. Notre Dame, IN: University of Notre Dame.

ECLAC (Economic Commission for Latin America and the Caribbean). 2004. *América Latina y el Caribe en la era global*. Bogotá: CEPAL/Alfaomega.

———. 2000. *Equity, Development and Citizenship*. Santiago, Chile: ECLAC.

Freeman, Christopher. 1963. "The Plastic Industry: A Comparative Study of Research and Innovation." *National Institute Economic Review* 26: 22–62.

Frenkel, Roberto, and Martín González. 1999. "Apertura comercial, productividad y empleo en Argentina." In *Productividad y empleo en la apertura económica*, eds. Víctor Tokman and Daniel Martínez. Lima, Peru: International Labour Organization.

Harrod, Roy. 1933. *International Economics*. Cambridge, UK: Cambridge University Press.

Hirsch, S. 1965. "The U.S. Electronics Industry in International Trade." *National Institute Economic Review* 34: 92–107.

Holland, Márcio, Flávio Vilela Vieira, and Otaviano Canuto. 2002. "Economic Growth and the Balance of Payments Constraint in Latin America." Paper presented at VII Encontro Nacional de Economia Politica, Sociedade Brasileira de Economia Politica, Universidade Federal do Paraná, Curitiba, Brasil, May 28–31.

Hufbauer, Gary C. 1966. *Synthetic Materials and the Theory of International Trade*. London: Buckworth.

Kaldor, Nicholas. 1975. "What Is Wrong with Economic Theory?" *Quarterly Journal of Economics* 89 (3): 347–57.

———. 1966. *Causes of the Slow Rate of Economic Growth in the United Kingdom*. Cambridge, UK: Cambridge University Press.

Katz, Jorge, and Giovanni Stumpo. 2001. "Regímenes sectoriales, productividad y competitividad internacional." *CEPAL Review* 75 (LC/G.2150-P): 131–52.

Kennedy, Charles, and Anthony P. Thirlwall. 1979. "Import Penetration, Export Performance and Harrod's Trade Multiplier." *Oxford Economic Papers* 31 (2): 302–23.

3

Four Sources of "De-Industrialization" and a New Concept of the "Dutch Disease"

José Gabriel Palma

USING KALDOR'S ANALOGY, ONE OF THE most notable "stylized facts" of the post-World War II (WWII) period is the rapid decline in manufacturing employment in most industrial countries and in many middle- and high-income developing countries. Although it is well known that over the long-term course of economic development, the structure of employment changes substantially, relative variations in the scale and speed of change during this period constitute a phenomenon without precedent.

In essence, during the long-term course of economic development, changes in the structure of employment are set in motion by an increase in the productivity of the agricultural sector.[1] This increase in productivity reduces the labor requirements of agriculture and, at the same

The author is Senior Lecturer, Faculty of Economics, Cambridge University. This chapter builds on Robert Rowthorn's influential work on this subject. I am extremely grateful to him for sharing his data and for many lengthy discussions on the subject. I would also like to thank Daniel Hahn, Richard Kozul-Wright, Carlota Pérez, Hashem Pesaran, Guy Standing, Fiona Tregenna, Ben Turok, and especially Stephanie Blankenburg and José Antonio Ocampo, and participants at seminars in Bangkok, Bilbao, Cambridge, Cape Town, Chicago, Geneva, Kuala Lumpur, Mexico City, and Santiago for their helpful comments on a previous draft. Last, I am very grateful to John Wells, with whom I had frequent discussions on the subject before his sudden death. The usual caveats apply.

time, raises both the demand for agricultural intermediate and capital inputs, and the demand for consumer goods by those benefiting from the increase in productivity in agriculture. As a result, two processes are set in motion: one in which labor begins to be released from agriculture; and one in which labor is progressively absorbed into other sectors of the economy—initially by those activities whose products benefited from higher demand from agriculture and later by the more general dynamics of economic growth. During this new phase, generally called the *industrialization* phase, labor is absorbed mainly by manufacturing and services. During the next phase, alongside a continuing contraction of employment in agriculture and an expansion of employment in services, comes a tendency for the share of manufacturing employment in total employment to stabilize. Finally, a new phase emerges in which employment in manufacturing begins to fall (first in relative terms and then, at least in some countries, in absolute terms); in the meantime, services continue to be the main source of labor absorption.[2] This last phase is commonly referred to as the *de-industrialization* phase.[3]

Most industrial countries reached this phase of de-industrialization around the end of the 1960s and the beginning of the 1970s, whereas some high-income developing countries (such as the rapidly industrializing economies of East Asia) began this phase in the 1980s. However, at about the same time (and for a number of different reasons that will be discussed in more detail below), some Latin American countries also began to de-industrialize rapidly, despite the fact that their level of income per capita was far lower than the levels found in other countries that had either de-industrialized earlier, or that were beginning to de-industrialize at the same time.

Among industrial countries, one group of countries in which the scale and speed of change were most remarkable was the European Union (EU), where manufacturing employment was reduced by almost a third in the last three decades of the 20th century.[4]

Figure 3.1 shows how, in the years between 1960 and the early 1970s, both output and productivity in the European Union's manufacturing sector were growing at similarly high speeds (with annual average rates of 5.9 percent and 5.3 percent in 1960–73, respectively). In the post-1973 period, both these rates fell drastically; however, the *production* rate dropped far more rapidly, ending up at just half that of productivity (1.4 percent and 2.8 percent, respectively). Therefore, the origins of the rapid fall in manufacturing employment in the European Union can be explained easily— at least in *arithmetic* terms. Because the growth in employment is equal to the growth in output less that of productivity, the result of the above asymmetry is a decline in employment. From this (arithmetic) standpoint, what happened in the European Union after 1973 should be considered as basically a case of "output-led" de-industrialization—that is,

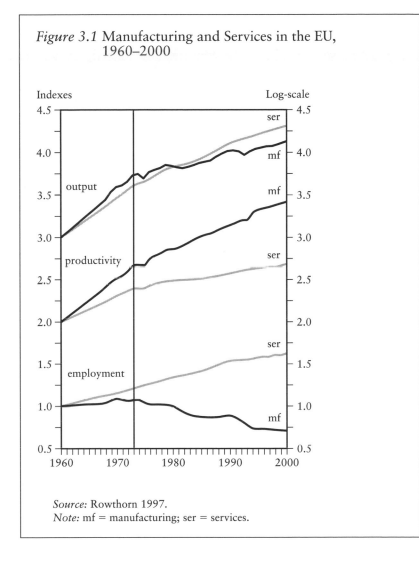

Figure 3.1 Manufacturing and Services in the EU, 1960–2000

Source: Rowthorn 1997.
Note: mf = manufacturing; ser = services.

the result of a rapid slowdown of the rate of growth of output—rather than a case of "productivity-led" (or a "new-technological-paradigm-led") de-industrialization.[5]

Figure 3.1 also shows that in the services sector the reverse phenomenon took place: Although in this sector the rate of growth of both output and productivity also began to fall sharply in the early 1970s, it was growth in *productivity* that fell much faster, with productivity growing at less than half the rate of output (1.1 percent and 2.6 percent, respectively).

This reversed asymmetry resulted in a rapid *increase* in employment. Consequently, after the early 1970s, both sectors—manufacturing and services—demonstrated significant contrasts in their capacity to absorb labor.

As a result, between 1973 and 2000 the European Union was able to raise its production of manufactures by about 50 percent while cutting employment by almost 30 percent. At the same time, in order to continue raising its output of services (even though this was done at a slow pace, and certainly much more slowly than in the preceding period), the European Union had to increase employment in this sector by more than 50 percent.

The literature on the subject has developed various hypotheses to explain the fall in manufacturing employment in industrial countries since the late 1960s. The four better-known hypotheses are the following:

1. The fall is no more than a "statistical illusion" (caused mainly by the reallocation of labor from manufacturing to services following a rapid increase in the number of activities being contracted out by manufacturing firms to specialist service producers, including transport, cleaning, design, security, catering, recruitment, and data processing).

2. The decrease is the result of a significant reduction in the income elasticity of demand for manufactures.

3. The decline is the consequence of the rapid productivity growth in (at least some sectors of) manufacturing, brought about by the propagation of the new technological paradigm of microelectronics. (This would have been a case of the new technology tending to produce "jobless growth.")

4. The fall is the result of a new international division of labor (including "outsourcing"), which is detrimental to manufacturing employment in industrial countries, especially as concerns its non-skilled labor.[6]

The main aim of this chapter is to study the trajectory of manufacturing employment in the post-WWII period—in particular, the "inverted-U" phenomenon of the process of economic development, in which, as income per capita increases, the percentage of employment in manufacturing first *rises*, then *stabilizes,* and finally *falls.* A sample of 105 countries will be used over the period 1970–98 (the same 105 countries throughout); for 1960, however, there was information for only 81 of those countries; see annex B). The sources of the data analyzed here are the International Labour Organization databank for manufacturing employment and the Penn Tables for income per capita.[7] Table 3.1 summarizes the employment data by region.

This chapter will illustrate that these data provide significant confirmation of this inverted-U relationship between manufacturing

Table 3.1 Employment in Manufacturing (% of total)

Region 1998	1960	1970	1980	1990	
Sub-Saharan Africa	4.4	4.8	6.2	5.5	5.5
Latin America and the Caribbean	15.4	16.3	16.5	16.8	14.2
Southern Cone and Brazil	17.4	17.2	16.2	16.6	11.8
West Asia and North Africa	7.9	10.7	12.9	15.1	15.3
Southeast Asia	8.7	9.2	10.7	13.0	13.9
East Asia (except China and Japan)	10.0	10.4	15.8	16.6	14.9
NIE-1s	10.5	12.9	18.5	21.0	16.1
China	10.9	11.5	10.3	13.5	12.3
Developing Countries	10.2	10.8	11.5	13.6	12.5
Industrial Countries	26.5	26.8	24.1	20.1	17.3

Source: Calculations made using statistics from the International Labour Organization databank.

Note: Regional averages are weighted by economically active population. Economies included under the heading "Developing Countries". *Sub-Saharan Africa*—Benin, Botswana, Burkina Faso, Cameroon, Central African Republic, Chad, Democratic Republic of the Congo, Côte d'Ivoire, Gabon, Ghana, Kenya, Lesotho, Malawi, Mali, Mauritania, Mauritius, Niger, Nigeria, Republic of the Congo, Rwanda, Senegal, South Africa, Togo, Zambia, and Zimbabwe. *Latin America and the Caribbean*—Argentina, Brazil, Chile, Colombia, Costa Rica, Dominican Republic, Ecuador, El Salvador, Guatemala, Honduras, Jamaica, Mexico, Nicaragua, Panama, Paraguay, Peru, and Uruguay (within this category, the subcategory "Southern Cone" includes Argentina, Chile, and Uruguay). *West Asia and North Africa*—Algeria, Arab Republic of Egypt, Morocco, Oman, Saudi Arabia, Tunisia, and Turkey. *Southeast Asia*—Bangladesh, India, Pakistan, and Sri Lanka. *East Asia*—Hong Kong (China), Indonesia, Malaysia, Philippines, Republic of Korea, Singapore, Thailand, and Taiwan (China) (within this category, the subcategory "NIE-1s" includes Hong Kong [China], Republic of Korea, Singapore, and Taiwan [China]). Economies included under the heading "Industrial Countries": Australia, Austria, Belgium, Canada, Denmark, Finland, France, Greece, Italy, Japan, Luxembourg, Netherlands, New Zealand, Norway, Portugal, Spain, Sweden, United Kingdom, and United States.

employment and income per capita. However, it will also show that this relationship has characteristics that are far more complex than has so far been recognized.

The Four Sources of De-Industrialization

Rowthorn (1994) defined de-industrialization as the decline in manufacturing employment that takes place when countries reach a certain level of income per capita. This section will establish that, in addition to this process—(henceforth called the *first source* of de-industrialization)—there are *three* further processes at work.

An Inverted-U Relationship Between Manufacturing Employment and Income Per Capita

The point of departure for this approach to de-industrialization is the inverted-U developed by Rowthorn (1994), who, having discussed and critiqued the above-mentioned hypotheses in detail (particularly the second and third ones), defined de-industrialization as the decline in manufacturing employment that takes place when countries reach a certain level of income per capita. In his cross-section regression for 1990 (built from a sample of 70 countries), this level is approximately US$12,000 in 1991 international dollars (see figure 3.2).

Although the analysis of our sample confirms Rowthorn's hypothesis, there are also grounds for arguing that the process of de-industrialization is a rather more complex phenomenon. De-industrialization, in fact, is not simply the result of a single process (the existence of a stable inverted-U relationship between manufacturing employment and income per capita), but a consequence of the interaction of four distinct phenomena.

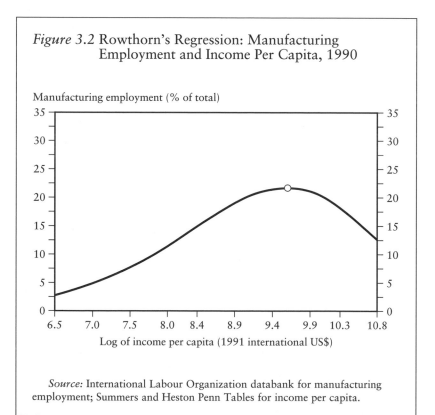

Figure 3.2 Rowthorn's Regression: Manufacturing Employment and Income Per Capita, 1990

Manufacturing employment (% of total)

Log of income per capita (1991 international US$)

Source: International Labour Organization databank for manufacturing employment; Summers and Heston Penn Tables for income per capita.

A Declining Relationship Between Income Per Capita and Manufacturing Employment

The first phenomenon to note is that Rowthorn's inverted-U relationship is not stable over time, but instead follows a continuous downward slope for middle- and high-income countries (see figure 3.3).

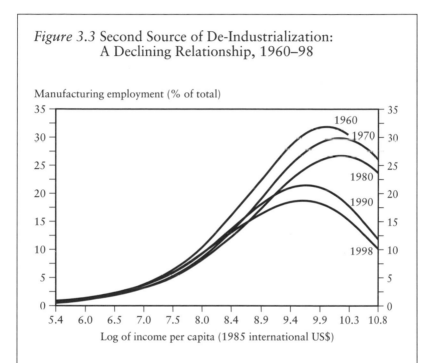

Figure 3.3 Second Source of De-Industrialization: A Declining Relationship, 1960–98

Manufacturing employment (% of total)

Log of income per capita (1985 international US$)

Source: International Labour Organization databank for manufacturing employment; Summers and Heston Penn Tables for income per capita.

Note: 1960—Cross-section regression for 1960, using a sample of 81 countries. 1970, 1980, 1990, and 1998—Cross-section regressions for the corresponding dates, using a sample of the *same* 105 countries. For the specification of the regressions, see annex A. The regression for 1998 corresponds to employment for that year, but income per capita is for 1992, the last year for which the Penn Tables offer information so far. Unfortunately, there were too few countries with reliable employment information for 1950 to construct a comparable regression. In the five regressions, all parameters are significant at the 1 percent level and the adjusted R^2 are between 57 percent and 72 percent (for point estimators and test statistics, see annex A). All regressions also pass the tests for homoscedasticity and for normality of residuals at the 5 percent level of significance.

This continuous decline over time in the relationship between manufacturing employment and income per capita is the second source of de-industrialization identified in this chapter. In essence, for middle- and high-income countries, *whether or not they had reached the turning point of the regression,* there was a declining level of manufacturing employment associated with each level of income per capita. Although the reasons for this steady decline (in particular, the big drop observed during the 1980s for industrial countries) still need to be fully understood, evidence so far indicates that it is the result of a combination of factors, including, at least in part, three of the hypotheses mentioned above: the statistical illusion hypothesis; (in an indirect way) the propagation of the new technological paradigm (microelectronics)[8]; and the increasingly significant process of breaking down the value chain being carried out by multiproduct transnational corporations, which is leading to the relocation to developing countries of the labor-intensive assembly-end part of the value chain. However, at least of equal (if not more) importance are the consequences of the new politics and economics of the 1980s—especially the sharp slowdown of economic growth that followed the implementation of those policies—and the massive institutional and financial transformations that characterized the world economy in this period.

Although a detailed analysis of the role that each of these factors has played in de-industrialization is outside the scope of this chapter, it is important at least to emphasize that the existing literature does not pay sufficient attention to the latter phenomenon: the role that the 1980s switch in the "policy regime" of most industrial countries (from post-WWII Keynesianism, broadly speaking, to the 1980s radical brand of monetarist-oriented deflationary policies) had on manufacturing employment. As is clear from figure 3.3, the combined effect that the latter had on manufacturing employment was devastating—in particular, the stagflation that followed the (barking-up-the-wrong-tree) sharp deflationary response to the second oil shock.

Monetarist-oriented deflationary policies became dominant after the failure of the Carter Administration's attempt to stimulate aggregate demand in the United States in 1977–78; as a result of these expansionary policies, the U.S. trade deficit reached the equivalent of one quarter of exports just at a time when the rest of the industrial countries were no longer willing to absorb "excess" dollars. The resulting weakness of the dollar, in tandem with rising inflation, set the stage for the Federal Reserve's radical monetarist era following the appointment of Paul Volker and his trebling of interest rates between 1979 and 1981. In turn, the election of Margaret Thatcher in 1979 consolidated this new radical monetarist era both in its neoliberal politics and in its deflationary economics; at around the same time, the "Chicago Boys" policies in Pinochet's

Chile signaled the (not very democratic) emergence of these policies in developing countries.

In the EU, for example, there was an immediate collapse of growth rates: In the United Kingdom, during Prime Minister Thatcher's first two years in office (1979–81), the growth rate of output fell from 3.7 percent to –2.2 percent (in fact, output declined by no less than 17 percent in just six quarters); in Germany, it dropped from 4.2 percent (1979) to –0.6 percent (1982); in France, from 3.2 percent (1979) to 0.8 percent (1983); and in Italy, from 6.0 percent (1979) to 0.3 percent (1983). This sharp slow-down had a major impact on unemployment—in the United Kingdom, it rose from 5.0 percent (1979) to 12.4 percent (1982); in Germany, from 3.2 percent (1979) to 8.0 percent (1983); and in France, from 5.9 percent (1979) to 10.2 percent (1985).

Manufacturing was particularly badly hit by these events. In the United Kingdom, for example, net manufacturing investment became highly negative in 1981 and 1982. The combination of these factors— massive reductions in private consumption (which fell from an annualized growth rate of 8.5 percent in the second quarter of 1979 to –3.7 percent in the same quarter of the following year), high interest rates, low levels of investment, and a sharp revaluation of the pound—caused manufacturing employment to fall by 20 percent in the first three years of Prime Minister Thatcher's Administration alone, and there was no significant recovery thereafter. Hence, there is little doubt that the remarkable decline in the relationship between income per capita and manufacturing employment in industrial countries during the 1980s (clearly evident in figure 3.3 above) had as much to do with "policy" as with other factors, such as the need for industrial restructuring, technological change, accounting issues, or the trend toward "financialization."[9]

A Decline in Income Per Capita Corresponding to the Turning Point of the Regression

The third source of de-industrialization to be identified concerns the huge drop in the *turning point* of the regressions that relate manufacturing employment to income per capita since 1980. As figure 3.4 shows, since the beginning of the 1980s there has been a dramatic reduction in the level of income per capita, from which the downturn in manufacturing employment began: from US$20,645 in 1980, to just US$9,805 in 1990 (and US$8,691 in 1998; all figures in 1985 international U.S. dollars).

This rapid lowering of the turning point of the regressions since 1980 is crucial to an understanding of one of the sources of the process that leads to de-industrialization. Until that date, *no country*—not even the United States, the country with the highest income per capita in the sample—had reached a level of income per capita anywhere near

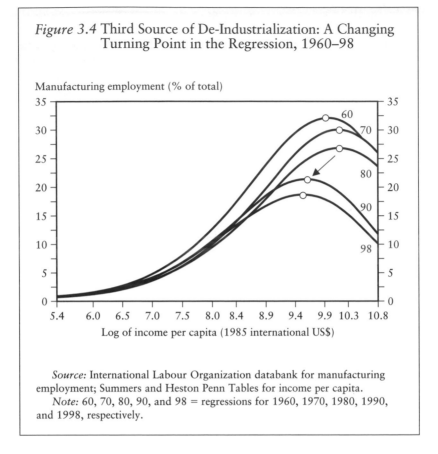

Figure 3.4 Third Source of De-Industrialization: A Changing
Turning Point in the Regression, 1960–98

Manufacturing employment (% of total)

Log of income per capita (1985 international US$)

Source: International Labour Organization databank for manufacturing
employment; Summers and Heston Penn Tables for income per capita.
    Note: 60, 70, 80, 90, and 98 = regressions for 1960, 1970, 1980, 1990,
and 1998, respectively.

the point where the curves begin to fall. In 1990, by contrast, there were
more than 30 countries whose income per capita was above that critical
point in the curve.[10]
    However, as is well known, the drop in manufacturing employment
in industrial countries began in the late 1960s—that is, well *before* any
industrial country was anywhere near the turning point in the curve.
This would suggest that the original impulse for de-industrialization was
not the fact that some countries had already reached the level at which
the curve begins to slope downward, but rather the remarkable fall in
time of the actual inverted-U relationship for middle- and high-income
countries (shown in figure 3.3). It would not be until the 1980s that the
de-industrialization phenomenon would include the additional element
of the downward slope of the curve as well (leading to an acceleration
of this process).

Working from a different perspective, this lowering of the turning point of the regressions had been predicted by Rowthorn and Wells (1987, pp. 329–32); according to them, because productivity catch-up is fastest in manufacturing, in developing countries de-industrialization was probably going to start at a lower level of income per capita than in early industrializers. Nevertheless, nobody could have predicted that the drop in the turning point of the regression could be of such a magnitude.

The Dutch Disease

Finally, in addition to the three sources of de-industrialization already mentioned, in several countries there is a fourth one: the so-called Dutch disease effect. Some countries, such as the Netherlands and a group of Latin American countries, registered a fall in their manufacturing employment that was clearly greater than would have been expected to result from the three sources of de-industrialization discussed above (see figure 3.5).

However, the following analysis will show that, rather than being simple cases of overshooting, the Dutch disease is associated with a specific *additional* degree of de-industrialization that is characteristic of some countries that have undergone at least one of three brands of transformations.

The origin of this "disease" lies in the fact that the relationship between manufacturing employment and income per capita tends to be different in countries that are following an industrialization agenda that seeks to generate a trade surplus in manufacturing than it is in those that are content just to aim at a trade deficit in manufacturing (such as countries rich in natural resources and thus able to generate a trade surplus in primary commodities that can finance their trade deficits in manufacturing). However, in reality, as will be shown below, what I will call here the "primary commodity effect" is a more general phenomenon that also applies to countries that generate a significant trade surplus in services, especially tourism and finance.

It is important to stress from the beginning that the first category of countries (the "manufacturing" category) includes some that are there out of *necessity* and others that are there because of their *growth policy*. That is, some countries are there because they have no option but to aim at a trade surplus in manufacturing in order to be able to cover their trade deficits in primary commodities and services; others are there because, even though they are able to generate a trade surplus in primary commodities or services, they are still trying to implement an industrialization agenda that aims to generate a trade surplus in manufacturing.

Following the Akaike regression-specification criterion, in this chapter the two types of countries ("manufacturing" and "primary commodity"

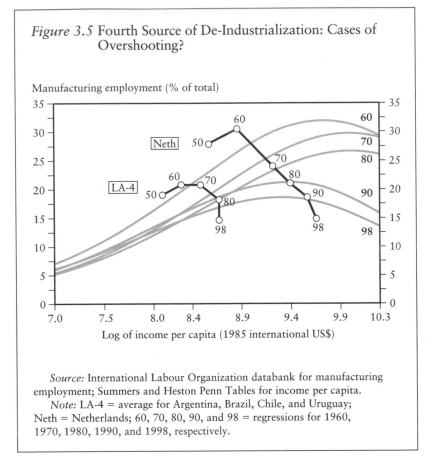

Figure 3.5 Fourth Source of De-Industrialization: Cases of Overshooting?

Manufacturing employment (% of total)

Log of income per capita (1985 international US$)

Source: International Labour Organization databank for manufacturing employment; Summers and Heston Penn Tables for income per capita.
  Note: LA-4 = average for Argentina, Brazil, Chile, and Uruguay; Neth = Netherlands; 60, 70, 80, 90, and 98 = regressions for 1960, 1970, 1980, 1990, and 1998, respectively.

countries) are differentiated by an intercept dummy in the above regressions. Countries are classified according to their position at the end of the period—and once classified, they stay in the same group in all regressions (to avoid circular-type arguments). Furthermore, as above, the cross-section regressions for 1970, 1980, 1990, and 1998 are based on the same sample of 105 countries (because of a lack of data, however, the regression for 1960 is based on a sample of only 81 countries, all of which are later included in the larger sample). The intercept dummy shows that the relationship between manufacturing employment and income per capita in the two groups of countries is located at different levels in all five regressions (1960, 1970, 1980, 1990, and 1998); this dummy is significant at the 1 percent level in all regressions.[11] Figure 3.6 shows this phenomenon for 1998.

Figure 3.6 Primary Commodity and Export Services Effects, 1998

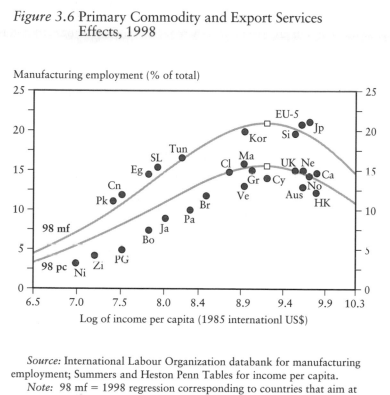

Manufacturing employment (% of total)

Source: International Labour Organization databank for manufacturing employment; Summers and Heston Penn Tables for income per capita.

Note: 98 mf = 1998 regression corresponding to countries that aim at generating a trade surplus in manufacturing; 98 pc = 1998 regression of countries that have a trade surplus in primary commodities (or services, such as tourism or finance). See annex B for the classification of countries in the sample. As mentioned above, the difference between the two types of regressions is an intercept dummy. Countries shown around the 98 mf regression are Cn = China; Eg = Arab Republic of Egypt; EU-5 = five continental countries of the European Union (Austria, Belgium, France, Germany, and Italy); Jp = Japan; Kor = Republic of Korea; Pk = Pakistan; SL = Sri Lanka; Tun = Tunisia; and Si = Singapore. Countries shown around the 98 pc regression are Aus = Australia; Bo = Botswana; Br = Brazil; Ca = Canada; Cl = Chile; Cy = Cyprus; Gr = Greece; HK = Hong Kong (China); Ja = Jamaica; Ma = Malta; Ne = Netherlands; Ni = Nigeria; No = Norway; Pa = Panama; PG = Papua New Guinea; UK = United Kingdom; Ve = República Bolivariana de Venezuela; and Zi = Zimbabwe.

Obviously, the main reasons for the different degrees of industrialization of these two groups of countries are their differences in resource
endowment and in growth policy; these factors end up being reflected in
their patterns of international trade and in their internal economic—and
employment—structures. However, as will be shown below, although
this primary commodity (or export services) effect is a necessary condition for developing Dutch disease, it is by no means a sufficient one.

Figure 3.7 shows a remarkable similarity in the decline of the relationship between manufacturing employment and income per capita in
both categories of countries between 1960 and 1998. One aspect of
these relationships must be emphasized: Although the primary commodity group of countries does tend to reach a lower level of industrialization
at any given point in time,[12] the primary commodity ("pc") effect does
not lead *per se* to a greater relative level of de-industrialization over
time. In fact, figure 3.7 illustrates that both categories of countries experience a similar drop in relative terms. Taking the highest point of the

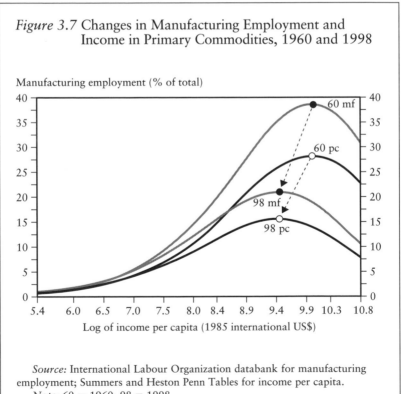

Figure 3.7 Changes in Manufacturing Employment and
Income in Primary Commodities, 1960 and 1998

Manufacturing employment (% of total)

Source: International Labour Organization databank for manufacturing
employment; Summers and Heston Penn Tables for income per capita.
  Note: 60 = 1960; 98 = 1998.

curves for each group of countries, it is noticeable that, in these four decades, both categories of countries lost about the same share of man-ufacturing employment—from 39 percent to 21 percent in manufactur-ing countries and from 29 percent to 16 percent in the others (that is, in the former, the 1998 inflection point of the regression is located at a share of manufacturing employment that is 45 percent below that of 1960, whereas, in the latter, the respective point is 46 percent below). In turn, from the point of view of the horizontal axis (income per capita), the turning points of both curves also fell to half their former levels: from about US$18,000 in 1960 to US$9,000 in 1998 (both figures in 1985 international dollars).[13]

After this (of necessity, lengthy) introduction on the differences between these two types of countries, it is now possible to explain my concept of Dutch disease properly. From the point of view of the methodology devel-oped here, what is most interesting about this "disease" is that, in the light of our analysis, it acquires a quite different connotation from the one that it has hitherto been associated with. This allows us to develop a new, more specific way of looking at it. There is a group of countries, both industrialized and developing (although the latter include only countries that have reached at least a middle-income level), that exhibits a specific *additional* de-industrialization phenomenon (additional to the three de-industrialization forces already discussed, that is). This phe-nomenon is associated either with a sudden surge in exports of primary commodities or services (particularly in countries that had not previ-ously developed these sectors) or, as in the Southern Cone of Latin America, with a sudden shift in economic policy. The Netherlands rightly gives its name to this phenomenon (see figure 3.8).[14]

From this perspective, the Dutch disease is a process in which the dis-covery of a natural resource (natural gas, in the case of the Netherlands) causes a country to switch from one group of reference to the other, that is, from the group of countries that aim at generating a trade surplus in manufacturing (type-mf regressions) to the group that is able to gener-ate a trade surplus in primary commodities (type-pc regressions). When this occurs, as figure 3.8a shows for the case of the Netherlands, the country experiencing this disease moves along *two* different paths of de-industrialization: The first, which is common to the countries in its original group (from 60 mf to 98 mf), consists of the three processes discussed above; and the second, which is *in addition to* this "common" path, corresponds to a second surge of de-industrialization resulting from the change in the reference group (from 98 mf to 98 pc). In this context, the Dutch disease should *only* be regarded as the "excess" degree of de-industrialization associated with the latter movement; that is, only with the difference between employment in manufacturing falling to 98 mf and falling to 98 pc. In the case of the Netherlands, then, it is the

Figure 3.8 a. The Netherlands: Unraveling the Dutch Disease,
            1960–98
         b. The United Kingdom: Catching the Dutch
            Disease, 1960–98
         c. The Netherlands and Five Countries of the EU,
            1960–98
         d. The Netherlands and Four Traditional Primary
            Commodity Exporters, 1960–98

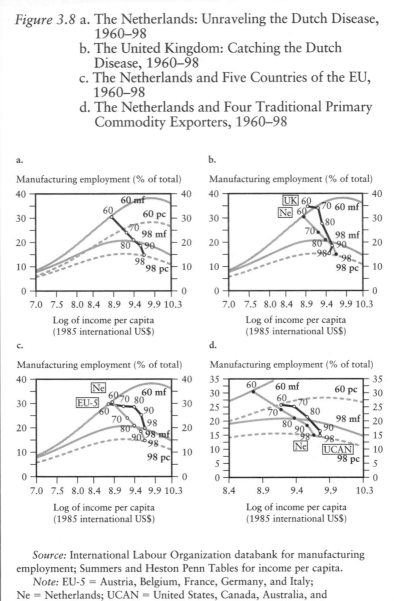

Source: International Labour Organization databank for manufacturing
employment; Summers and Heston Penn Tables for income per capita.
   Note: EU-5 = Austria, Belgium, France, Germany, and Italy;
Ne = Netherlands; UCAN = United States, Canada, Australia, and
New Zealand; and UK = United Kingdom; 60, 70, 80, 90, and
98 = regressions for 1960, 1970, 1980, 1990, and 1998, respectively.

difference between having fallen from 30.5 percent in 1960 to 19.8 percent in 1998 (in this hypothetical non-Dutch disease scenario, this is the predicted level of manufacturing employment in the mf regression, given the actual 1998 level of income per capita) and from 30.5 percent to 14.8 percent, between those same years (actual Dutch disease situation).[15]

When thus perceived, it becomes clear that the Dutch disease is not a phenomenon limited to the Netherlands, because it has also occurred in other industrial countries, such as the United Kingdom, where there were both a significant discovery of natural resources (North Sea oil) and an increase in the trade surplus for financial-services exports (see figure 3.8b). In the United Kingdom, the improvement in the trade balance in oil between 1979 and 1984 (from a deficit of £2.2 billion to a surplus of £6.6 billion)[16] in fact mirrored the decline in the trade surplus in manufactures (from a surplus of £3.6 billion to a deficit of £6.3 billion between those same years). It is hardly surprising that the United Kingdom's economic and employment structure switched from one category of countries (and from one industrialization agenda) to the other.

A comparison between the degree of de-industrialization of the Netherlands and other continental European Union countries can also help to explain the special nature of Dutch disease. Figure 3.8c shows how, while the share of manufacturing employment in the five European Union countries fell according to the trade-surplus-in-manufacturing regression (from 60 mf to 98 mf), the Netherlands suffered an *added* fall (from 98 mf to 98 pc, which is equivalent to an extra five percentage points, in this case).

As is clear from the graph, the major portion of the fall in manufacturing employment in the Netherlands took place in the first half of this period (following the discovery of natural gas), whereas in the other five European Union countries, manufacturing employment began to fall only after 1980. As mentioned above, the latter drop was greatly influenced by a shift in the political and economic policy regime of these countries. The rapid decline in domestic demand (which resulted from high interest rates, the shift in income distribution toward capital, the breaking up of the trade unions' power, and so forth) meant that productivity growth had much stronger negative effects on manufacturing employment than it would have had otherwise. In the case of Germany, for example, although its machine-tool industry did not suffer significantly (mainly because the relevant markets were characterized by a combination of high income and low price elasticity of demand), other segments of its manufacturing sector (such as steel) were badly hit by the effects of having to cope with rapid technological change in the context of demand-constrained domestic markets.[17]

At the same time, figures 3.8b and 3.8c indicate the remarkable difference between the United Kingdom and the "EU-5" (Austria, Belgium, France, Germany, and Italy) during the 1980s: In the former, the fall in the share of manufacturing employment during this decade amounted to 9.2 percentage points; in the latter, it totaled 3.3 points. In the United Kingdom, the more unrelenting deflationary policies not only affected manufacturing more intensely (than in the EU-5), but also the discovery of oil and the strengthening of the financial-services export sector meant that manufacturing in the United Kingdom had the added problem that export markets were being lost (mainly, but certainly not exclusively) as a result of the revaluation of the pound sterling. As mentioned above, between 1979 (the year that Prime Minister Thatcher was first elected and when oil exports began) and 1984, the United Kingdom's trade balance in manufactures switched from a surplus of £3.6 billion to a deficit of £6.3 billion. In the EU-5 (and, in particular, in Germany), on the other hand, success in export markets was crucial in mitigating their de-industrialization.

A further comparison between the Netherlands and four other industrial countries (in this case, countries that have been major primary commodity exporters *throughout* the period: United States, Canada, Australia, and New Zealand [UCAN]) will also help to illustrate the specific nature of the Dutch disease (as understood in this chapter). Figure 3.8d shows that, although these four UCAN countries also ended up in the "primary commodity" relationship in 1998 (98 pc), they did *not* suffer from the Dutch disease (as the Netherlands did) because they had also started out in that type of relationship back in 1960 (60 pc). Consequently, although both the EU-5 and the UCAN countries did experience a large (and similar, in relative terms) drop in the share of total employment accounted for by manufacturing employment during this period (9.2 and 10.5 percentage points, respectively), they each began and ended this four-decade period in the same reference group that they had started in; the Netherlands, on the other hand, switched from one to the other as a result of the Dutch disease (with an overall manufacturing employment loss of no less than 15.1 percentage points).

Moreover, as already indicated, the phenomenon of the Dutch disease was not limited to those industrial countries that discovered natural resources, but also occurred in countries that developed important service export sectors, such as tourism (for example, Cyprus, Greece, and Malta) and financial services (for example, Hong Kong [China], Luxembourg, and Switzerland) (see figure 3.9).

The countries shown in figures 3.9a and 3.9b also began this period in the manufacturing regression (or to the left of it, in the cases of Hong Kong [China] and Malta), but they all ended it in (or very close to) the 98 pc regression (rather than in their corresponding 98 mf regression).

Figure 3.9 a. Greece, Cyprus, and Malta: A Tourism Dutch
          Disease?
       b. Luxembourg, Hong Kong (China), and
          Switzerland: A Financial Dutch Disease?

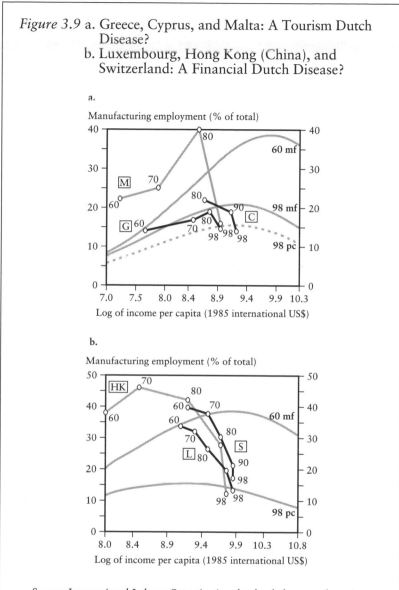

Source: International Labour Organization databank for manufacturing
employment; Summers and Heston Penn Tables for income per capita.
   Note: C = Cyprus (for the sake of clarity, the trajectory of Cyprus is only
shown from 1980; at that point in time, this country had a level of manufacturing
employment corresponding to 80 mf regression); G = Greece; HK = Hong
Kong (China); L = Luxembourg; M = Malta; and S = Switzerland; 60, 70, 80,
90, and 98 = regressions for 1960, 1970, 1980, 1990, and 1998, respectively.

Finally, this disease also spread to some Latin American countries. But the key issue in this case is that it was not brought about by the discovery of natural resources or the development of a service export sector, but instead occurred mainly because of a drastic switch in their economic policy regime. Basically, it was the result of a drastic process of trade and financial liberalization in the context of a radical process of institutional change, leading to a sharp reversal of their previous (State-led) import-substituting industrialization (ISI) agenda. Despite the well-known abundance of natural resources in the countries of the region, ISI had brought many of them to a level of industrialization characteristic of the mf group (see figure 3.10). This shift in policy regime, although in many ways similar to that of most industrial countries during the 1980s, hit their level of manufacturing employment more drastically because it brought their process of industrialization down from their policy-induced mf heights to a Ricardian resource-rich pc level. Brazil and the three Southern Cone countries (Argentina, Chile, and Uruguay) were the Latin American countries that experienced the highest levels of de-industrialization following their economic reforms, while also being among the countries of the region that had previously industrialized the most and that had implemented such reforms most rapidly and drastically (see figure 3.10).

These four Latin American countries began this period (as did the Netherlands) with a level of manufacturing employment typical of countries aiming at a trade surplus in manufacturing (60 mf), although obviously for different reasons. For the Netherlands, it was a matter of the most likely Ricardian position, given its resource endowments and level of income per capita. For the four Latin American countries, in contrast, it was the deliberate result of a structuralist ISI agenda. They had shifted to this development model in the hope of improving their chances of catching up with industrial countries by promoting specialization in products with higher productivity growth potentials that were more likely to move them up the technology ladder.[18] Moreover, both the Netherlands and these four Latin American countries reached 1998 with a level of manufacturing employment corresponding to the *other* category of countries (98 pc). Again, the reasons vary. In the case of the Netherlands, it was because of the effects of the discovery of natural resources in a "mature" manufacturing economy, whereas in the four Latin American countries, it was generated by the previously mentioned sharp reversal of ISI policies. The end of industrial and trade policies, together with changes in relative prices, in real exchange rates, in the institutional framework of the economies, in the structure of property rights, and in market incentives in general led them back to their "natural" Ricardian position—that is, one more in accordance with their traditional resource endowment.[19]

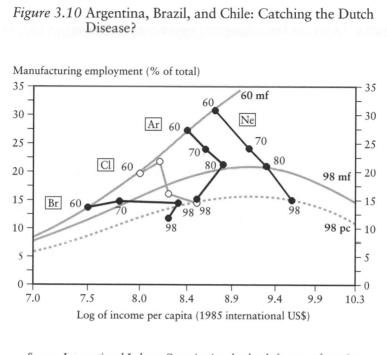

Figure 3.10 Argentina, Brazil, and Chile: Catching the Dutch Disease?

Source: International Labour Organization databank for manufacturing employment; Summers and Heston Penn Tables for income per capita.

Note: Ar = Argentina; Br = Brazil; Cl = Chile; and Ne = the Netherlands. For the sake of clarity, Uruguay is not included (its trajectory is similar to that of the other three Latin American counties, located between those of Argentina and Chile). The numbers 60, 70, 80, 90, and 98 = regressions for 1960, 1970, 1980, 1990, and 1998, respectively.

From this point of view, the major difference between Latin America and continental Europe is that, in the latter, the crucial transformations took place in industrial relations, the welfare State, public corporations, and so forth, whereas in Latin America, because these countries were hit by the new policies at a much lower level of income per capita, these new policies also obstructed their transition toward a more mature—that is, self-sustaining (in a Kaldorian sense)—form of industrialization.[20]

In terms of the future prospects for manufacturing employment, the situation in the four Latin American countries that have already experienced the Dutch disease seems to be fairly straightforward, as figure 3.10 shows. With the drastic switch in economic policies, these four countries have not only returned to their expected Ricardian position, but their middle-income level in per capita terms has already carried them almost as far as the *leveled-out* part of the curve (Argentina, Chile, and Uruguay, in particular). Furthermore, it is also important to remember that this curve has been continuously falling since the 1960s, and there is no reason to suspect that this downward tendency has run its full course: The regressions and their turning points could easily keep getting lower. Therefore (and with the necessary strong caveats regarding the use of this type of cross-section regression for purposes of prediction, in particular due to the "homogeneity conditions" it required),[21] in the absence of any new and imaginative industrial and trade policies (that would rescue these countries' pro-industrialization agenda by adapting it to their new export-led strategy), the framework developed here would suggest that, at their absolute best, these countries will be able to maintain their present levels of manufacturing employment. More likely, the decline will continue, even if their income per capita increases rapidly—a prospect that at the time of writing seems (at best) rather unlikely, at least in the immediate future.[22]

In sum, in this chapter the Dutch disease is perceived to be not just a simple "overshooting" of de-industrialization, but a specific type of excess, which is associated with the movement from a process of de-industrialization typical of countries following an industrialization agenda aiming at generating a trade surplus in manufacturing to a process of de-industrialization typical of countries able (and content) to generate a trade surplus in primary commodities or services. In general, the shift between the two types of de-industrialization processes has taken place for one of three different reasons: (1) the discovery of natural resources (for example, the Netherlands); (2) the development of service export activities, particularly tourism and finance (for example, Greece in the former, and Hong Kong [China] in the latter); and, finally, (3) changes in economic policy, which brought countries that were above their natural Ricardian position back to their traditional (static) comparative advantage place (for example, Argentina, Brazil, and Chile).

Therefore, in analytical terms, (policy-induced) Dutch disease in Latin America should be understood more as a case of "downward" de-industrialization than in the other Dutch disease countries discussed above, where it was the result of the emergence of other productive activities. In turn, all Dutch disease cases should be distinguished from more "normal" processes of de-industrialization, such as those seen in many industrial countries after they have reached the level of income per capita associated with the inflection point of the manufacturing employment-income per capita relationship. The latter should be understood more as processes of "upward" de-industrialization—that is, mature economies switching employment from manufacturing into other activities (mainly services) in their normal process of economic development.

Finally, one should also distinguish all the above types of de-industrialization from that found in the late 1980s and 1990s in many Sub-Saharan African economies, including South Africa, and in some countries of the former Soviet Union and Eastern Europe, which have been associated with a fall in income per capita. Because all these countries had levels of income per capita below the turning point of the curve, a decline in income per capita was associated with a reduction in manufacturing employment along the *same* relationship among these two variables: a case of "reverse" de-industrialization.

Thus, in all, we have at least four different types of de-industrialization: upward de-industrialization (continental Europe, Japan, and traditional primary commodity exporting industrial countries); normal Dutch disease (the Netherlands and countries with newly developed service export activities); downward Dutch disease (Latin America); and reverse de-industrialization (Sub-Saharan Africa and countries of the former Soviet Union).

Trying to Swim Against the De-Industrialization Tide

Finland, Sweden, and some Southeast Asian countries rich in natural resources are cases that, despite having abundant natural resources, did not follow the de-industrialization tide.

Finland and the Diversity of the Nordic Countries

Figure 3.11a shows the diversity of the process of de-industrialization in three Nordic countries. The most interesting case is that of Finland, which follows an industrialization path that runs opposite to the path associated with the Dutch disease. This country is rich in natural resources, and in 1960 held a position that corresponded to that comparative advantage, given its income per capita (that is, manufacturing employment accounted for 21.6 percent of total employment, or 7.3 percentage points below what would have been its expected position had it then already been in the "manufacturing-trade-surplus" category of countries). However, through a greater processing of the primary commodities that it exports and the development of sectors such as the mobile phone industry (Nokia being the paradigmatic case), it managed to move in the opposite direction to the path associated with the Dutch disease—starting in 1960 in the 60 pc regression but finishing in 1998 on the 98 mf regression (with a 20 percent share of manufacturing

Figure 3.11 a. Nordic Countries: Three Different Industrialization Paths, 1960–98
b. Finland and Chile: An Anti-Dutch Disease and
a Dutch Disease Industrialization?
c. Finland: Changing Vertical Integration in
Timber-Based Exports, 1963–2000

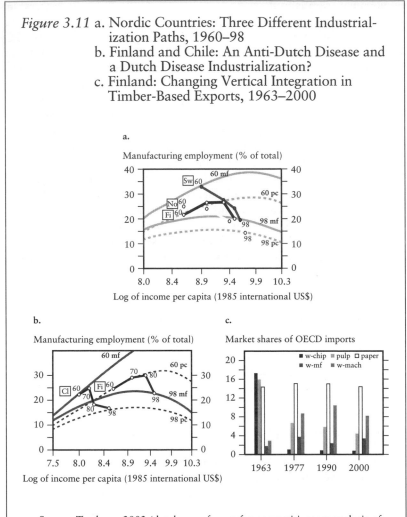

Source: Tradecan 2002 (database software for competitiveness analysis of
nations; created by ECLAC and the World Bank). Regarding 3.11c, see also
Palma (1996).
Note: Cl = Chile; Fi = Finland; No = Norway; Sw = Sweden;
w-chip = wood-chips; w-mach = machinery for the production of wood-
chips, pulp, and paper; w-mf = wood manufactures; 60, 70, 80, 90, and
98 = regressions for 1960, 1970, 1980, 1990, and 1998, respectively.

employment, well above the 15.4 percent conditional expectation had it continued in the pc group of countries).

Norway is another interesting case. In 1960 it was situated between the 60 mf and 60 pc regressions. In fact, its position in 1960 corresponded exactly to its conditional expectation in the original "average" 1960 regression—that is, the one that did not differentiate between "primary commodity" and "manufacturing" countries (see figure 3.3). The main reason for this was that, at the time, Norway had a mixed composition of exports, combining manufactures with primary commodities and services (the latter coming from its strong maritime fleet). However, the discovery of oil and further development of primary commodity exports (such as those produced by its flourishing fishery industry) brought Norway fully into the primary commodity exporting family of countries (98 pc). In this context, although Norway has not suffered from full-fledged Dutch disease, it does present what could be called a "mild" case. From the beginning of this period, however, Sweden, despite its abundance of primary commodities, followed a systematic industrialization path corresponding to the "manufacturing-track" group of countries (such as the EU-5), moving from 60 mf to 98 mf.

Returning to the case of Finland, when this country is compared with Chile, for example, the contrasting paths of the "anti-Dutch disease" and Dutch disease industrialization processes become even more clear (see figure 3.11b). Whereas Finland was able to redirect the course of its industrialization toward a path characteristic of a country aiming at a trade surplus in manufacturing (going from 60 pc to 98 mf), Chile did the opposite by moving from 60 mf to 98 pc. After Chile had spent many years following strong ISI-type industrial and commercial policies, in the 1970s it abandoned its pro-industrialization agenda and embarked on a drastic process of trade and financial liberalization and economic reform. This led it back to its more natural Ricardian position. Despite Chile's rapid economic growth for about half of the period that had elapsed since the beginning of its economic reforms, the comparative advantage associated with this position not only resulted in the reduction of the relative size of this country's manufacturing sector in general, but even ended up drastically reducing the overall share of manufacturing value added in its main primary commodity export (copper). This took the form of a steep drop in the share of refined copper and an increase in the share of exports accounted for by the more primitive copper "concentrates." In fact, the share of total exports of copper represented by copper concentrates increased from 3 percent at the time of trade and financial liberalization in the early 1970s, to 17 percent in 1990 and to 40 percent in 2002.[23] Figure 3.11c shows how Finland instead moved in the opposite direction—one characterized by an increasingly higher degree of processing of the primary commodities it exported—thus enabling the country to manage this anti-Dutch disease form of industrialization.

Finland, Sweden, and, as we will see below, some Southeast Asian countries rich in natural resources therefore prove that from the perspective of manufacturing employment, there is no such thing as the so-called curse of natural resources.[24] It seems blatantly clear that countries that export primary commodities (and services) have sufficient degrees of freedom to allow them to end up having a manufacturing sector that, in terms of relative size, is more typical of countries that aim at a trade surplus in manufacturing.[25] However, as the Latin American experience in particular shows, it would seem that as globalization progresses, there are fewer and fewer countries wishing to take advantage of such degrees of freedom.[26]

East Asian and Southeast Asian Industrialization

Starting with the second-tier newly industrialized economies (NIE-2s) of Southeast Asia, the most important feature common to all of them is that they are following a "mixed" path toward industrialization; this mixed path keeps them near or above the original "average" regressions (see figure 3.3 above); that is, those that did not differentiate between primary and nonprimary commodity countries. Figure 3.12 shows that Malaysia is another country that clearly swam against the de-industrializing tide by sharply raising the proportion of employment located in its manufacturing sector. Despite being a country rich in natural resources, it moved from a position corresponding to the average regression to one in the manufacturing regression. In fact, by 1998, its level of manufacturing employment was even higher than that of the conditional expectation in 98 mf for a country with its level of income per capita. As for the other NIE-2s, they clearly follow the intermediate or average course (between 98 mf and 98 pc) characterized by the original regressions (figure 3.3). In other words, despite being rich in natural resources, these three countries (Indonesia, the Philippines, and Thailand) had a level of manufacturing employment as of 1998 that was higher than would be indicated by a traditional Ricardian integration into the international division of labor. However, unlike Malaysia (and Finland and prereform Latin America), the industrialization agenda of these countries does not seem to aim at a level of manufacturing employment similar to that of the "manufacturing" ones, but only at an intermediate level (somewhere in between the two types of countries).

In contrast, NIE-1s did industrialize (and very successfully) in a way that corresponds to their condition of being "poor" in primary commodities; the exception, of course, as shown in figure 3.9b above, is Hong Kong (China), which, having developed a powerful financial service economy

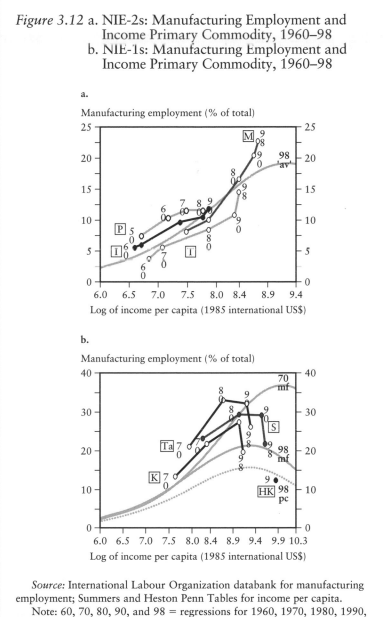

Figure 3.12 a. NIE-2s: Manufacturing Employment and
Income Primary Commodity, 1960–98
b. NIE-1s: Manufacturing Employment and
Income Primary Commodity, 1960–98

Source: International Labour Organization databank for manufacturing
employment; Summers and Heston Penn Tables for income per capita.
Note: 60, 70, 80, 90, and 98 = regressions for 1960, 1970, 1980, 1990,
and 1998, respectively; 98 av = cross-section regression for 1998 for the whole
sample; HK = Hong Kong (China); I = Indonesia; K = Republic of Korea;
M = Malaysia; NIE-1s = first-tier NIEs; NIE-2s = second-tier NIEs;
P = Philippines; S = Singapore; Ta = Taiwan (China); and T = Thailand.

in the 1980s, suffered probably the worst case of Dutch disease of them all; its manufacturing employment collapsed, from 42.1 percent of total employment in 1980 to just 12.2 percent in 1998, which led it to end up the period at a point even lower than the 98 pc regression.

An important issue that emerges from figure 3.12b is that the characteristic component of the industrialization of the Republic of Korea, Singapore, and Taiwan (China) is not their *level* of industrialization as measured by their manufacturing employment at the end of the period (although in 1998 the latter did, in fact, have approximately 5 percentage points of manufacturing employment above the value suggested by regression 98 mf for a country with its level of income per capita). What is unique about their process of industrialization is the extremely steep rise in income per capita associated with that industrialization process. In other words, the real "miracle" in these countries is not found in their levels of industrialization but in the income multipliers and export linkages they were able to develop in parallel with this process. This contrasts sharply with developments in the maquila-based process seen in Central America and Mexico.

Mexico and Central America's Maquila (or Labor-Intensive Assembly Activities) Industrialization Process

One noticeable characteristic of Latin American industrialization in the post-WWII period was the homogeneity of the countries' industrialization agendas during the period of ISI (or State-led industrialization). Now, however, one of its most conspicuous characteristics (after these countries' economic reforms) is the diversity of the countries' respective agendas. As discussed above, their initial degree of similarity was associated with the fact that most of them were clearly more industrialized than countries rich in primary commodities would be expected to be. However, what were relatively similar economic reforms and processes of trade and financial liberalization in fact led to a marked diversity in the industrialization agenda of the region. In general, three distinct patterns of industrialization were developed: (1) the Dutch disease path followed by Brazil and the Southern Cone countries, with higher incomes per capita and more advanced industrialization processes (Argentina, Chile, and Uruguay), as illustrated in figure 3.10 above; (2) the route taken by Central America and Mexico (see figure 3.13); and (3) the pattern exhibited by the Andean countries, which displayed little variation with respect to their earlier patterns, thus giving the impression that, as of 1998, they had still not decided which path to take (see figure 3.14).

As can be seen in figure 3.13, Central America and Mexico present a very different picture than Brazil and the Southern Cone countries do in terms of manufacturing employment, and a remarkably different

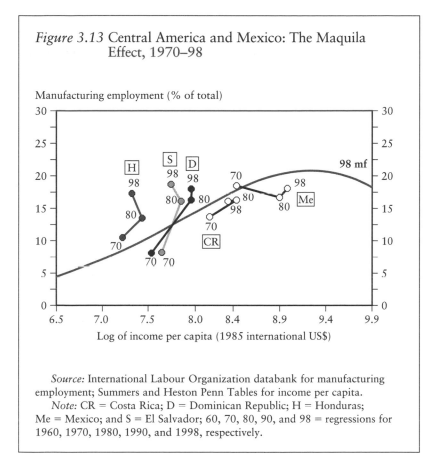

Figure 3.13 Central America and Mexico: The Maquila Effect, 1970–98

Source: International Labour Organization databank for manufacturing employment; Summers and Heston Penn Tables for income per capita.

Note: CR = Costa Rica; D = Dominican Republic; H = Honduras; Me = Mexico; and S = El Salvador; 60, 70, 80, 90, and 98 = regressions for 1960, 1970, 1980, 1990, and 1998, respectively.

one from that of East Asian countries in terms of the income multipliers and export linkages associated with their export-led industrialization processes.

No other country in our sample shows such steep growth in manufacturing employment as do the Dominican Republic, El Salvador, and Honduras; in turn, no other country shows such poor manufacturing export income multipliers. In these countries, maquila industrialization for exports increased manufacturing employment very dramatically, but this is in no way associated with the same income growth as in East and Southeast Asia. In fact, particularly in El Salvador and Honduras, income per capita hardly grew at all during these three decades![27]

At the same time, figure 3.13 shows the contrasting patterns of growth in Mexico between the (ISI) 1970s, on the one hand, and the export-led

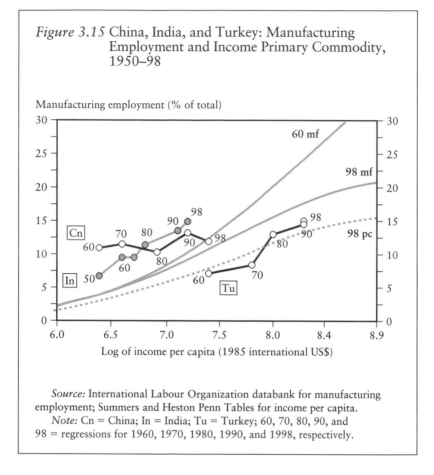

Figure 3.15 China, India, and Turkey: Manufacturing
Employment and Income Primary Commodity,
1950–98

Manufacturing employment (% of total)

Log of income per capita (1985 international US$)

Source: International Labour Organization databank for manufacturing
employment; Summers and Heston Penn Tables for income per capita.
Note: Cn = China; In = India; Tu = Turkey; 60, 70, 80, 90, and
98 = regressions for 1960, 1970, 1980, 1990, and 1998, respectively.

industrialization has been associated with a particularly rapid increase in
income per capita; (2) in the case of India, its industrialization has been
characterized by an especially high level of manufacturing employment[33]; and (3) in the case of Turkey, its industrialization process has
succeeded only in raising this country above the primary commodity
track, despite the fact that it has provided a large volume of manufactures for exports.

De-Industrialization—Does It Matter?

One of the consequences of the process of de-industrialization has
been to reopen one of the age-old debates in economics: Is a unit value

added in manufacturing equal to one in primary commodities or services? In particular, is this so from the point of view of the level and sustainability of long-term growth? This debate has re-emerged because, even though it is a well-known fact that, over the long-term course of economic development, the structure of employment changes substantially, relative changes in scale and speed occurring since the 1960s in most industrial countries and in many middle- and high-income developing countries constitute a phenomenon without precedent.

Although a detailed discussion of this issue is beyond the scope of this chapter, from the point of view of this debate one can basically classify growth theories into three basic camps. However, in order to do this it is first necessary to introduce a distinction between two concepts: "activity" and "sector." Examples of the former are research and development (R&D) and education; examples of the latter are manufacturing and agriculture. Taking this distinction into account, the three "growth camps" are (1) those (mainly traditional neoclassical models) that treat economic growth as a process that is both "activity indifferent" and "sector indifferent"; (2) those (mainly new growth models) that instead postulate that growth is "activity specific" but "sector indifferent"; and, finally, (3) those (mainly post-Keynesian and Latin American structuralist theories) that argue that economic growth is "activity neutral" but "sector specific."

In the first camp (growth as activity and sector indifferent), one finds the Solow-type growth models (both the traditional ones, including the Krugman-type critique of the Korean model, and the later "augmented" models) and the branch of endogenous growth theories that associates growth with increasing returns that are activity indifferent. This would include, for example, early "AK" models (in which production is defined as a function of technology [A] and capital [K], although this would depend on how one interprets them), as well as more recent endogenous growth models in which changes in the rate of growth are the result of the cumulative effect of market imperfections arising in the process of technical change. However, these imperfections, and the associated increasing returns, are somehow seen as stemming directly from within the production function (rather than being based—as is characteristic of the new growth theories classified here as belonging in the second camp—on any specified mechanism, such as the use of R&D or the production of human capital).[34]

In the second camp (growth as an activity-specific but sector-indifferent phenomenon in new endogenous growth models), one finds, in particular, the now classic examples of Romer (1990) and the neo-Schumpeterian version of Aghion and Howitt (1998). In these models, as well as in some of the later endogenous growth models, increasing returns, though generated by research-intensive activities, are explicitly not associated with the size, depth, or strength of the manufacturing sector as such, or with the process of capital accumulation within the manufacturing sector; nor do they allow for specific effects from the manufacturing sector on R&D activities.

Essentially, growth models in this second camp are similar to the general new growth-theory approach of the first camp—namely, they model growth as a function of market imperfections that somehow create increasing returns in the process of technical change. However, the crucial difference between them and the more general models of the first camp is simply that they explicitly attribute the increasing returns to R&D, whereas more general models do not address this issue. This is why the Romer et al. models are classified here as activity specific (for example, R&D specific, human capital specific, and so forth); however, these models are explicitly non-sector specific, because they do not allow for any way in which capital accumulation in the manufacturing sector might have a feedback effect on R&D (other than via exchange between the two, but not via a Kaldorian-style argument of capital accumulation embedding or embodying technical change).

Thus, Aghion and Howitt, for example, accommodated (physical) capital accumulation by arguing that it is "complementary" to innovation (that is, knowledge production) through its effect on the profitability of research. They admitted, however, that "there are many reasons for thinking that policies that favor capital accumulation will generally also stimulate innovation and raise the long-run growth rate," adding in a footnote that "[a]nother reason, *which does not however fit easily into the present framework*, is that capital goods embody technologies" (1998, p. 102; emphasis added). Although the effect of research on profitability is a very particular concept that they develop, the quote clearly indicates that "embodiment" à la Kaldor, Thirlwall, and other (mainly post-Keynesian) models of the third camp cannot be accommodated in their framework. They are, therefore, different from both the first and third camps because, while paying attention to R&D (as somehow being the main source of growth), they do not link it specifically with manufacturing.

In the third camp (activity-neutral but sector-specific growth theories), the approaches to economic growth found in Kalecki, Hirschman, Kaldor, Thirlwall, Pasinetti, Prebisch, and (arguably) Schumpeter stand out.[35] In these sector-specific growth theories—which continue a long tradition that goes all the way back to Smith and Hume[36]—there are specific capital accumulation effects on growth stemming from the manufacturing sector. In these models, the pattern of growth, increasing returns, and the whole dynamics of economic growth are crucially dependent on the economic activities being developed (that is, on the structure of output). The crucial difference between this camp and the previous two (but, in particular, between it and the first) is that in its more classical theories, issues such as the capacity to generate and diffuse technological change, productivity growth potentials, ability to move up the technology ladder, externalities, synergies, balance of payments sustainability, gains from trade, and, in the case of developing countries, ultimately their capacity for catching up were directly linked to the size, strength, and depth of the manufacturing sector. In the more recent theories of this economic growth camp, increasing returns, "indivisibilities," complementary capital, public goods, property rights, entrepreneurial capacity, transaction costs, and the structure of incentives are also (directly or indirectly, explicitly or implicitly) related to the structure of output.

Therefore, from the point of view of the possible growth effect of de-industrialization, the first growth camp does not look at de-industrialization as a particularly relevant growth issue, other than in relation to the question of whether other sectors of the economy would be able to absorb the labor force that is displaced from manufacturing. Furthermore, for these growth theories, even if the discovery of natural gas did produce some structural changes in the Dutch economy, to label these transformations a "disease" must be seen as, at the least, a misleading dramatization!

From the point of view of the second camp, de-industrialization in *mature* economies may or may not have a specific impact on growth; it would all depend on the specific form that this de-industrialization takes. For example, it could actually result in a *stimulus* for growth if the dynamic of the "upward" de-industrialization is characterized by the reallocation of resources within manufacturing into more R&D-intensive products. However, in the case of de-industrialization in middle-income countries, it is difficult to imagine how this approach to growth can view "premature" (or "downward") de-industrialization—particularly when it includes a reversion in the level of processing of primary commodities for export, as in some Latin American countries—could in any way be good for long-term growth.

Finally, it goes without saying that in the third approach to economic growth both de-industrialization—especially if it has the additional component related to the Dutch disease—*and* the present difficulties involved in generating and implementing new and imaginative "palliative" trade and industrial policies (given the current international ideological and institutional climates) are unambiguously major issues for growth in industrial and developing countries alike. For example, based on this approach, one interpretation of the industrial countries' remarkable slowdown in productivity growth since the mid-1970s would be that it could be precisely the result of "wrong" policies (particularly in the 1980s) and "wrong" structural change (for example, "financialization") that have over-intensified the otherwise natural processes of de-industrialization. Another obvious example would be the likely damaging long-term growth effects for developing countries of premature de-industrialization (such as in Brazil and in the Southern Cone of Latin America)—not just in terms of the speed of their economic growth but also (crucially) in relation to its sustainability.

Conclusions

If one makes a distinction between "relative" and "absolute" de-industrialization, it should be noted that this chapter deals systematically only with the former—that is, the analysis has concentrated on the study of the shrinkage of the manufacturing sector (in terms of employment), relative to the rest of the economy, in the context of a process of structural change brought about either by endogenous forces (for example, a movement toward service industries in mature economies) or by exogenous ones (for example, changes in economic policy in middle-income countries and the discovery of natural resources). For reasons of space, it has not been possible to properly analyze recent experiences of "absolute" de-industrialization—that is, the decline of the manufacturing sector within the context of a collapse in national income, such as the one that took place in the former Soviet republics and in parts of Sub-Saharan Africa.[37]

The data and analysis presented here have provided significant confirmation of the inverted-U type of trajectory of manufacturing employment with respect to income per capita. However, it has also been shown that this relationship has causes that are far more complex than has thus far been recognized. First, the relationship between these two variables is not stable over time. Moreover, there is convincing evidence that the original impulse for de-industrialization was not the fact that some countries had already reached the level at which the curve begins to slope downward, but was instead closely related to a continuous fall over time of the actual inverted-U relationship for middle- and high-income countries. Furthermore, the radical monetarism of the 1980s exerted strong downward pressure on the relationship between manufacturing employment and income per capita in industrial economies.[38]

Second, the regressions presented above have also identified a huge drop in the turning point of the regressions that relate manufacturing employment to income per capita since the 1980s. Since the beginning of that decade, there has been a dramatic reduction in the level of income per capita from which the downturn in manufacturing employment begins: from US$21,000 in 1980 to less than US$10,000 in 1990 (both measured in 1985 international U.S. dollars). This rapid lowering of the turning point of the regressions since 1980 is crucial to an understanding of the evolving nature of de-industrialization: Whereas in the 1980s no country—not even the United States, the country with the highest income per capita in the sample—had reached a level of income per capita anywhere near the inflection point of the inverted-U curve, by 1990 there were more than 30 countries (including first-tier NIEs) whose income per capita was beyond that critical point in the respective curve.

Third, the data and analysis presented in this chapter have allowed us to develop a new, more specific (and, it is to be hoped, more useful) way of looking at the Dutch disease. There is a group of countries that exhibits a specific additional degree of de-industrialization (additional to the de-industrialization caused by the three de-industrializing sources mentioned above, that is). This added de-industrialization is associated either with a sudden surge in exports of primary commodities or with the development of a successful service export sector (mainly tourism or finance). From this perspective, the Dutch disease is a process in which a country undergoes a change in its group of reference, switching from one corresponding to countries that need to generate a trade surplus in manufacturing to one corresponding to those able to generate a trade surplus in primary commodities or services. When this is the case, the country experiencing this disease moves along two different paths of de-industrialization: the first, which is common to the countries in the original group; and a second surge of de-industrialization resulting from the change in reference group. In this context, the Dutch disease should be regarded only as the "excess" degree of de-industrialization associated with the latter movement.

Fourth, although this disease also spread to some Latin American countries, the key issue in this case is that it was not brought on by the discovery of natural resources or the development of a service export sector, but rather by a drastic switch in the economic policy regime.[39] This was basically the result of a radical program of trade and financial liberalization within the context of an overall process of economic reform and institutional change that led to a sharp reversal of these countries' (State-led) ISI strategy. Brazil and the three Southern Cone countries with the highest incomes per capita (Argentina, Chile, and Uruguay) were the Latin American countries that experienced the highest levels of de-industrialization while also being among the countries in the region that had previously industrialized most rapidly and had implemented the most drastic policy reforms. From this point of view, the major difference in the consequences of neoliberal policies and deflationary economics between Latin America and industrial countries is that in the former—because they were hit at a much lower level of income per capita—they also hampered the transition toward a more mature form of industrialization (that is, self-sustaining in a Kaldorian sense).

To begin with, ISI policies had achieved a degree of manufacturing employment that "normally" corresponds to a situation in which the countries concerned seek to generate a trade surplus in manufacturing (although Latin American countries were never actually able to achieve this). In turn, a radical shift in the policy regime (mostly implemented after the 1982 debt crisis) brought about the end of industrial and trade policies and, in particular, changes in relative prices, in real exchange rates, in the institutional framework of the economies, in the structure of property rights, and in market incentives in general. This shift led them to abandon their industrialization agenda, bringing them back to their "natural Ricardian position"; that is, a position associated with comparative advantages more in accordance with their traditional resource endowment.

Fifth, Finland, Sweden, Malaysia, and, to a lesser extent, other Southeast Asian countries rich in natural resources (such as Indonesia, the Philippines, and Thailand) prove that, from the perspective of manufacturing employment, there is no such thing as the so-called curse of natural resources. It seems patently clear that countries rich in natural resources or having a high potential for developing strong export services activities have sufficient degrees of freedom to allow them to pursue trade and industrial policies aimed at continuing to develop a strong manufacturing sector—let alone to implement policies designed to avoid the Dutch disease. However, as the Latin American experience, in particular, shows, it would seem that as globalization progresses, there are fewer and fewer countries left with the political will to take advantage of such degrees of freedom and undertake policies that promote or maintain manufacturing capacity. This is not only because the new international institutional order is rapidly trying to narrow down these degrees of freedom, but also because of the obvious role of ideology in economic policy making and the fact that the newly developed structure of property rights has (at least so far) been perfectly capable of generating alternative (nonmanufacturing) rents from which domestic elites have been able to profit.

However, whether a process of structural change that includes premature de-industrialization can ever deliver rapid and sustainable economic growth is another matter altogether; so is the issue of whether the current premature de-industrialization taking place in Brazil and in the Southern Cone of Latin America contains an important component of policy-induced "uncreative destruction."

Annex A: Econometric Results—Ordinary Least Squares Estimation

Parameters' Point Estimation

	Regression 1	Regression 2	Regression 3	Regression 4	Regression 5
Intersect	−16.71	−15.96	−14.98	−17.78	−16.47
Ln Y pc	4.189	3.889	3.660	4.491	4.204
Ln Y pc sq	−0.218	−0.195	−0.183	−0.242	−0.228

Note: Regression 1 corresponds to the "average" regression for 1960 (see figure 3.3); regression 2 corresponds to the regression for 1970; regression 3 to the regression for 1980; regression 4 to the regression for 1990; and regression 5 to 1998. Ln Y pc = log of income per capita; Ln Y pc sq = square of the log of income per capita.

"T" Values

	Regression 1	Regression 2	Regression 3	Regression 4	Regression 5
Intersect	−3.5	−4.9	−4.3	−5.5	−5.0
Ln Y pc	3.3	4.5	4.1	5.5	5.0
Ln Y pc sq	−2.6	−3.5	−3.2	−4.7	−4.3

"P" Values

	Regression 1	Regression 2	Regression 3	Regression 4	Regression 5
Intersect	0.001	0.000	0.000	0.000	0.000
Ln Y pc	0.002	0.000	0.000	0.000	0.000
Ln Y pc sq	0.011	0.001	0.002	0.000	0.000

Regression Statistics

	Regression 1	Regression 2	Regression 3	Regression 4	Regression 5
R-bar-sq	0.65	0.72	0.67	0.64	0.57
F (2, 78)	75.1	—	—	—	—
F (2, 102)	—	135.5	107.0	92.2	70.1
p of F	0.000	0.000	0.000	0.000	0.000

Note: R-bar-sq is the adjusted coefficient of determination; F is the F statistic. All regressions pass the tests for homoscedasticity and for the normality of residuals at the 5 percent level of significance.

— Not available.

(Annex A continues on the following page.)

Annex A (continued)

Parameters' Point Estimation

	Regression 6	Regression 7	Regression 8	Regression 9	Regression 10
Intersect	−14.65	−15.35	−14.82	−17.90	−16.73
pc dummy	−0.334	−0.434	−0.419	−0.274	−0.243
Ln Y pc	3.724	3.848	3.760	4.637	4.401
Ln Y pc sq	−0.189	−0.196	−0.194	−0.255	−0.245

Note: Regression 6 corresponds to the regression for 1960 when an intercept dummy is added for countries able to generate a trade surplus in primary commodities or export services (see figures 3.7 and 3.8); regression 7 corresponds to the regression for 1970; regression 8 to the regression for 1980; regression 9 to 1990; and regression 10 to 1998. Ln Y pc = log of income per capita; Ln Y pc sq = square of the log of income per capita; pc dummy is the intercept dummy.

"T" Values

	Regression 6	Regression 7	Regression 8	Regression 9	Regression 10
Intersect	−3.2	−5.2	−5.0	−7.2	−6.9
pc dummy	−2.9	−4.1	−4.0	−2.8	−2.5
Ln Y pc	3.1	4.9	5.0	7.3	7.2
Ln Y pc sq	−2.4	−3.9	−4.0	−6.4	−6.4

"P" Values

	Regression 6	Regression 7	Regression 8	Regression 9	Regression 10
Intersect	0.002	0.000	0.000	0.000	0.000
pc dummy	0.006	0.000	0.000	0.000	0.014
Ln Y pc	0.003	0.000	0.000	0.000	0.000
Ln Y pc sq	0.020	0.000	0.000	0.000	0.000

Regression Statistics

	Regression 6	Regression 7	Regression 8	Regression 9	Regression 10
R-bar-sq	0.67	0.77	0.74	0.74	0.70
F (3, 77)	55.1	—	—	—	—
F (3, 101)	—	114.1	99.9	99.4	81.3
p of F	0.000	0.000	0.000	0.000	0.000

Note: All regressions pass the tests for homoscedasticity and for the normality of residuals at the 5 percent level of significance.
— Not available.

Annex B: Country Classification

The classification of countries was based on their 1998 positions; all Latin American countries are classified in the primary commodity group (including those that export maquila manufactures, as a result of the problems discussed above—in particular, these exports' low levels of domestic value added).

Countries	Non-primary commodity (and export services) group		Primary commodity (and export services) group	
Present in all samples	Austria	Korea, Rep. of	Argentina	Malawi
	Belgium	Malaysia	Australia	Malta
	Denmark	Morocco	Bolivia	Mauritius
	Egypt, Arab Rep. of	Pakistan	Botswana	Mexico
	Finland	Philippines	Brazil	Mozambique
	France	Portugal	Canada	Namibia
	Germany	Singapore	Chile	Netherlands
	India	Spain	Colombia	New Zealand
	Indonesia	Sri Lanka	Congo, Rep. of	Nicaragua
	Ireland	Sudan	Costa Rica	Niger
	Israel	Sweden	Côte d'Ivoire	Norway
	Italy	Taiwan (China)	Cyprus	Panama
	Japan	Thailand	Dominican	Paraguay
	Jordan	Tunisia	Republic	Peru
			Ecuador	Puerto Rico
			El Salvador	Reunion
			Gabon	South Africa
			Ghana	Switzerland
			Greece	Tanzania
			Guatemala	Turkey
			Guyana	Uganda
			Haiti	United
			Honduras	Kingdom
			Iceland	United States
			Kenya	Uruguay
			Liberia	Venezuela, R. B. de
Missing in the 1960 sample, but present in all other samples	Bangladesh		Algeria	Guinea-Bissau
	China		Angola	Lesotho
	Syrian Arab Rep.		Burkina Faso	Luxembourg
			Burundi	Madagascar
			Cameroon	Mali
			Cape Verde	Mauritania
			Central African Republic	Myanmar
			Chad	Nigeria
			Comoros	Rwanda
			Ethiopia	Senegal
			Gambia, The	Swaziland
			Guinea	Zimbabwe

Endnotes

1. In some historical experiences, like that of Great Britain, this process starts with what is usually called the "agrarian revolution."

2. Often, more labor is released by one sector than can be absorbed by others, leading to problems such as the growth of unemployment, informality, and so on.

3. Throughout this chapter, de-industrialization will be analyzed solely from the point of view of manufacturing employment.

4. In the United Kingdom, the fall was even more dramatic, with the level dropping by half in the same period (see figure 3.10).

5. Of course, in order to understand this process not just simply in arithmetic terms but in its proper macro and micro frameworks, one would have to go more deeply into the causal relationships between the trends in output, employment, and productivity growth. Furthermore, at the risk of stating the obvious, surely the issue is not to determine whether the de-industrialization was the result of rising productivity growth *or* of falling output growth, but more critically the result of focus on the actual relationship between productivity growth and output growth. Unfortunately, the study of this relationship falls outside the scope of this chapter.

6. For a detailed analysis, critical discussion, and bibliographical references on these hypotheses, see Rowthorn (1997, 1999) and Rowthorn and Ramaswamy (1999).

7. In addition, the ECLAC Statistical Division has provided data on manufacturing employment in Latin America during the 1960s.

8. See, in particular, Pérez (2002).

9. "Financialization" includes, inter alia, the rise in size and dominance of the financial sector relative to the nonfinancial sector, as well as the diversification toward financial activities in nonfinancial corporations.

10. Inasmuch as Rowthorn (1994) used data for 1990 for his regression (see figure 3.2), this particular effect was already clearly in operation.

11. In the five regressions, all parameters are significant at the 2 percent level (or less), and the adjusted R^2 are between 67 percent and 77 percent (see annex A). All regressions also pass the tests of homoscedasticity and normality of residuals at the 5 percent level of significance.

12. From now on, the primary commodity *and* export services countries will be referred to simply as the "primary commodity group" (pc).

13. The drop in the level of income per capita at which the inflection points are located is not surprising, however, because the difference in the regressions is just the dummy in the intercept. As indicated before, in 1960 no country had reached the income per capita associated with the turning point of both regressions.

14. On this point, I disagree with my friend, Dutch economist Willem Buiter, who always remarks that the so-called Dutch disease is just a "slander" on the Dutch economy! The literature on the general macro-mechanisms at work in the Dutch disease is extensive; see, for example, Pieper (2000), Ros (2000), and Rowthorn and Wells (1987).

15. An alterative form of measuring the Dutch disease along these lines would be to have a growth model for the Netherlands that somehow included the effect of the discovery of natural resources as an explanatory variable and to use this regression to predict what would have been the expected level of income per capita in 1998, had this country not discovered natural gas. In this case, the Dutch disease effect could be measured as the difference between the actual and predicted levels of manufacturing employment in 1998 in the mf regression, given the hypothetical income per capita of a non-Dutch disease scenario.

16. A billion is 1,000 million.

17. See, in particular, Solow (1997).

18. Although Latin America's "structuralist" industrialization agenda did not succeed (as East Asia's did) in creating a trade surplus in manufacturing, import-substituting industrialization in Latin America at least did lead to a significant reduction in the trade deficit in manufactures (as well as in the trade surplus in primary commodities); see Palma (2003).

19. It should be emphasized that, in these countries, it was policy rather than a surge in primary commodity exports that brought about their Dutch disease. In fact, these exports only surged in these countries *after* their respective (post-economic reform) financial crises and subsequent devaluations; therefore, by 1998, only in Chile had there been a rapid expansion of unprocessed primary commodities exports (generating, in this case, an additional impetus for its de-industrialization).

20. See, in particular, Kaldor (1967).

21. See, for example, Pesaran et al. (2000).

22. The signing of new bilateral free trade treaties with the United States, such as that recently signed by Chile, is unlikely to help promote industrialization. In fact, as is well known, other than for agricultural products, the treaty between Chile and the United States has little to do with trade issues, but is instead focused on restricting Chile's capacity to implement trade and industrial policies and controls in the capital account of the balance of payments; on this issue, see, in particular, Bhagwati (2003) and Stiglitz (2003).

23. On this subject, see, in particular, Caputo (1996), *Economist* (2001), Lavanderos (2001), and Tomić (1985).

24. This concept is very popular these days in some of the most simplistic "new-institutionalist" literature that seeks to explain the development failure of resource-rich countries. For a critical review of this literature, see Di John (2003).

25. For policies for avoiding the Dutch disease, see, in particular, Pesaran (1984); for an analysis of the specific experience of a developing country that avoided the Dutch disease in the late 19th century (despite the fact that its level of exports of primary commodities suddenly more than doubled), see Palma (2000); for a comparative analysis of trade and industrial policies in East Asia and Latin America, see Palma (2004, 2005).

26. As Stiglitz keeps reminding us, "Washington Consensus"-type of thinking is not renowned for its flexibility or its imagination (see, for example, Stiglitz [2002]).

27. For a detailed discussion of this issue, see Palma (2002).

28. In a study of the television industry in Tijuana, for example, Carrillo (2002) clearly showed both sides of Mexico's manufacturing export-led success. On the one hand, in 2001 Mexico produced about 30 million television sets, 90 percent of which were exported to the United States (representing 78 percent of all imports of television sets into the United States). On the other hand, Carrillo's calculations showed that, in value terms, 98 percent of inputs for the Mexican television industry are either direct imports or indirect ones (that is, inputs that are supplied by foreign firms in Mexico, which themselves import practically all of their inputs). In fact, Mexican companies only supply the remaining 2 percent of inputs (mostly cardboard boxes and plastic sheets needed for packaging and the printing of some manuals).

29. In 2001, for example, Mexico exported roughly the same amount of manufactures as the Republic of Korea (about US$150 billion); however, its overall manufacturing sector generated less than half the latter country's level of value added and absorbed more than twice the level of imports; see UNCTAD (2002) and Palma (2002).

30. See, for example, ECLAC (2002), Mortimore (2000), and Palma (2002).

31. See, in particular, Di John (2003); see also Palma (2003). It must have taken some doing for oil-rich República Bolivariana de Venezuela to manage to have a

level of income per capita today that is well below what it had at the time of the first oil-price shock three decades ago!

32. For important insights on China's economic success, see Sen (1999).

33. See, for example, Bhaduri and Nayyar (1996).

34. See Barro and Sala-i-Martin (1995) and Blankenburg (2000, 2004) for overviews of new growth theories.

35. It could be argued that these growth theories are also activity specific rather than just activity neutral; however, in Kaldor's work and in the work of the other authors mentioned above (with some exceptions), the internal organization of manufacturing—for example, the role of R&D versus that of other (what has here been called) "activities"—is usually not central to their analysis.

36. "Husbandry [...] is never more effectively encouraged than by the increase of manufactures" (Hume, 1767, vol. III, p. 65; quoted in Reinert, 2003, pp. 451–78).

37. In the third section of this chapter, "absolute" de-industrialization was also called "reverse" de-industrialization.

38. The former aimed at rolling back the welfare state, the radical transformation of industrial relations (in order to "discipline" labor), and the creation of a new stream of rents (for example, privatizations) in order to give a new impetus to capitalist accumulation (or, perhaps, just as part of the long-awaited revenge of the rentier); the latter was necessary for dealing with the newly discovered Friedman-type obsession with inflation.

39. See, for example, ECLAC (2003) and Palma (2003).

Bibliography

Aghion, Philippe, and Peter Howitt. 1998. *Endogenous Growth Theory*. Cambridge, MA: MIT Press.

Barro, Robert, and Xavier Sala-i-Martin. 1995. *Economic Growth*. New York: McGraw-Hill.

Bhaduri, Amit, and Deepak Nayyar. 1996. *The Intelligent Person's Guide to Liberalization*. New Delhi, India: Penguin Books.

Bhagwati, Jagdish. 2003. "Testimony to the Subcommittee on Domestic and International Monetary Policy, Trade and Technology, US House of Representatives Committee on Financial Services." Washington, DC, April 1.

Blankenburg, Stephanie. 2004. "Knowledge in the 'New Endogenous Growth Theory': A Factor of Production, a Good and an Externality." PhD diss., Cambridge University.

———. 2000. "Knowledge, Economic Growth and the Role of Policy." Working Paper 185, ESRC Centre for Business Research, Department of Applied Economics, Cambridge University, Cambridge, UK.

Caputo, Orlando. 1996. "La sobreproducción mundial de cobre creada por Chile. Su impacto en la economía nacional." Working paper, University of Arts and Social Science (ARCIS)/Centro de Estudios sobre Transnacionalización, Economía y Sociedad (CETES), Santiago, Chile.

Carrillo, Jorge. 2002. "Foreign Direct Investment and Local Linkages: Experiences and the Role of Policies. The Case of the Mexican Television Industry in Tijuana." Geneva: United Nations Conference on Trade and Development (UNCTAD).

Chang, Ha-Joon, ed. 2003. *Rethinking Development Economics*. London: Anthem Press.

Di John, J. 2003. "Growth as Interactive Process of Political and Economic Strategy: The Political Economy of Industrial Policy and State Capacity in Venezuela, 1920–2000." PhD diss., Cambridge University.

ECLAC (Economic Commission for Latin America and the Caribbean). 2003. *A Decade of Light and Shadow: Latin America and the Caribbean in the 90s.* Santiago, Chile: ECLAC.

———. 2002. *Foreign Investment in Latin America and the Caribbean, 2002.* Santiago, Chile: ECLAC.

The Economist. 2001. "Chile Could Do More to Become Less Dependent on Copper." December 1.

Hume, David. 1767. *History of England.* Vol. 3. Cambridge, UK: Cambridge University Press. http://www.ilo.org.

Kaldor, Nicholas. 1967. "Problems of Industrialization in Underdeveloped Countries." In *Strategic Factors of Economic Development,* ed. N. Caldor. New York: Cornell University Press.

Lavanderos, Jorge. 2001. *El cobre NO, es de Chile, el cobre no es de Chile.* Valparaíso, Chile: University of Santiago.

Mortimore, Michael. 2000. "Libre comercio, integración y el futuro de la industria maquiladora. Producción global y trabajadores locales." Unpublished paper. Tijuana, Mexico: Colegio de la Frontera Norte.

Palma, Gabriel. 2005. "Flying-Geese and Waddling-Ducks: The Different Capabilities of East Asia and Latin America to 'Demand-Adapt' and 'Supply-Upgrade' Their Export Productive Capacity." In *Industrial Policy in Developing Countries,* eds. M. Cimoli, G. Dosi, and J. Stiglitz. Oxford, UK: Oxford University Press.

———. 2004. "The Economic Consequences of Different Regional Leadership: The Role of the US and Japan in the Economic Development of Latin America and East Asia." In *O Poder Americano,* ed. J. L. Fiori, 393–454. Rio de Janeiro, Brazil: Editora Vozes.

———. 2003. "Latin America During the Second Half of the Twentieth Century: From the 'Age of Extremes' to the Age of 'End of History' Uniformity." In *Rethinking Development Economics,* ed. H.-J. Chang, 125–51. London: Anthem Press.

———. 2002. "Trade Liberalization in Mexico: Its Impact on Growth, Employment and Wages." ILO Employment Paper 55. http://www.ilo.org.

———. 2000. "Trying to 'Tax and Spend' Oneself out of the Dutch Disease. The Chilean Economy from the War of the Pacific to the Great Depression." In *An Economic History of Twentieth-Century Latin America: The Export Age. The Latin American Economies in the Late Nineteenth and Early Twentieth Centuries,* vol. 1, eds. E. Cárdenas, J. A. Ocampo, and R. Thorp, 217–48. Oxford, UK: Palgrave/St. Antony's College.

———. 1996. "Does It Make a Difference to Export Micro-Chips Rather Than Potato-Chips? Comparing Export Structures in East Asia and Latin America." Unpublished paper. Cambridge, UK: University of Cambridge.

Pérez, Carlota. 2002. *Technological Revolutions and Financial Capital. The Dynamics of Bubbles and Golden Ages.* Cheltenham, UK: Edward Elgar.

Pesaran, Hashem. 1984. "Macroeconomic Policy in an Oil-Exporting Economy with Foreign Exchange Controls." *Economica* 51: 253–70.

Pesaran, Hashem, Nadeem U. Haque, and Sunil Sharma. 2000. "Neglected Heterogeneity and Dynamics in Cross-Country Savings Regressions." In *Panel*

Data Econometrics—Future Direction: Papers in Honour of Professor Pietro Balestra, eds. J. Krishnakumar and E. Ronchetti, 53–82. Contributions to Economic Analysis Series. Amsterdam: Elsevier Science.

Pieper, U. 2000. "De-Industrialization and the Social and Economic Sustainability Nexus in Developing Countries: Cross-Country Evidence on Productivity and Employment." *Journal of Development Studies* 36 (4): 66–99.

Reinert, Eril S. 2003. "Increasing Poverty in a Globalized World: Marshall Plans and Morgenthau Plans As Mechanisms of Polarisation of World Incomes." In *Rethinking Development Economics,* ed. H.-J. Chang, 451–78. London: Anthem Press.

Romer, Paul M. 1990. "Endogenous Technical Change." *Journal of Political Economy* 98 (5): S71–S102.

Ros, Jaime. 2000. *Development Theory and Economic Growth.* Ann Arbor: University of Michigan Press.

Rowthorn, Robert. 1999. "The Political Economy of Full Employment in Modern Britain." The Kalecki Memorial Lecture, Department of Economics, University of Oxford, United Kingdom, October 19.

———. 1997. "Manufacturing in the World Economy." *Economie Appliquée* 1 (4): 63–96.

———. 1994. "Korea at the Cross-Roads." Working Paper 11, ESRC Centre for Business Research, Cambridge University, Cambridge, UK.

Rowthorn, Robert, and R. Ramaswamy. 1999. "Growth, Trade and De-Industrialization." *IMF Staff Papers* 46 (1): 18–41.

Rowthorn, Robert, and J. Wells. 1987. *De-Industrialization and Foreign Trade.* Cambridge, UK: Cambridge University Press.

Sen, Amartya. 1999. *Beyond the Crisis: Development Strategies in Asia.* Singapore: Institute of Southeast Asian Studies.

Solow, Robert. 1997. "What Is Labour Market Flexibility? What Is It Good For?" Keynote Lecture. *Proceedings of the British Academy* (October).

Stiglitz, Joseph. 2004. "Chile perdió soberanía al firmar TLC con EE.UU." *El Mostrador* (December 19). http://www.elmostrador.cl.

———. 2003. "Whither Reform? Toward a New Agenda for Latin America." *CEPAL Review* 80: 7–38.

———. 2002. *Globalization and Its Discontents.* New York: W. W. Norton.

Tomić, Radomiro. 1985. *La política minera chilena.* Santiago, Chile: Centre for Public Studies.

UNCTAD (United Nations Conference on Trade and Development). 2002. *Trade and Development Report.* Geneva: United Nations.

World Bank/ECLAC . 2002. "International Commodity Trade Data Base (COMTRADE)." CD-ROM version. Washington, DC: World Bank.

4

Globalization, Rising Labor Inequality, and Poverty in Latin America

Rob Vos

A STRIKING ASPECT OF ECONOMIC POLICY in developing economies during the last 10 to 15 years has been the spread of packages aimed at liberalizing the balance of payments current and capital accounts. Dramatic leaps toward external openness took place throughout Latin America, Eastern Europe, Asia, and parts of Africa. Together with large but highly volatile foreign capital movements (often but not always in connection with privatization of State-owned enterprises), this wave of trade and financial deregulation redefined the external environment for a major part of the nonindustrialized developing world. In Latin America, the stabilization and structural adjustment efforts immediately following the debt crisis of the early 1980s had focused mainly on fiscal and monetary adjustment and realignment of exchange rates. Then, in the late 1980s and early 1990s, came drastic reductions in trade restrictions and domestic and external financial liberalization, almost simultaneously in most countries. Steps were also taken toward restructuring tax systems and deregulating labor markets.

All these changes are very recent. It will take time before their full effects on growth, employment, income distribution, and poverty can be fully assessed. Still, external liberalization marks a dramatic switch in development policies away from the traditional regime of widespread

The author is Professor of Finance and Development at the Institute of Social Studies, The Hague. I am grateful to José Antonio Ocampo for comments and suggestions regarding a previous version of this chapter.

State controls and import-substituting industrialization. Accordingly, one would expect to see major consequences. The old regime, to a large extent, was built upon the infant-industry argument to create "learning-by-doing" externalities and enhance Hirschman-type domestic linkages so as to lay the foundations for a sustainable growth process. Import substitution did yield moderate to high growth for a prolonged period of time, as gross domestic product (GDP) growth averaged over 6 percent per annum and productivity (measured as output per worker) doubled between 1950 and 1970 (Stallings and Peres 2000). Despite this relatively successful growth performance, however, the pioneers of development economics who gave the theoretical justification for a government-supported industrialization strategy were among the first to observe the flaws of the policy regime, even before the economies ran out of steam and macroeconomic problems started to mount.[1] The protectionist regime was rightfully criticized for failing to promote efficient and competitive industrial production (and thereby providing a source of "structuralist inflation"), for creating insufficient employment, and for failing to reduce income inequality. Sectoral balance and income distribution formed a central element in the critique: The protectionist policies had biased relative prices in favor of capital-intensive industrial production, causing employment creation to lag behind population growth and skewing income distribution against wage earners and farmers. Widening inequalities placed a limit on the growth of the domestic market and thus on further growth in general. The solutions had to be found in redistribution policies as much as in economic opening. As noted, full economic liberalization ultimately became the dominant paradigm of the new policy regime, thus marking the end of classical development economics as an influential factor in shaping development policies.

A fundamental question that is now being asked is whether the liberalization of trade and capital flows will be better at meeting the development goals of growth, equity, and poverty reduction. Will a world system in which national economies are highly integrated in commodity and capital markets (in terms of increased transaction flows and tendencies toward price equalization) promote equality and reduce poverty? In answering this question, I will draw heavily on the findings of a set of 16 Latin American country studies that analyzed the distribution and poverty effects of trade and capital account liberalization (see Ganuza et al. 2001; Ganuza, Morley, Robinson, and Vos 2004, forthcoming; and Vos, Taylor, and Paes de Barros 2002). The first section of the chapter raises some analytical issues that suggest that there are no easy answers to the question as to whether the reforms will promote poverty reduction. The second section provides a summary of some of the main findings of the Latin American country studies. The third section draws some conclusions for policy making and further research.

Analytical Issues

The reforms have been justified by expected increases in efficiency and output growth. The governments and international institutions promoting them have been less explicit, however, about their distributional consequences. During the 1990s the predominant view has been that liberalization is likely to lead to better economic performance, at least in the medium-to-long run. According to this view, even if there are adverse transitional impacts, they can be cushioned by social policies and, in any case, after some time has passed they will be outweighed by more rapid growth. Both theory and empirical evidence are less conclusive about this. In the following discussion I will review some of the main issues, but no attempt will be made at comprehensiveness.

The Supply-Side Story

The new policy view basically stemmed from supply-side arguments. The purpose of trade reform is to switch production away from nontradables and inefficient import substitutes toward exportables in which countries have a comparative advantage. Presumed full employment of all resources—labor included—permits such a switch to be made painlessly. Standard trade theory based on the Heckscher-Ohlin model and Stolper-Samuelson theorem (HOS) would predict, further, that workers in developing countries would benefit from freer trade because this would lead such nations to specialize in types of production that make more intensive use of the most abundant factor, which would presumably be (unskilled) labor. Under the given assumptions, this should be conducive to greater income equality.

Opening up the capital account is supposed to attract financial inflows that will stimulate investment and productivity growth. In a defense based on cross-country regressions for Latin America, Londoño and Székely (1998) argued that equity is positively related to growth and investment. In turn, these variables are asserted to be positively related to structural reforms, and liberalization is therefore seen as being supportive of low-income groups.

This story contrasts with findings of many other studies, however, which, referring in particular to the effects of trade reforms, found that the opening of domestic markets to external competition in Latin America is associated with greater wage inequality (Berry 1998; Beyer, Rojas, and Vergara 1999; Cragg and Epelbaum 1996; Feenstra and Hanson 1997;

Hanson and Harrison 1999; Ocampo and Taylor 1998; Robbins 1996; Robbins and Gindling 1999; Wood 1994, 1997). Much of the increase in wage inequality and unemployment in several countries over the last two decades has been attributed to the change in the structure of labor demand in favor of skilled workers. This is reflected in the overall increase in the returns to education for skilled labor and, in some countries, in the rise of unemployment among less skilled individuals (Freeman 1995; Gottschalk and Smeeding 1997). Márquez and Pages (1997) estimated labor demand models with panel data for 18 Latin American countries and found that trade reforms had a negative effect on employment growth. Meanwhile, Currie and Harrison (1997), Revenga (1997), and Ros and Bouillón (2002) have analyzed the cases of Morocco and Mexico and found that reductions in tariff levels and import quotas have had a modest but negative impact on employment, which has partly been the result of firms' efforts to cut margins and raise productivity.

This developing-country evidence stands in stark contrast to that of East Asia, where many studies have observed an improvement in income equality after a strong export-led strategy was introduced in the 1960s and 1970s. In line with this view, Wood (1994, 1997) has found evidence of rising demand for unskilled labor and a decline in wage inequality in the Republic of Korea, Taiwan (China), and Singapore following trade liberalization. These cases are consistent with the hypothesis that the integration of developing countries into the international economy is accompanied by a reduction in income inequality and greater employment, as claimed by Krueger (1983, 1988).

This apparent contrast between experiences could suggest that the issue is an empirical matter rather than a theoretical puzzle. Economists, however, do not agree on the causes of the change in the structure of labor demand.

The controversy is based mainly on the HOS model and interpretations of the recent wave of technological innovations, which has had strong impacts on the structure of labor demand.[2] Because developing countries tend to have abundant unskilled labor, the increasing inequality is puzzling. According to the HOS model, developing countries should specialize in the production of goods that are intensive in unskilled labor, thus increasing the relative demand for this factor and reducing wage differentials.

The question has been raised, however, as to whether the empirical evidence of rising inequality is sufficient to challenge the relevance of the Stolper-Samuelson theorem, because Latin America's comparative advantage may not be to specialize in labor and low-skill-intensive production. This possibility has been brought up not only because of Latin America's abundant endowment of natural resources, but also because the predominance of low-skilled workers (say, with fewer than nine years of education) is probably less marked in the region's labor force than in much of Asia and Africa.[3] These conditions will change the expected outcomes of trade liberalization. Latin America's abundant endowment of land (relative to labor) and its unequal distribution has been shown to drive up income inequality following trade liberalization.[4] Other factors, such as China's growing presence in world markets, for instance, may also depress wage improvements in Latin America's export sectors (De Ferranti et al. 2002; Wood 1994). These conditions are probably only part of the explanation for rising inequality following trade liberalization. An alternative hypothesis suggests that the recent opening to trade observed in various developing countries may have unleashed a simultaneous process of technological modernization and an increase in capital stock that have had a positive impact on the demand for skilled labor. These developments would then drive up the returns to human capital and intensify the dispersion of wages.

Demand-Side Issues

Although trade reforms may have important supply-side effects, aggregate demand also has an impact on growth and distribution, just as capital inflows have an impact on relative prices. The import-substitution model relied on the expansion of internal markets with rising real wages as part of its strategy. Under the new regime, the question of controlling wage costs has taken center stage. As long as there is enough productivity growth and no substantial displacement of workers, wage restraints need not be a problem because the expansion of output can create room for the growth of employment and real incomes. But if wage levels are seriously reduced and/or workers with high consumption propensities lose their jobs, then the resulting contraction of domestic demand could cut labor income in sectors that produce for the domestic market. Income inequality could then rise if displaced unskilled workers end up in informal services for which there is a declining demand.

Larger inflows of capital following liberalization tend to lead to real exchange rate appreciation, which can offset liberalization's incentives for the production of traded goods and force greater reductions in real wage costs. On the demand side, though, capital inflows may stimulate aggregate spending through increased domestic investment (either directly or through credit expansion) and lower saving (credit expansion triggering a consumption boom). Furthermore, although macroeconomic stabilization policies that use the exchange rate as a nominal anchor may exacerbate real exchange rate appreciation, inflation can be brought under control, thereby allowing a recovery of real wages. Poverty, and in particular urban poverty, may decline, because much of the short-run economic expansion will be in nontraded goods. The expansion of aggregate demand may quite likely prove to be short-lived if the consequent widening of the external balance is not sustainable and if volatility in short-term capital inflows and a lack of regulatory control put the domestic financial system at risk. However, even if a financial crisis can be avoided, the economy may be pushed onto a deflationary path. A stop in capital inflows, as happened in the late 1990s, may not trigger a strong export drive in response, if there has been an earlier erosion of competitiveness and aggregate demand, and in this case imports will have to be slashed. Morley and Vos (forthcoming) showed that exports became the main driving force of aggregate output growth in most Latin American countries in the second half of the 1990s, even though the export sector was not very dynamic and virtually none of the economies managed to increase their penetration in world markets. For sure, this is export-led growth on a slippery path.

The thrust of these observations is that the effects of balance of payments liberalization on growth, employment, and income distribution arise out of a complex set of interactions involving both the supply and the demand sides of the economy. Income redistribution and major shifts in relative prices are endogenous to the process, and there are no simple conclusions about the effects of liberalization.

A Simple Analytical Framework

A more comprehensive approach for analyzing the effects of balance of payments liberalization could start with a simple model for traded and nontraded goods, because large shifts in price and quantity relationships between the two sectors have been observed in practice. Direct effects of the removal of barriers to trade and capital movements show up first in the traded (or tradable) goods sector, but spillovers in both directions with nontraded goods have been immediate and substantial. Taylor and Vos (2002) pointed out the major connections in a stylized fashion.

Assume traded goods are produced under imperfect competition. The simplest model involves a discriminating monopolist that manufactures goods that can be both exported and sold at home, as in Ocampo and Taylor (1998). Households at home buy both domestically made and imported consumer goods. Prior to liberalization, firms have established markup rates over variable costs in both markets (their levels will depend on the relevant elasticities). The market prices and productivity levels of unskilled labor and intermediate imports determine variable cost; skilled labor and physical capital are fixed factors in the short run. The traded goods' price level P_t follows from the markup over variable cost.

With stable markup rates, traded goods comprise a Hicksian fix-price sector with a level of output X_t determined by effective demand. The level of production of nontraded goods is also determined by demand, but the sector may well have decreasing returns to unskilled labor in the short run. A higher production level X_n is made possible by greater unskilled employment L_n. However, cost-minimizing producers will hire extra workers only at a lower real product wage w/P_n, where w is the unskilled nominal wage and P_n is the price of nontraded goods. In other words, a higher price-wage ratio P_n/w is associated with greater nontraded goods production and employment and, if there are decreasing returns, reduced labor productivity. If P_n/w is free to vary, then nontraded goods aggregate into a flex-price sector (which we assume in the basic version of the model). With stable markup rates in the traded goods sector, the intersectoral price ratio P_t/P_n will fall as P_n/w rises; that is, rising prices for nontraded goods are associated with real appreciation as measured by the ratio of traded to nontraded goods price indexes.

Figure 4.1 provides a graphic presentation of the model. The extreme northeast quadrant is the key one because it shows how prices and output in the two sectors are determined. Along the schedule for "nontraded goods equilibrium," a higher traded goods output level X_t is assumed to generate additional demand for nontraded goods. Because it is met by an increase in supply, the nontraded price-wage ratio P_n/w will rise. In the market for traded goods, a higher level of P_n/w can be associated with either higher or lower demand, depending on income effects. The "traded goods equilibrium" schedule illustrates the former case: Demand for X_t is stimulated by an increase in P_n/w. As drawn in the figure, the short-run macro equilibrium defined by the intersection of the two curves is stable.

As indicated above, in most Latin American economies the current and capital accounts of the balance of payments were liberalized nearly simultaneously in the late 1980s to early 1990s. Given this history, the two policy regime shifts have to be considered together. However, for the sake of analytical clarity, it is useful to dissect them one at a time. A full analysis would need to consider the effects of other reforms as well (in particular domestic financial, tax, and labor market deregulation), but for the present purpose the analysis is limited to the effects of capital and current accounts liberalization.

Capital Account Liberalization. Upon removing restrictions on capital movements, most countries received a surge of inflows from abroad. These inflows were subject to the accounting restriction that an economy's net foreign asset position (total holdings of external assets minus total external liabilities) can only change gradually over time through a deficit or surplus on the current account. Hence, when external liabilities increased as foreigners acquired securities issued by national governments or firms, external assets had to rise sharply as well. The new assets typically showed up on the balance sheets of financial institutions

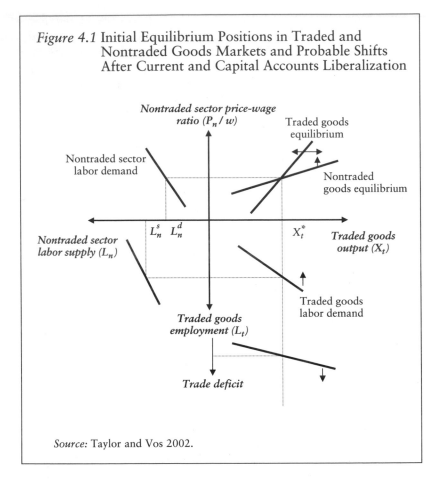

Figure 4.1 Initial Equilibrium Positions in Traded and
          Nontraded Goods Markets and Probable Shifts
          After Current and Capital Accounts Liberalization

Source: Taylor and Vos 2002.

and included the larger international reserves of the central bank. Unless a concerted effort was made to "sterilize" the inflows, they set off a domestic credit boom. Poorly regulated financial systems ran a high risk of lapsing into a classic mania-panic-crash sequence along the lines described by Kindleberger (1996). The events in Latin America's Southern Cone around 1980 were only the first of many such disasters.

When the credit expansion was allowed to work itself through, it was possible for interest rates to settle at low levels. However, other factors entered to push both levels and the spread between borrowing and lending rates upward. One source of widening spreads was related to asset price booms in housing and stock markets, which forced rates to rise on interest-bearing securities such as government debt. Another source that sometimes played a role was the efforts made by the countries' central banks to sterilize capital inflows, because this pushed up interest rates as well. Finally, in noncompetitive financial markets, local institutions often found it easy to raise spreads. High local returns pulled in more capital inflows, thereby worsening the overall disequilibrium.

Not surprisingly, exchange rate movements complicated the story. As indicated, in many countries the exchange rate was used as a nominal anchor in anti-inflation programs. Its nominal level was devalued at a rate lower than that of inflation, leading to real appreciation. In several cases the effect was rapid, with traded goods' variable costs in dollar terms jumping immediately after the rate was frozen. At the same time, interest rates would be driven upward (a tendency that would be amplified if real appreciation was expansionary in the short run), providing a disincentive to investment and long-run productivity growth. Abandoning capital controls made this trade-off far more difficult to manage. Some countries did succeed in keeping their exchange rates relatively weak, but they were in a minority during the first half of the 1990s when capital inflows were booming. There was an initial "sudden stop" in capital flows to the region following the Mexican peso crisis in 1995 and a more forceful one after 1997 with the Asian and Russian crises. This made it impossible to continue the nominal-exchange-rate-based stabilization policies, and a fair number of countries were forced to switch exchange rate regimes from fix to flex (such as Mexico in 1995, Ecuador and Brazil in 1999, and Argentina in 2002) and back (such as Ecuador, which introduced full dollarization in 2000).

To summarize, capital account liberalization, when combined with a boom in external inflows, could easily trigger an "excessive" credit expansion. Paradoxically, the credit boom could be associated with relatively high interest rates and a strong local currency. These were not the most secure foundations for the liberalization of the current account, as subsequent events would prove.

Current Account Liberalization. Current account deregulation basically took the form of the conversion of quota restrictions (where they were significant) into tariffs, followed by the consolidation of tariff rates into a fairly narrow band (for example, between zero and 20 percent). With a few exceptions, export subsidies were also removed. These measures had visible effects on the level and composition of effective demand and on patterns of employment and labor productivity.

Demand composition typically shifted in the direction of imports, especially when there was real exchange rate appreciation. In several cases, national savings rates also declined. This shift can be partly attributed to an increased supply of imports at low prices (increasing household spending, aided by credit expansion following financial liberalization) and partly to a profit squeeze (cutting retained earnings) in industries producing traded goods. The subsequent decline in private saving was sometimes partially offset by rising government saving in cases where fiscal policy became more restrictive. Many countries displayed "stop-go" cycles in government taxing and spending behavior.

Especially when it was combined with a real appreciation, current account liberalization pushed traded goods producers toward workplace reorganization (including greater reliance on outsourcing) and downsizing; cases in point include the Mexican and Argentine manufacturing sectors. If, as assumed above, unskilled labor is a major component of variable cost, then these workers would bear the brunt of such adjustments via job losses. In other words, traded goods enterprises that stayed in operation had to cut costs by generating labor productivity growth. Thus, depending on demand conditions, their total employment levels could very easily fall.

The upshot of these effects often took the form of increased inequality between groups of workers—in particular, between the skilled and unskilled. This outcome is not only at odds with the predictions of the simple two-factor Stolper-Samuelson theorem (assuming unskilled labor would be the abundant production factor); it is also analytically different, because the adjustment involves more than mere responses to relative factor and commodity prices. There are macroeconomic effects, such as the impact of exchange rate movements and capital flows on remunerations and interest rates. The analysis also departs further from the standard Heckscher-Ohlin trade theory framework underlying Stolper-Samuelson by working with more than two production factors and allowing for factor immobility and product market imperfections. These considerations, along with changes in the sectoral composition of output as emphasized in figure 4.1, are important factors in determining the distributive effects of trade liberalization. With liberalization stimulating productivity increases in some tradables, which, in turn, led to a reduction of labor demand from modern, traded-goods production, primary income differentials widened between workers in such sectors and those employed in nontraded, informal activities (for example, informal services) and the unemployed.

Graphic Illustration of the Possible Effects of Balance of Payments Liberalization. It is easy to trace through the implications of these changes in figure 4.1, beginning with the traded-goods equilibrium schedule in the northeast quadrant. The sector may be subject to several conflicting forces:

• By shifting demand toward imports, current account liberalization tends to reduce output X_t. This demand loss is strengthened by real appreciation and weakened—or even reversed—by devaluation. Removal of export subsidies may hurt manufacturing and raw materials sectors in some cases.

- Domestic credit expansion and a falling savings rate stimulate demand for both sectors, although high interest rates may hold back spending on luxury manufactured items, such as consumer durables and automobiles (in countries where they are produced).

The outcome is that the shift in the traded-goods equilibrium schedule is likely to be ambiguous, as shown by the double-headed arrow in the diagram. The contractionary forces that have just been mentioned do not impinge directly on nontraded goods; as shown, the corresponding market equilibrium schedule is shifted upward. The likely results after both schedules adjusted were a higher nontraded price-wage ratio P_n/w, a fall in the intersectoral terms of trade P_t/P_n, and an ambiguous change in X_t.

Turning to employment and productivity changes, a fair share of new jobs may be created in the nontraded sector, owing to aggregate demand expansion; that is, L_n^d moves up along the demand schedule in the northwest quadrant. With overall decreasing returns in the sector, its real wage w/P_n and labor productivity level X_n/L_n^d could be expected to fall.

Increased labor productivity in the traded sector means that the traded goods labor demand schedule in the middle quadrant on the right moves toward the point of origin. Regardless of what happened to their overall level of activity, traded goods producers generate fewer jobs per unit of output. Reading through the lower quadrant on the left, L_n^s or unskilled labor supply in nontraded goods tends to rise. The effect on overall unemployment $(L_n^s - L_n^d)$ is unclear. During the expansionary phase of the business cycle, unemployment may fall enough to generate strong upward wage pressure. However, in practice, wage dynamics are driven by institutional circumstances in partially segmented labor markets, with details differing from one country to another. In many cases, stable or rising unemployment and unresponsive wages cause the overall income distribution to become more concentrated. A typical case found in several instances has been that surplus labor was absorbed by the informal sector. This puts downward pressure on the mean incomes of the self-employed in that sector, generating a widening differential between wage and nonwage labor incomes. The differential between skilled and unskilled wage rates tends to rise as well, because the productivity switch was associated with more skill-intensive production.

The last curve to shift is the one corresponding to the trade deficit in the extreme southeast quadrant: Higher import demand and typically lagging exports cause it to move away from the point of origin. The trade deficit thus increases for a given output level. The corresponding increase in "required" capital inflows feeds into the shifts in the capital account discussed above.

Growth, Distribution, and Poverty in Latin America: Recurring Problems

Although there are no simple conclusions, evidence from a set of comparative studies of the postliberalization performance of 16 Latin American and Caribbean economies during the 1990s suggests that diverging outcomes are closely associated with the issues described above.[5] Most Latin American countries achieved moderate growth rates in the 1990s. However, a few exceptions aside, it is hard to speak of a strong and sustained recovery from the dismal performance of the 1980s. What is more, toward the end of the decade, growth tapered off in many countries as a result of emerging domestic financial crises and/or external events. Adverse foreign shocks included the impact of the Asian crisis on capital flows to Brazil with spillover effects on neighboring countries, particularly Argentina, and falling export earnings for most primary exporting economies as a result of plummeting commodity prices. Whereas it is also true for Latin America that poverty falls with growth (see figure 4.2), significant deviations from the trend line are strongly

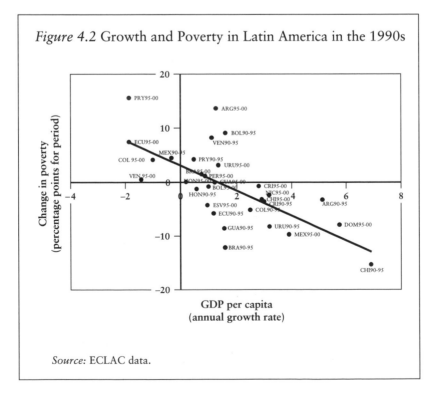

Figure 4.2 Growth and Poverty in Latin America in the 1990s

Source: ECLAC data.

associated with specific macroeconomic conditions and, more specifically, with the pattern of growth.

Macroeconomic Conditions

Let us first look at some of these macroeconomic conditions. Particularly in the first half of the 1990s, capital inflows to most countries increased substantially, prompting both aggregate demand growth and real exchange rate appreciation (with a few exceptions, as noted below). The latter outcome was consistent with reductions in inflation, which helped support higher average real wages in most countries. The surge in capital inflows produced expansionary macroeconomic cycles, and the associated real wage increases lifted domestic market constraints. Growth accelerated and poverty declined during such episodes, but rather than constituting a "big push" à la Rosenstein-Rodan (1943, 1984), the overall picture was one of macroeconomic stop-go cycles along the lines of what is shown in figure 4.1, with wages and aggregate demand strongly contracting as capital inflows slowed down. In most cases, private spending proved to be the major source of growth (though typically in conjunction with expanding trade), with consumption growth more often than investment being the major driving force (table 4.1). As indicated above, by the end of the 1990s, exports started playing a larger role in output growth—however, in a context of faltering growth dynamics (Morley and Vos forthcoming). Remarkably, the countries that managed to stay on a more dynamic export-led growth path throughout the decade maintained either relatively competitive exchange rates or a credible system of export incentives, or both. However, export stimulus through competitive exchange rates is not necessarily a guarantee of higher aggregate output growth and poverty reduction. Furthermore, as indicated earlier, volatility and sudden stops in capital inflows pushed many economies onto a deflationary path as it became necessary to squeeze aggregate demand in order to compress imports and thus compensate for a lack of export dynamism.

Observed Patterns of Growth and Inequality

Even if we concentrate our attention on the period of more rapid GDP growth in the 1990s, liberalization efforts yielded only modest aggregate productivity increases in most Latin American countries (see table 4.2). In a majority of cases, as was to be expected, there was greater productivity growth in traded than in nontraded sectors. Changes in aggregate productivity are the result of the sum of productivity changes in the various sectors, weighted by sectoral output shares, plus the reallocation of

Table 4.1 Factors of Growth in Latin American Countries in the 1990s

GDP Growth/Leading Factor	Export-Led		Public Spending Driven (Years)	Private Spending Driven (Years)
	Exports with Private Spending (Years)	Exports Only (Years)		
Negative or zero GDP growth (<0.5%)	Jamaica, –/+ (1995–2000) Paraguay, +/– (1995–2000)	Venezuela, R. B. de (1995–2000)		Colombia (1995–2000) Ecuador (1995–2000) Venezuela, R. B. de (1995–2000)
Low GDP growth (0.5–4.0%)	Brazil (1990–4) Ecuador (1990–4) Nicaragua (1990–4) Venezuela, R. B. de (1990–4)	Argentina (1995–2000) Brazil (1995–2000) El Salvador (1995–2000) Mexico (1990–4) Paraguay (1990–4) Peru (1995–2000) Uruguay (1990s)	Honduras (1995–2000)	Bolivia (1995–2000) Honduras (1990–4) Jamaica (1990–4)
Moderate to high GDP growth (>4.0%)	Bolivia (1990–4) Chile (1990–4) Dominican Republic (1995–2000) El Salvador (1990–4) Guatemala (1990s) Mexico (1995–2000) Nicaragua (1995–2000)	Chile (1995–2000) Costa Rica (1990s) Dominican Republic (1990–4)	Argentina (1990–4)	Colombia (1990–4) Peru (1990–4)

Source: Morley and Vos (forthcoming), based on a decomposition method of the Keynesian multiplier by final demand categories.

Table 4.2 Productivity Growth

| Country | Years | Periods | Productivity Growth | | | Sector Reallocation Effects: Employment |
			Overall	Traded Goods Sectors	Nontraded Goods Sectors	
Bolivia	1980–92	Destabilization/stabilization	−2.8	−2.9	−3.0	Large (toward agriculture, informal trade)
	1992–7	Postliberalization	1.0	1.0	0.8	Large (toward urban informal trade)
Brazil	1982–6	Prereform	0.7	2.0	−0.4	
	1987–91	Liberalization	−4.0	−2.4	−5.1	
	1992–4	Postliberalization I	4.4	2.4	4.6	
	1994–7	Postliberalization II	0.9	4.4	−1.2	
Chile	1970–4	Demand expansion, hyperinflation	0.8	0.1	1.3	Small
	1976–81	Liberalization	2.6	3.7	1.9	Small (−)
	1985–9	Readjustment	0.1	−1.2	0.9	Small (−)
	1990–7	Free trade agreements	3.9	4.8	3.5	Small (−)
Colombia	1992–5	Liberalization and boom	2.6	2.7	2.9	Small
	1995–8	Stagnation	2.0	2.8	1.9	Small
Costa Rica	1987–91	Trade liberalization	1.5	2.3	0.9	Small
	1992–8	Further opening	0.6	3.0	−1.0	Small

(Table continues on the following page.)

Table 4.2 (continued)

Country	Years	Periods	Productivity Growth			Sector Reallocation Effects: Employment
			Overall	Traded Goods Sectors	Nontraded Goods Sectors	
Cuba	1989–93	Opening for exchange market	-8.3	-13.7	-5.0	0
	1994–8	Fiscal adjustment, flexibilization informal activity	4.1	11.1	0.1	0
Dominican Republic	1991–6	Postliberalization	3.5	5.7	2.3	Small
Ecuador	1992–7	Postreform	0.1	1.3	-0.9	Large (away from nontraded goods sectors)
El Salvador	1991–5	Balance of payments and financial liberalization	14.3	-0.6	31.3	Large
	1995–6	Demand contract	9.6	4.4	14.0	Small
Guatemala	1987–92	Balance of payments liberalization	0.4	-0.4	1.1	Large
	1992–7	Balance of payments with domestic financial liberalization	0.3	-1.3	0.8	Large
Jamaica	1980–9	Preliberalization	3.2	1.7	0.9	Small
	1990–2	Financial liberalization	3.7	1.2	2.1	Small
	1993–8	Trade liberalization	-1.0	0.5	-1.6	Small

Mexico	1988–93	Financial liberalization	0.6	6.0	−0.5	Small
	1994–7	Peso crisis, NAFTA	−0.8	−0.2	−2.1	Small
Panama	1991–4	Stabilization and recovery	0.2	4.3	−2.0	Large (out of agriculture)
	1994–8	Trade reform	0.2	1.2	−0.5	Fair (into informal services)
Paraguay	1982–92	Trade and exchange rate reform	−0.4	1.2	−2.5	Large (away from traded goods sectors)
	1992–7	MERCOSUR and financial liberalization	−5.7	−2.1	−8.7	Large (away from traded goods sectors)
Peru	1986–90	High Inflation period	0.7	1.1	0.6	
	1991–8	Balance of payments liberalization	0.6	1.1	0.5	
Uruguay	1986–90	Pre-MERCOSUR	0.4	−0.7	0.6	
	1990–4	MERCOSUR (I)	3.8	0.0	2.2	
	1994–7	MERCOSUR (II)	2.7	6.5	2.4	

Source: Taylor and Vos 2002.

Note: MERCOSUR Common Market of the South/*Mercado Común del Sur*; NAFTA North American Free Trade Agreement. Productivity growth = annual rate of change of productivity.

labor from low- to high-productivity sectors (see Taylor and Vos 2002). Findings from the country studies indicate that within-sector productivity shifts and output growth rates largely determined the aggregate outcomes; that is, there was not enough of a shift from low- to high-productivity sectors to drive overall productivity growth. Typically, relatively small employment reallocation effects were found, but in a few cases—Ecuador, Guatemala, Mexico, and Panama—there were major labor reallocation effects, with low-productivity agriculture or urban informal services acting as "employers of last resort." Hence, productivity growth has remained rather sector specific and is not "lifting all boats," as had been hoped.

Turning to the pattern of growth and income distribution, in most countries of the region one can observe a rise in the inequality of primary incomes during the 1990s (see table 4.3). There is only a small number

Table 4.3 Growth and Inequality in Latin America in the 1990s

Growth After Liberalization	Inequality in Overall Primary Incomes		
	Rising Inequality (Years)	Decreasing Inequality (Years)	Unchanged (Years)
High (>5%)	Argentina (1991–4, 1996–8) Chile (1976–81, 1984–92) Colombia (1991–5) Dominican Republic (1991–8) Peru (1991–7)	Chile (1992–7) El Salvador (1991–7) Panama (1990–4)	Uruguay (1990–7)
Moderate (2–5%)	Bolivia (1989–97) Brazil (1987–94) Costa Rica (1992–8) Ecuador (1990–7) Mexico (1988–94) Panama (1994–8) Paraguay (1988–91, 1992–4)	Brazil (1994–7) Costa Rica (1987–92) Cuba (1994–8)	Uruguay (1986–90)
Low (0–2%)	Colombia (1995–8) Ecuador (1995–9) Mexico (1985–7) Paraguay (1995–8)		
Negative (<0%)	Cuba (1989–93) Mexico (1994–5)		

Source: Taylor and Vos 2002.

of episodes after the liberalization process in which income inequality has been decreasing. Trade liberalization and capital account opening appear to have come with a "skill twist." Looking more deeply into sectoral adjustment patterns, it becomes clear that the drive toward efficiency gains has led to the adoption of more skill-intensive technologies, in many instances driving the abundant supply of unskilled workers into unemployment or low-paid informal sector employment along the lines shown in figure 4.1. Virtually without exception, wage differentials between skilled and unskilled workers rose in Latin America during the postliberalization period. Excess labor was typically absorbed into the nontraded, informal trade, and services sectors (as in Bolivia, Colombia, Costa Rica, Ecuador, Panama, and Peru), or—as happened in a few cases—traditional agriculture served as a sponge for the labor market (Guatemala, Mexico, and, in the late 1980s, Panama).

The sectoral patterns have not been uniform. In Argentina, for instance, productivity increases in the traded goods sector affected workers of all skill levels. Wage rigidity being greater for unskilled workers, there was a reduction in earnings inequality in the sector, but overall the greater inequality in Argentina resulted from rising income concentration in the nontraded sector, combined with the greater skill intensity of new investment, and from rising unemployment in the traded goods sector. By contrast, in Mexico, reorganization of manufacturing production was found to be a major source of greater skill demand, pushing up wage inequality in the traded goods sector, while many of the displaced workers were absorbed by agriculture, at least until 1994. In Brazil, productivity growth produced employment losses in the manufacturing sector. Labor demand fell for everyone in modern manufacturing, but skilled workers suffered the most. Real hourly wages also fell for both skilled and unskilled workers in modern industry, but, here again, slightly less for unskilled workers, showing—as in Argentina—greater rigidity in wage adjustment at the lower end; hence, skilled-unskilled income differentials showed a slight decline. As indicated, in most other cases such productivity growth in traded goods sectors pushed up skill differentials in the sector and widened the gap between formal- and informal-sector workers.

As shown in figure 4.3, rising per-worker differentials do not necessarily translate into rising inequality and poverty at the household level. Cases of rising inequality clearly predominate (east of the vertical axis), but so do episodes in which poverty fell during the 1990s (south of the horizontal axis). Economic growth evidently helped reduce poverty, even in cases in which liberalization tended to heighten the degree of inequality. As a result, most cases of poverty reduction occurred in the first half of the 1990s, and those of poverty increases occurred in the period

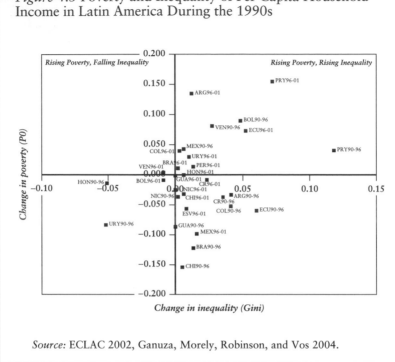

Figure 4.3 Poverty and Inequality of Per Capita Household
Income in Latin America During the 1990s

Change in inequality (Gini)

Source: ECLAC 2002, Ganuza, Morely, Robinson, and Vos 2004.

of growth slowdown thereafter. Only in a few cases—particularly, Chile, El Salvador, and Guatemala—was poverty reduction associated with moderate to strong export-led growth and falling inequality. In most other cases, the resumption of growth following a surge in capital inflows paved the way for an expansion of aggregate demand and sufficient overall employment growth, or a rise in real wages, to bring about a reduction in poverty. In Argentina and Mexico, the rise in inequality has been associated with labor demand shifts favoring skilled workers and employment shifts whereby unskilled workers are absorbed into informal activities or unemployment. On balance, these effects have led to a rise in poverty despite positive per capita growth. In other cases, changing labor market conditions have triggered strong labor supply responses, including rising female participation, as in urban areas of Ecuador and in Panama. Elsewhere, emigrant remittances (Central America, Cuba, Dominican Republic, and Ecuador after 2000) or social security transfers (Costa Rica) have a strong positive influence in terms of the reduction of poverty and inequality at the household level.

The Effects of Trade Reforms on Skill Intensity and Labor Income Inequality

In the above analysis, we looked at observed patterns of growth and changes in inequality. Because countries introduced trade reforms in conjunction with stop-go macroeconomic policies, it is difficult to discern the precise impact of each of these factors. Ganuza, Morley, Robinson, and Vos (2004) thus tried to disentangle their differential effects by simulating the effects with the help of a "top-down" multiple modeling framework with the computable general equilibrium (CGE) model as the first layer and a methodology of microsimulations as the second layer. The latter translates the general equilibrium effects of trade reform on the labor market onto household incomes, allowing one to derive an estimate of the impact of macroeconomic changes on poverty and inequality, making use of the full income distribution from micro (household survey) data.

This methodology seems particularly useful for analyzing the implications for skill intensity and wage gaps of trade reforms when taken in isolation. The short answer is that these effects essentially depend on whether the traded goods sector is relatively skill intensive and on how wage rates are set in the labor market. In about one third of the country cases analyzed, import liberalization leads to higher overall skill intensity of production and widening wage gaps. In another one third of the cases, skills differentials decline, and in the final group there is little change. According to CGE models, if countries apply a unilateral, uniform tariff cut, the earnings gap between skilled and unskilled workers is expected to increase in six country cases (Brazil, Costa Rica, Cuba, Dominican Republic, Ecuador, and El Salvador), whereas a smaller earnings gap is expected in Honduras, Mexico, and Uruguay and, to a lesser extent, in Argentina and Colombia. In all other countries, the simulation of further unilateral trade opening shows no substantial shifts in skill inequality.

Hence, rising skill intensity resulting from import liberalization does not seem to explain all of the rising labor income inequality observed in table 4.3. Technology changes associated with capital inflows should also be considered . The modeling analysis suggests that at least as much, if not most, of the rise in earnings gaps that may be associated with trade reform originates from sectoral labor shifts, along the lines discussed earlier; that is, with many more workers shifting to lower-paid jobs in informal sectors and fewer benefiting from higher-paid new jobs in modern sectors (manufacturing or nontradables). Trade reform has not only come with a skill twist, as mentioned above, but also, at least as importantly, it has come with a "sectoral twist" inducing greater labor income inequality.

Conclusions

The core issue of economic development involves the movement of resources (labor, in particular) from low- to high-productivity sectors, thereby creating new growth dynamics. This is what structural adjustment should be about. This is not a one-time process, but rather a revolving one. Nor is it likely to be a smooth and continuous process; instead, it will tend to occur in spurts ("big pushes"). If, as in postliberalization Latin America, the spurt lacks dynamism or is hampered by macroeconomic volatility, new development traps may emerge. The country evidence reviewed in this chapter shows that trade liberalization and capital account opening have generated efficiency gains in some sectors (particularly manufacturing and modern services) but at the cost of an expulsion of labor to low-productivity sectors (traditional agriculture or informal services). Such labor reallocations have been a major source of widening income gaps. Skill intensity has increased in most parts of the modern sector of the economy, despite the predominance of unskilled workers in the labor force. Perhaps unskilled labor is not Latin America's comparative advantage after all, but, clearly, shifts in macro prices (the real exchange rate and interest rates, in particular) and the opening of the capital account have provided strong incentives for the importation of more skill-intensive technologies. These results cannot be fully attributed to the trade reforms conducted in the 1990s. CGE model simulations suggest that there are as many cases in which import liberalization has fomented greater skill intensity as there are cases in which unskilled labor has benefited and cases in which there is not much of an effect on average skill intensity and skill-related wage inequality.

Surges in capital inflows, rather than export drives, have been the major tools for overcoming demand constraints. Volatility in capital markets thus has directly affected growth, because the trends toward employment growth, real wage increases, and poverty reduction seen in the expansionary phase of the cycle are reversed again during downswings in capital inflows. These factors, which to a large extent act upon the demand side of the economy, appear to have predominated among the observed inequality and poverty outcomes of trade and capital account liberalization in Latin America during the 1990s. Because of the financial volatility and the stop-go pattern of macroeconomic policies, growth performance and poverty outcomes have been positive during some episodes and negative during others, but on the whole, they have been rather disappointing.

Structural reforms have thus interacted poorly with short-term macroeconomic adjustment mechanisms. Policy reforms in Latin America have focused too much on eliminating protection and domestic price distortions and too little on the need for active government policies to provide adequate levels of social overhead capital (infrastructure, education, market institutions) and to promote the creation of vertical technological linkages. In the empirical discussion, a few concrete policy issues came to the fore, such as the use of credible export promotion policies as a potential element in promoting certain technological externalities in various countries (for example, Chile, the Central American nations, and the Dominican Republic). Rising skill-based earnings differentials hint at insufficient human capital investment, and financial opening in most countries preceded establishment of adequate regulatory frameworks and mechanisms to limit volatility in capital inflows. These issues, along with a greater concern about income distribution and poverty reduction, are now surfacing as "second-stage reforms" on the liberalization agenda (Kuczynski and Williamson 2003), but clearly they ought to have been part of the reform process right from the start. Belated as their placement on the agenda may be, these issues should now be pursued aggressively and should become the focus of research and policy recommendations.

Endnotes

1. See, for instance, Hirschman (1968) and Prebisch (1961, 1963).

2. In the literature, this is known as the skill-biased technological change (SBTC) hypothesis. It is claimed that labor demand in many advanced economies has shifted away from unskilled workers and toward skilled workers as a consequence of technologies that require fewer workers but higher skill levels. The SBTC hypothesis has no *direct* link with trade, at least in the case of industrial countries, although the same does not seem to be true for developing countries. The SBTC hypothesis is seen as the main theoretical alternative to the view that trade is the key cause of rising wage inequality.

3. Spilimbergo, Londoño, and Székely (1999) and Wood (1997) provided some evidence on this point.

4. See Birdsall and Londoño (1997), Fischer (2001), and Leamer et al. (1999).

5. The findings reported below are based on two rounds of studies. The first looks at the broader set of reforms, but particularly current and capital accounts liberalization. These results have been published in Spanish (see Ganuza et al. 2001) and in English (see Vos, Taylor, and Paes de Barros 2002). The second source focused in greater detail on the impact of trade liberalization and export promotion on poverty and inequality. These findings are in Ganuza, Morley, Robinson, and Vos (2004, forthcoming).

Bibliography

Berry, Albert, ed. 1998. *Poverty, Economic Reform, and Income Distribution in Latin America*. London: Lynne Rienner.

Beyer, Harald, Patricio Rojas, and Rodrigo Vergara. 1999. "Trade Liberalization and Wage Inequality." *Journal of Development Economics* 59 (1): 103–23.

Birdsall, Nancy, and Juan Luis Londoño. 1997. "Asset Inequality Does Matter: Lessons from Latin America." OCE Working Paper 344, Inter-American Development Bank, Washington, DC.

Cragg, Michael I., and Mario Epelbaum. 1996. "Why Has Wage Dispersion Grown in Mexico? Is It the Incidence of Reforms or the Growing Demand for Skills?" *Journal of Development Economics* 51 (1): 99–116.

Currie, Janet, and Ann Harrison. 1997. "Sharing Costs: The Impact of Trade Reform on Capital and Labor in Morocco." *Journal of Labor Economics* 15 (3): S44–S72.

De Ferranti, David, Guillermo Perry, Daniel Lederman, and William F. Maloney. 2002. *From Natural Resources to the Knowledge Economy: Trade and Job Quality*. Washington, DC: World Bank.

ECLAC (Economic Commission for Latin America and the Caribbean). 2002. *Social Panorama of Latin America, 2001–2002*. Santiago, Chile: ECLAC.

Feenstra, Robert C., and Gordon H. Hanson. 1997. "Foreign Direct Investments and Relative Wages: Evidence from Mexico's Maquiladoras." *Journal of International Economics* 42 (3/4): 371–93.

Fischer, Ronald. 2001. "The Evolution of Inequality After Trade Liberalization." *Journal of Development Economics* 66 (2): 555–79.

Freeman, Richard B. 1995. "Are Your Wages Set in Beijing?" *Journal of Economic Perspectives* 9 (3): 15–32.

Ganuza, Enrique, Samuel Morley, Sherman Robinson, and Rob Vos, eds. Forthcoming. *Who Gains from Free Trade? Export-Led Growth and Poverty in Latin America*. London: Routledge.

———. 2004. *¿Quién se beneficia del libre comercio? Promoción de exportaciones y pobreza en América Latina y el Caribe en los 90*. Bogotá, Colombia: Alfaomega Publishers.

Ganuza, Enrique, Samuel Morley, Sherman Robinson, Valeria Pineiro, and Rob Vos. 2004. "¿Son buenas la promoción de exportaciones y la liberalización comercial para los pobres de América Latina? Un análisis comparativo macromicro CEG." In *¿Quién se beneficia del libre comercio? Promoción de exportaciones y pobreza en América Latina y el Caribe en los 90*, eds. E. Ganuza, S. Morley, S. Robinson, and R. Vos, 49–105. Bogotá, Colombia: Alfaomega Publishers.

Ganuza, Enrique, Lance Taylor, Ricardo Paes de Barros, and Rob Vos, eds. 2001. *Liberalización, equidad y pobreza. América Latina y el Caribe en los noventa*. Buenos Aires: Ediciones Universidad de Buenos Aires.

Gottschalk, Peter, and Timothy M. Smeeding. 1997. "Cross-National Comparisons of Earnings and Income Inequality." *Journal of Economic Literature* 35 (2): 633–87.

Hanson, Gordon, and Ann Harrison. 1999. "Trade, Technology and Wage Inequality." *Industrial and Labor Relations Review* 52 (2): 271–88.

Hirschman, Albert O. 1968. "The Political Economy of Import-Substituting Industrialization in Latin America." *Quarterly Journal of Economics* 83 (1): 1–32.

Kindleberger, Charles P. 1996. *Manias, Panics and Crashes*. New York: John Wiley & Sons.

Krueger, Anne O. 1988. "The Relationship Between Trade, Employment, and Development." In *The State of Development Economics: Progress and Perspectives*, eds. Gustav Ranis and Theodore Schultz, 357–85. Cambridge, UK: Basil Blackwell.

———. 1983. *Trade and Employment in Developing Countries—Synthesis and Conclusions*. Chicago: Chicago University Press.

Kuczynski, Pedro-Pablo, and John Williamson, eds. 2003. *After the Washington Consensus. Restarting Growth and Reform in Latin America*. Washington, DC: Institute for International Economics.

Leamer, Edward, and others. 1999. "Does Natural Resource Abundance Increase Latin American Income Inequality?" *Journal of Development Economics* 59 (June Special Issue): 3–42.

Londoño, Juan Luis, and Miguel Székely. 1998. "Sorpresas distributivas después de una década de reformas." *Pensamiento Iberoamericano-Revista de Económica Política* (Special Issue): 195–242.

Márquez, Gustavo, and Carmen Pages. 1997. "Trade and Employment: Evidence from Latin America and the Caribbean." Unpublished paper. Washington, DC, Inter-American Development Bank.

Morley, Samuel, and Rob Vos. Forthcoming. "Bad Luck or Wrong Policies? External Shocks, Domestic Adjustment and the Growth Slowdown in Latin America." In *Who Gains from Free Trade? Export-Led Growth and Poverty in Latin America*, eds. E. Ganuza, S. Morley, S. Robinson, and R. Vos. London: Routledge.

Ocampo, José Antonio, and Lance Taylor. 1998. "Trade Liberalization in Developing Economies: Modest Benefits But Problems with Productivity Growth, Macro Prices and Income Distribution." *Economic Journal* 108 (8): 1523–46.

Prebisch, Raúl. 1963. *Towards a Dynamic Development Policy for Latin America*. New York: United Nations.

———. 1961. "Economic Development or Monetary Stability: A False Dilemma." *Economic Bulletin of Latin America* 6 (1): 1–26.

Revenga, Ana. 1997. "Employment and Wage Effects of Trade Liberalization: The Case of Mexican Manufacturing." *Journal of Labor Economics* 15 (3): S20–S43.

Robbins, Donald J. 1996. "HOS Hits Facts: Facts Win; Evidence on Trade and Wages in the Developing Countries." Development Discussion Paper 557, Harvard Institute for International Development, Cambridge, MA.

Robbins, Donald J., and Thomas H. Gindling. 1999. "Trade Liberalization and the Relative Wages for More-Skilled Workers in Costa Rica." *Review of Development Economics* 3 (2): 140–54.

Ros, Jaime, and César Bouillón. 2002. "Mexico: Trade Liberalization, Growth, Inequality and Poverty." In *Economic Liberalization, Distribution and Poverty: Latin America in the 1990s*, eds. R. Vos, L. Taylor, and R. Paes de Barros, 347–89. Cheltenham, UK: Edward Elgar.

Rosenstein-Rodan, Paul. 1984. "Natura Facit Saltum: Analysis of the Disequilibrium Growth Process." In *Pioneers in Development*, eds. Gerald M. Meier and Dudley Seers, 221. New York: Oxford University Press.

———. 1943. "Problems of Industrialization in Eastern and Southeastern Europe." *Economic Journal* 53 (June–September): 201–11.

Spilimbergo, Antonio, Juan Luis Londoño, and Miguel Székely. 1999. "Income Distribution, Factor Endowments, and Trade Openness." *Journal of Development Economics* 59 (1): 77–101.

Stallings, Barbara, and Wilson Peres. 2000. *Growth, Employment, and Equity. The Impact of Economic Reforms in Latin America and the Caribbean.* Washington, DC: Brookings Institution Press.

Taylor, Lance, and Rob Vos. 2002. "Balance of Payments Liberalization in Latin America: Effects on Growth, Distribution and Poverty." In *Economic Liberalization, Distribution and Poverty: Latin America in the 1990s*, eds. R. Vos, L. Taylor, and R. Paes de Barros, 1–53. Cheltenham, UK: Edward Elgar.

Vos, Rob, Lance Taylor, and Ricardo Paes de Barros. 2002. *Economic Liberalization, Distribution and Poverty: Latin America in the 1990s.* Cheltenham, UK: Edward Elgar.

Wood, Adrian. 1997. "Openness and Wage Inequality in Developing Countries: The Latin American Challenge to East Asian Conventional Wisdom." *World Bank Economic Review* 11 (1): 33–57.

———. 1994. *North-South Trade, Employment and Inequality: Changing Fortunes in a Skill-Driven World.* Oxford, UK: Clarendon Press.

II

Macroeconomic Vulnerabilities

5

Developing-Economy Cycles

Lance Taylor

THE TOPIC OF BUSINESS CYCLES IN ECONOMICS is ancient, but rarely addressed in the context of developing or transition economies. To a degree, the absence of theory fits the reality. Although they are buffeted by frequent and at times substantial macroeconomic disturbances, nonindustrial economies often do not seem to generate their own endogenous fluctuations. But cyclical phenomena do still appear. For example, devaluation/appreciation cycles, oscillating capital inflows and outflows, and investment/excess capacity swings have occurred in many countries over the years.

This chapter sets out simple formal models for the sorts of cycles just mentioned. Three simple principles are employed: Output is determined by effective demand; demand is influenced by shifts in the income distribution; and there are strong, potentially destabilizing interactions between the real and financial sides of the economy. We begin with a memory-refreshing glance at Richard Goodwin's (1967) predator-prey growth cycle, which deals with interactions between distribution and demand, and then go on to the other three models, pointing out policies that might be used to dampen cyclical fluctuations, or even be put to better use. In particular, intelligent ways to manage exchange rate, capital market, and investment policy are discussed.

The author is Arnhold Professor of International Cooperation and Development, New School University, New York. The analysis in this chapter draws on Taylor (2004). Comments by José Antonio Ocampo are gratefully acknowledged.

Preliminaries

The formal specifications presented here all boil down to sets of two differential equations with a similar mathematical form. Consider the Jacobian J of the two equations evaluated at a stationary point:

$$J = \begin{bmatrix} j_{11} & j_{12} \\ j_{21} & j_{22} \end{bmatrix}, \qquad (5.1)$$

where $TrJ = j_{11} + j_{22}$ and $DetJ = j_{11} j_{22} - j_{12} j_{21}$. We will be considering systems in which the first variable has stable own dynamics, $j_{11} < 0$, whereas the second feeds back positively into itself, $j_{22} > 0$, creating a potential instability. If the system is to avoid a saddle point with $DetJ < 0$ and instead generate cycles, it has to be damped by oppositely signed off-diagonal entries—$j_{12} j_{21} < 0$ and $|j_{12} j_{21}| > |j_{11} j_{22}|$. That is, an increase in the second variable sets off a response in the first that drives the second back down. If this effect is strong enough, the destabilizing positive feedback from $j_{22} > 0$ can be overcome.

This sort of specification is especially relevant to economic variables set up as ratios of quantities (for example, output-capital) or as real prices (exchange rate-price level), which in practice often behave in a quasi-stationary fashion, rather than trending over time. When they form a stable system, differential equations involving such variables will generate a convergent spiral around the stationary point in a two-dimensional phase diagram. Continuing exogenous "shocks" would be required to keep the damped cycle going over time. The spiral may also tend toward a "limit cycle" approaching a "closed orbit," or else it may diverge in an expanding spiral. In the following discussion, we will not be greatly concerned with which of these possible outcomes happens. To find out, one has to resort to relatively sophisticated mathematics, which would take too much time to develop here.[1] Rather, the emphasis will be on describing economic mechanisms that can make the potentially destabilizing positive value of j_{22} and damping through j_{21} and j_{12} show up in the first place.

Goodwin's Model

The Goodwin model is a simplified version of this setup. As noted above, it is based on distributive conflict between capitalists and workers. The workers, as it turns out, are economic predators, with output and employment as their prey. The original model presupposed full utilization of capital and savings-determined investment, but Taylor (2004) showed how such un-Keynesian hypotheses can easily be relaxed. Let $K = \kappa X$, with κ as a "technologically determined" capital-output ratio. The employed labor force is $L = bX$. If N is the total population, then the employment ratio λ is given by $\lambda = L/N = b(K/\kappa)/N$. The growth rate of N is n. The wage share is Ψ, and if all profits are saved and depreciation ignored, the growth rate g of the capital stock becomes $g = (1 - \Psi) X/K = (1 - \Psi)/\kappa$.

Over time, the evolution of the employment ratio is determined by growth in output and population,

$$\dot\lambda = \lambda(g - n) = \lambda\{[(1 - \Psi)/\kappa] - n\}, \tag{5.2}$$

where $\dot\lambda = d\lambda/dt$. Along Phillips curve lines, the wage share is assumed to rise in response to the employment ratio,

$$\dot\Psi = \Psi (\ A + B\lambda). \tag{5.3}$$

At a stationary point where $\dot\lambda = \dot\Psi = 0$, the Jacobian of (5.2) – (5.3) takes the rather extreme form,

$$J = \begin{bmatrix} 0 & -\lambda/\kappa \\ B_\Psi & 0 \end{bmatrix}. \tag{5.4}$$

The two variables basically damp fluctuations in one another, with no dynamics of their own. Hirsch and Smale (1974, p. 262) showed that with zeros along the diagonal of the Jacobian, λ and Ψ chase each other endlessly around a counterclockwise closed orbit in the (λ, Ψ) plane that encircles the stationary point (λ^*, Ψ^*). See figure 5.1, in which the particular orbit that the variables trace is set by initial conditions. The labor share is the predator because it rises with λ. The employment ratio, in turn, is the prey because a higher value of Ψ squeezes profits and cuts back accumulation and growth.

A Contractionary Devaluation Cycle

The real wage or wage share is by no means the only object of distributive conflict, especially in developing economies open to international trade. In part because it affects the real wage, the real exchange rate $z = e/P$ often is a bone of contention (e stands for the nominal exchange rate in units of the local currency against the foreign currency, and P is the national price level). Its movements can set off cycles, especially when real devaluation has contractionary effects on output—apparently

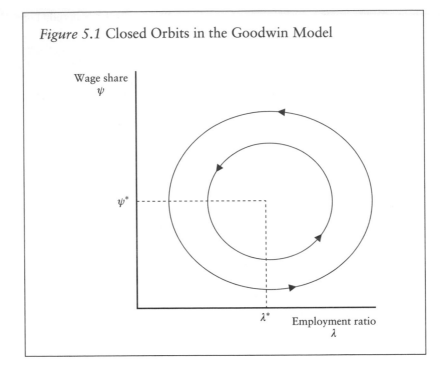

Figure 5.1 Closed Orbits in the Goodwin Model

the case historically in many developing countries. With a lag, devaluation may lead to an export push, followed by wage increases that cut back on exports and ultimately on demand and real wages themselves. Following Larraín and Sachs (1986), it is easy to model such interactions over time.

Let $\varepsilon = E/K$ be the export-capital ratio. A lagged response of ε to changes in z is a realistic assumption,

$$\dot{\varepsilon} = \alpha[\varepsilon^*(z) - \varepsilon], \qquad (5.5)$$

where $\varepsilon^*(z)$ is the "long-run" export level corresponding to a given value of z. Because of preexisting contracts, the need to search for new foreign outlets, and so on, exports do not immediately respond to price signals. Rather, their foreign currency value ε/e is likely to follow a J-curve as a function of time. After a nominal devaluation, ε/e first drops as e jumps up, and then gradually rises according to (5.5).

It is convenient to gauge economic activity by the output-capital ratio $u = X/K$. Suppose that the money wage rate w changes according to a simple Phillips curve, $\dot{w} = \beta bw(u - \bar{u})$, in which β is a response coefficient, b the labor-output ratio, and $\bar{u}$ a long-term level of the output-capital ratio.[2] From this equation, higher activity will make money wages begin to rise. Suppose that the price level is set as a markup over labor and import costs, $P = (1 + \tau)(wb + ea)$, in which a is the import-output ratio. Then $\dot{w} > 0$ means that the real exchange rate will start to appreciate (move downward), leading export expansion to slow.

One can show that real exchange rate dynamics are given by

$$\dot{z} = z(1 - \phi)[\hat{e} - \beta b(u - \bar{u})], \tag{5.6}$$

where $\phi = ea/(ea + wb)$ is the share of imports in variable costs, and $\hat{e} = \dot{e}/e$ is an exogenous growth rate of the spot exchange rate. If devaluation is contractionary, an increase in z pushes u down, making $\partial \dot{z}/\partial z > 0$ and creating a potential instability.

Around a steady state with $\dot{\varepsilon} = \dot{z} = 0$, with positive ε and z, the signs of the entries in the Jacobian of (5.5) and (5.6) are as follows:

$$
\begin{array}{ccc}
 & \varepsilon & z \\
\dot{\varepsilon} & - & + \\
\dot{z} & - & +
\end{array}
\tag{5.7}
$$

The off-diagonal terms have offsetting signs and can stabilize the system. In contrast to the Goodwin model, it is now the "prey" variable z with unstable own dynamics—instead of rapidly reproducing wage-share foxes, think of real exchange rate rabbits.

Figure 5.2 illustrates the resulting cycles. The "export response" curve corresponds to $\dot{\varepsilon} = 0$ and the "rate dynamics" corresponds to $\dot{z} = 0$. Starting from an initial equilibrium, a maxi-devaluation followed by an exchange rate freeze displaces the real rate upward. There is further depreciation until a trajectory crosses the rate dynamics schedule. As a result of the lag in the export response, ε keeps growing until the spiral crosses that curve. A downswing follows, setting off a clockwise spiral with oscillating exports and real exchange rate (not to mention output and inflation), or else cyclical divergence. A closed orbit would be an intermediate case.

An alternative policy could involve a steady depreciation at a rate $\hat{e}$. Via (5.6), this would shift the rate dynamics schedule to the right, leading to a long-term export gain but a lower real wage. If higher profits and more exports stimulated technical advance, the economy could jump to a higher growth path. Amsden (1989) emphasized that such a strategy contributed to the Republic of Korea's export miracle around the three-quarter mark of the 20th century. Because of capital account complications of the sort about to be discussed, Ocampo (2003) suggested

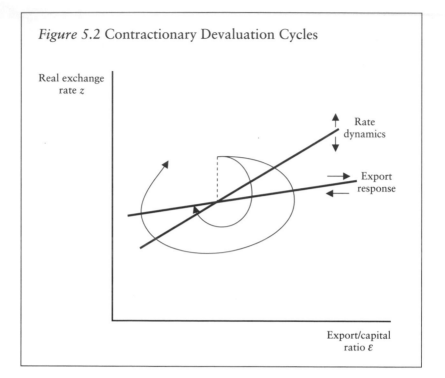

Figure 5.2 Contractionary Devaluation Cycles

that an appropriately managed floating rate is the corresponding contemporary alternative.

A Developing-Country Debt Cycle

The instability in (5.6) is the result of interactions between the real wage and effective demand. Another story can be built around capital movements and "confidence" in the home country's ability to manage its external debt, bringing in interactions between the real and financial sides of the economy, as discussed above. Such effects have been important in the debt cycles observed in many developing countries in the 1990s. A simple formal model emphasizing short- to medium-term dynamics follows, drawing heavily on ideas proposed by Frenkel (1983) and Neftci (2002).

We can begin by stating the familiar "uncovered interest rate parity" equation relating home and foreign interest rates and exchange rate expectations in the form

$$i = i^* + (\varepsilon/e) + \sigma. \tag{5.8}$$

The new symbols include i for the home interest rate and i^* for the foreign rate. It is assumed that there is a "credible" forecast ε (redefined from last section) of the expected instantaneous change in the nominal rate e, perhaps based on a crawling peg being pursued by the central bank. But even taking that into account, there is an observed "spread" between the home and foreign interest rates, with the former being substantially higher (as much as 1,000 or 2,000 basis points). In effect, at least some market participants believe that there is a possibility of a large devaluation at some future time, and thereby insist on a return far exceeding $i^* + (\varepsilon/e)$ if they are to hold home's securities. The magnitude of the spread is measured by σ, and its dynamics have been crucial in observed crises. Falling well short of the drama of the real world, a simple example is presented below, based on the potentially unstable dynamics of foreign investor confidence in the home exchange rate.

A post-Keynesian wrinkle is that (5.8) can be interpreted as fixing (at least a floor under) the home interest rate on loans. That is, on the right-hand side of (5.8), the total cost of funds for a firm borrowing abroad to finance a project at home will be the foreign rate + expected cost from depreciation + spread. Lending rates at home are unlikely to fall below this sum. But with (5.8) setting i, the home supplies of credit and money will have to be endogenous along post-Keynesian lines. We forego the analytical details here.

To set up equations for foreign borrowing, we can begin by letting Ω and Ω^* stand for home and foreign private sector wealth, respectively. Let T and T^* be the stocks of bonds ("T-bills") issued by the two countries' governments, and let qPK and $q^*P^*K^*$ be the asset values of their capital stocks (q and q^* are "valuation ratios" or levels of "Tobin's q"). Then total world wealth is $\Omega + e\Omega^* = (qPK + T) + e(q^*P^*K^* + T^*)$. Expressions for the two countries' individual levels of wealth will be presented momentarily.

With regard to foreign borrowing, assume that the home private sector holds no foreign assets (we thus ignore interesting issues of "dollarization" and "capital flight"), and that the foreign country does not bother to hold home's securities as reserves. Home's net foreign assets N then become $N = eR^* - T_f$, with eR^* as the domestic value of home's international reserves R^*, and T_f as foreign private sector holdings of the home country's bonds. If bond markets clear and both countries satisfy their balance sheets, it is easy to show that $\Omega = qPK + T + N$ and $\Omega^* = q^*P^*K^* + T^* - N/e$. Let η^* be the share of the foreign private sector's portfolio assigned to home bonds, or

$$T_f = e\eta^*\Omega^* = e\eta^*(q^*P^*K^* + T^* - N/e). \tag{5.9}$$

We concentrate on the dynamics of home's external debt T_f and reserves eR^*. The coefficient η^* in (5.9) will be determined in temporary equilibrium by the interest rates, the expected rate of depreciation, and the spread, so to see what happens to T_f over time, we can just examine the behavior of the equation $\dot{T}_f = e\eta*\dot{\Omega}^*$. Substituting through the relevant income/expenditure and flows of funds relationships gives

$$\dot{T}_f = \eta^*[eA^* + (eP^*auK - Pa^*u^*K^*) + iT_f] \qquad (5.10)$$

with

$$A^* = (q^*g^* + \gamma^*)P^*K \qquad (5.11)$$

and a and $a*$ and u and $u*$, respectively, standing for import-output and output-capital ratios in the two countries.

The term $eA*$ represents the increase in demand for home's T-bills induced by growth in foreign wealth (with $q*$ as the foreign country's asset valuation ratio, $g*$ as its capital stock growth rate, and $\gamma*$ its primary fiscal deficit as a share of the value of the capital stock P^*K^*). The term $(eP^* auK - Pa^*u^*K^*)$ in (5.10) is the home trade deficit that must be financed by external borrowing, and the last term iT_f shows that the home country is pursuing Ponzi finance in the sense that it is running up more external debt to meet existing interest obligations.

The change in home's foreign reserves (ignoring its interest receipts $ei^* R^*$ as being trivial) is $e\dot{R}^* = \dot{T}_f - (eP^* auK - Pa^*u^*K^*) - iT_f$, or flow capital inflows minus the trade deficit and interest payments abroad. Substituting (5.10) into this expression shows that

$$e\dot{R}^* = e\eta^*A^* - (1 - \eta^*)[(eP^*auK - Pa^*u^*K^*) + iT_f]. \qquad (5.12)$$

So reserves grow faster with "autonomous" capital inflows $e\eta^*A^*$, and otherwise are eroded by the trade deficit and interest payments (with the term $1 - \eta^*$ taking spillovers into growth of foreign wealth into consideration).

Reserve increases are likely to lead to an expansion of money and credit. In the real economy, both activity u and the trade deficit $(eP^*auK - Pa^*u^*K^*)$ should rise, reducing the growth of reserves: $\partial(e\dot{R}^*)/\partial(eR^*) < 0$ in (5.12). A higher rate spread σ will push up the interest rate i from (5.8). The cost of external debt service iT_f will increase, but the trade deficit is likely to fall. We assume the latter effect dominates, so $\partial(e\dot{R}^*)/\partial\sigma > 0$. The "stable reserves" schedule in figure 5.3 corresponds to the condition $eR^* = 0$. Suppose that $\eta*$ increases in a foreign portfolio shift toward home bonds. Because in (5.12) we have $\partial(e\dot{R}^*)/\partial(eR^*) < 0$, eR^* would have to rise to hold $e\dot{R}^* = 0$; that is, the stable reserves schedule shifts outward.

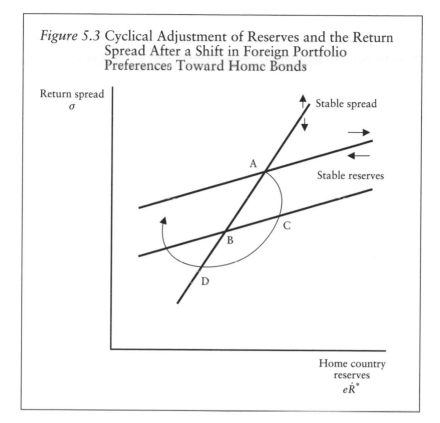

Figure 5.3 Cyclical Adjustment of Reserves and the Return Spread After a Shift in Foreign Portfolio Preferences Toward Home Bonds

Turning to the evolution of the spread over time, it is likely that higher reserves reduce anxiety in forward markets, so that $\partial\dot\sigma/\partial(eR^*) < 0$. On the other hand, there may be positive feedback of expectational changes into themselves, $\partial\dot\sigma/\partial\sigma > 0$, because a fall in the spread induces less perceived risk to holding home securities (and a rise creates greater preoccupations). We get the differential equation

$$\dot\sigma = f(eR^*, \sigma), \tag{5.13}$$

with the partial derivatives just indicated. The stable reserves schedule in figure 5.3 represents the condition $\dot\sigma = 0$.

Figure 5.3 shows local dynamics for the system (5.12) – (5.13). As in figure 5.2, the dynamic system generates clockwise spirals. By shifting the stable reserves schedule outward, an increase in η^* moves the steady-state equilibrium from A to B. With the capital inflow, reserves start to increase, in turn making $\dot{\sigma} < 0$. These trends continue until the economy reaches point C, where an increasing trade deficit makes $e\dot{R}^* < 0$. At point D, reserve losses become severe enough to force the return spread to start to rise, pushing up the interest rate as well. In the diagram, a stable or unstable cycle may ensue. In practice, in the 1990s, rising rates and currency imbalances in developing-country balance sheets (with assets mostly denominated in local currencies and liabilities in foreign currencies) forced σ to jump upward and crises followed. But the cyclical dynamic path that led into the collapses was exactly the one illustrated in the transition from points A through D in figure 5.3.

What could be done to avoid such a destabilizing spiral? Restrictions on capital inflows as applied in Chile and Colombia in the 1990s could mitigate the effects of an upward jump in η^*. "Liability policies" aimed at improving private and public sector debt profiles would operate in the same direction, as would better prudential regulation of the domestic financial system. In some countries, partial sterilization of capital inflows has been feasible for the central bank; countercyclical fiscal policy may be another option. For more detailed analysis of such policy moves, see Ocampo (2003).

Excess Capacity, Corporate Debt Burden, and a "Cold Shower"

Sticking to a stable interest rate in a generally post-Keynesian world, it is interesting to ask how animal spirits and corporate (as opposed to fiscal) debt interact over the cycle—some diagnoses of the East Asian financial crises come to mind. Cycles imposed on a growth model introduced by Lavoie and Godley (2000) help illustrate the dynamics. Several questions can be addressed:

1. Is there a tendency for industrialized economies (such as Korea's) to generate excess capacity and/or a rising organic composition of capital, to prime the plumbing for a Schumpeterian "cold shower"?[3]

2. If investment continues to rise while capacity utilization is falling, how does the implied "realization crisis" work itself out?

3. In particular, how long can investors' optimism persist when overcapacity begins to raise its head?

Such questions were hotly debated in Left U.S. policy circles around the latest turn of the century (see, for example, Greider [1997] and many subsequent pieces). They obviously cannot be fully answered by contemplating a clockwise spiral in a two-dimensional phase plane, but perhaps the construct to follow can shed some light.

The key state variable for Lavoie and Godley is λ, redefined from the second section above as the ratio of corporate debt to the replacement value of the capital stock. That is, $\lambda = L/PK$, with L as business debt currently outstanding. For simplicity, we assume that business firms borrow only from banks, and that the banking system balance sheet takes the "Wicksellian" form $M = L$, with M as the money supply. Basically, "loans create money" in the story to follow. The firms also issue equity to the household sector. They practice markup pricing over wage costs at a constant rate, implicitly setting the profit rate r. Like r and λ, several other variables in the model are normalized by PK.

A key distinction centers on the effect of λ on the output-capital ratio u. Is effective demand "debt burdened" ($\partial u/\partial \lambda < 0$) or "debt led" ($\partial u/\partial \lambda > 0$)? Second, if the debt ratio behaves in self-stabilizing fashion ($d\lambda/d\lambda < 0$ in a total derivative through the dynamic system), then what about the sign of $d\lambda/du$? Lavoie and Godley called a negative value "normal." A positive "Minskyan" response of debt growth to economic activity is not a bad label.[4]

In a bit more detail, macro equilibrium can be described in terms of saving and investment functions. The growth rate of the capital stock permitted by available saving, g^s, follows from the flow of fund balances for firms and households. Firms save a proportion s_f of their income net of interest payments $r - j\lambda$ (with r as the profit rate and j as the predetermined real rate of interest). Their other sources of funds are new borrowing $\lambda\hat{L}$ and issuance of equity. A working hypothesis is that they finance a share χ of their capital formation $g = I/K$ (I is gross investment and we ignore depreciation) with new shares. If V is the stock of equity outstanding and P_v its price, we get $P_v\dot{V}/PK = \chi g$.

Investment g equals the sum of business retained earnings $s_f(r - j\lambda)$ and new issues of securities. The overall business flow of funds is $s_f(r - j\lambda) + \lambda\hat{L} + P_v\dot{V} - g = 0$, which can be restated as

$$s_f(r - j\lambda) + \lambda\hat{L} - (1 - \chi)g = 0. \tag{5.14}$$

A post-Keynesian or "endogenous money" twist in this equation is the term for the growth of bank credit, $\lambda\hat{L}$. The profit rate r and growth rate g are determined on the real side of the model, so the supply of bank loans has to be endogenous to allow firms to carry through their investment plans.

Total primary wealth in the economy is $\Omega = qPK$, all held by households. Their consumption $\gamma_h = PC/PK$ is assumed to depend on (normalized) income ξ_h and wealth, $\gamma_h = (1 - s_h)\xi_h + \phi q$.

Household income comprises the wage bill per unit of capital stock $(u - r)$, loan interest paid by firms that is assumed to be transferred to the household sector by banks $(j\lambda)$, and the part of earnings not retained by firms that flows to households as dividends $(1 - s_f)(r - j\lambda)$. With $\xi_h = u - r + j\lambda + (1 - s_f)(r - j\lambda) = u - s_f(r = j\lambda)$, the household flow of funds is

$$s_h[(u - s_f)(r - j\lambda)] - \phi q - \chi g - \lambda \hat{M} = 0. \qquad (5.15)$$

Because $L = M$ and $\hat{L} = \hat{M}$ from the banking system's balance sheet, accounting consistency ensures that households obligingly pick up the new deposits $\lambda \hat{M}$ that bank lending creates.

The growth rate of the capital stock permitted by available saving, g^s, follows from the sum of (5.14) and (5.15),

$$s_h u + s_f(1 - s_h)(r - j\lambda) - \phi q - g^s = 0. \qquad (5.16)$$

Post-Keynesian investment functions emphasize cash-flow considerations. If the interest burden $j\lambda$ increases, firms are likely to cut back on capital formation g^i. For symmetry with the saving function (5.16), it is convenient to make g^i depend on q, and we also carry a term in capacity utilization:

$$g^i = g_0 + \beta u + \eta q - \Psi j\lambda. \qquad (5.17)$$

The short-term macro equilibrium condition is $g^i - g^s = 0$, or

$$g_0 + (\eta + \phi)q + [s_f(1 - s_h) - \Psi]j\lambda - [s_f(1 - s_h)\pi + s_h - \beta]u = 0, \qquad (5.18)$$

where the profit rate $r = \pi u$, with π as the share of profits in total income (assumed constant for simplicity).

The usual stability condition is a positive value for the term in brackets multiplying u in (5.18), $s_f(1 - s_h)\pi + s_h - \beta > 0$. Assuming that it is satisfied, note the ambiguous effect of $j\lambda$ on u. A bigger debt burden reduces investment demand through the coefficient $-\Psi$ but also cuts into firms' saving. Filtered through profits distributed to households, lower retained earnings create a net leakage reduction of $s_f(1 - s_h)j\lambda$. If this term exceeds Ψ, effective demand is debt led. When $\Psi > s_f(1 - s_h)j\lambda$, demand is debt burdened. The remaining term in (5.18) involves q. Through both investment and saving effects, a higher q increases the level of economic activity.

To set up a cycle model around λ, we can bring in investment confidence. The straightforward approach is to make the intercept term g_0 in the investment function (5.17) a dynamic variable,

$$\dot{g}_0 = f_g(\lambda, g_0). \qquad (5.19)$$

Positive feedback can be introduced by making the second partial derivative of the function f_g positive; a degree of caution on the part of investing firms (borrower's and lender's risks, and so forth) suggests that the first partial should be negative.

From the business sector's flow of funds (5.14), a differential equation for λ can be written as

$$\dot{\lambda} = (s_f j - g)\lambda + (1 - \chi)g - s_f \pi u. \tag{5.20}$$

As noted above, $d\dot{\lambda}/du$ from this equation can take either sign, whereas we assume that $d\dot{\lambda}/d\lambda < 0$. The short-term macro variables g and u will both respond positively to g_0, so (5.20) can be restated as

$$\dot{\lambda} = f_\lambda(\lambda, g_0). \tag{5.21}$$

Given the signs of the partial derivatives of f_g postulated in connection with (5.19), the existence of a cyclical solution to (5.19) and (5.21) requires that $d\dot{\lambda}/dg_0 > 0$; that is, a Minskyan debt growth response to rising animal spirits. Figure 5.4 shows the dynamics, with the "growth"

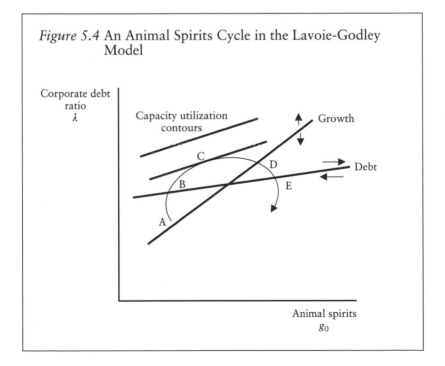

Figure 5.4 An Animal Spirits Cycle in the Lavoie-Godley Model

schedule corresponding to $\dot{g}_0 = 0$ and the "debt" curve corresponding to $\lambda > 0$. The familiar clockwise spiral appears.

An initial low-level temporary equilibrium at A will be associated with a falling debt burden and improving animal spirits until the (g_0, λ) trajectory crosses the debt schedule at B. Then λ begins to rise, while g_0 still increases until the growth schedule is crossed (point D). Autonomous investment begins to fall, and the cycle bottoms out as the debt ratio declines after the trajectory crosses the corresponding schedule again at E. Around that point, presumably, the cold shower kicks in.

What happens to capacity utilization while this spiral uncoils? Almost certainly, u responds positively to g_0. It is also likely that effective demand is debt burdened. On these assumptions ($\partial u / \partial g_0 > 0$ and $\partial u / \partial \lambda < 0$), we can sketch the positively sloped "capacity utilization" contours in figure 5.4. Each curve shows combinations of g_0 and λ that hold u constant, with its level increasing across contours toward the southeast. On this accounting, a realization crisis occurs at point C, where the trajectory is tangent to a contour line. Thereafter, u falls while animal spirits continue increasing until point D—growing overcapacity precedes a fall in optimism in this scenario. Together with a rising debt burden, a lower level of u slows investment demand; ultimately, output $X = uK$ will begin to fall as well.

One argument in the late 1990s was that a cycle of the sort sketched in the diagram was especially threatening because industrial capacity had been growing worldwide since the mid-1980s, under the stimulus of globalization. Instead of just one country's macro system, the whole world's was supposed to be going through a confidence squeeze. Apparent over-investment in capital goods supporting information technology (excess capacity for computer components) and infrastructure for the Internet (thousands of miles of unused fiberoptic cable) only made the situation worse.

Second, inflation had slowed almost everywhere, so that falling markup rates resulting from rising interest costs and decreasing capacity utilization were beginning to cause price levels to decline. Following Palley (1996), it would be straightforward to add a more complete treatment of the financial system to the present setup to show how debt deflation could further cut into economic activity.

Third, wage increases as advocated by people on the Left could restore aggregate demand—as may be the case in many developing countries—is wage led.[5] It is also true that demand is not stimulated by higher interest rates. So attempts to push rates down make sense in terms of the present model. Whether such a move would forestall massive worldwide output contraction combined with severe price deflation may still be an open question.

Final Thoughts

There are numerous oscillatory processes at work in the real economy, out there. Moreover, their importance changes over time. Simple little two-dimensional models cannot begin to cope with all the fluctuations (and fluctuations of fluctuations) that exist.

Nevertheless, they can focus attention on key oscillations. Devaluation and external debt cycles in developing economies surely happen. In both rich and poor countries, distributive and some sort of Lavoie-Godley-Minsky financial oscillations are visibly present. Trying to put the whole set of motions into a plausible package is the challenge, which neither econometrics nor computer simulation is likely to meet fully. But at least the toy models and their fancier cousins give a modicum of insight into some of the mechanisms underlying the intrinsic fluctuations of capitalism. In the future, of course, new models will have to be developed to track novel forms of cycles when they inevitably begin to spiral.

Endnotes

1. In continuous time, oscillating variables appear in a two-dimensional system when its eigenvalues are conjugate complex (as opposed to real); that is, they can be written in the form $\lambda = \alpha + \beta i$ and $\bar{\lambda} = \alpha + \beta i$, with $\alpha = TrJ - 2$. For the oscillations to converge locally, the real part α of the eigenvalues has to be negative. Steady cycles show up when the real part equals zero, and there are divergent spirals when it is positive. The two standard methods to investigate the properties of such systems are Hopf bifurcations and the Poincaré-Bendixson theorem. The former analyzes the changing nature of cycles as the real part of the eigenvalues shifts through the value zero. The latter sets out global conditions for convergence to a closed orbit. Hirsch and Smale (1974) is a classic text on these matters, and Lorenz (1989) offered economic intuition.

2. As stated, the Phillips curve presupposes the existence of a "natural" level $\bar{u}$ of u at which there is zero wage inflation. This unpalatable assumption can be relaxed, but to set up a simple cycle model it is convenient to employ it here.

3. The reference is to Schumpeter's famous 1930s pronouncement to credulous Harvard undergraduates that the Great Depression was an unavoidable capitalist "cold shower" (Heilbroner 1999).

4. There is an obvious parallel between using debt and a distributive variable, such as the wage share or profit rate, as a shift variable for effective demand. The literature on wage-led or profit-led demand shifts originated with Rowthorn (1982) and Dutt (1984), and was reviewed by Blecker (2002) and Taylor (2004). Similarly, normal and Minskyan responses of debt growth to economic activity run parallel to "forced saving" and "profit-squeeze" responses of the wage share. Minsky (1975) seemed to point to the label adopted here.

5. One symptom of wage-led demand is contractionary devaluation. Analytical linkages between the cycles discussed in the second and fourth sections of this chapter would be interesting to explore.

Bibliography

Amsden, Alice S. 1989. *Asia's Next Giant: South Korea and Late Industrialization.* New York: Oxford University Press.

Blecker, Robert A. 2002. "Distribution, Demand, and Growth in Neo-Kaleckian Macro Models." In *Demand-Led Growth: Challenging the Supply-Side Vision of the Long Run,* ed. Mark Setterfield, 129–52. Cheltenham, UK: Edward Elgar.

Dutt, Amitava Krishna. 1984. "Stagnation, Income Distribution, and Monopoly Power." *Cambridge Journal of Economics* 8 (1): 25–40.

Frenkel, Roberto. 1983. "Mercado financiero, expectativas cambiarias y movimientos de capital." *El Trimestre Economico* 50 (4): 2041–76.

Goodwin, Richard M. 1967. "A Growth Cycle." In *Socialism, Capitalism, and Growth,* ed. C. H. Feinstein, 34–58. Cambridge, UK: Cambridge University Press.

Greider, William. 1997. *One World, Ready or Not: The Manic Logic of Global Capitalism.* New York: Simon & Schuster.

Heilbroner, Robert. 1999. *The Worldly Philosophers.* 7th rev. ed. New York: Simon & Schuster.

Hirsch, Morris W., and Stephen Smale. 1974. *Differential Equations, Dynamical Systems, and Linear Algebra.* New York: Academic Press.

Larraín, Felipe, and Jeffrey Sachs. 1986. *Contractionary Devaluation, and Dynamic Adjustment of Exports and Wages.* Cambridge, MA: NBER.

Lavoie, Marc, and Wynne Godley. 2000. *Kaleckian Models of Growth in a Stock-Flow Monetary Framework: A Neo-Kaldorian Model.* Annandale-on-Hudson, NY: Jerome Levy Economics Institute, Bard College.

Lorenz, Hans-Walter. 1989. *Nonlinear Dynamical Economics and Chaotic Motion.* Berlin: Springer-Verlag.

Minsky, Hyman P. 1975. *John Maynard Keynes.* New York: Columbia University Press.

Neftci, Salih N. 2002. "FX Short Positions, Balance Sheets, and Financial Turbulence: An Interpretation of the Asian Financial Crisis." In *International Capital Markets: Systems in Transition,* eds. John Eatwell and Lance Taylor, 277–96. New York: Oxford University Press.

Ocampo, José Antonio. 2003. "Developing Countries' Anti-Cyclical Policies in a Globalized World." In *Development Economics and Structuralist Macroeconomics: Essays in Honour of Lance Taylor,* eds. Amitava Dutt and Jaime Ros, 374–405. Cheltenham, UK: Edward Elgar.

Palley, Thomas I. 1996. *Post Keynesian Economics.* New York: St. Martin's Press.

Rowthorn, Robert E. 1982. "Demand, Real Wages, and Economic Growth." *Studi Economici* 18: 2–53.

Taylor, Lance. 2004. *Reconstructing Macroeconomics: Critiques of the Mainstream and Structuralist Alternatives.* Cambridge, MA: Harvard University Press.

6

Fiscal Policy Efficacy and Private Deficits: A Macroeconomic Approach

Manuel Marfán

THE ANALYSIS IS INSPIRED BY THE Chilean economic situation throughout the 1990s, in which a disciplined fiscal policy and an independent central bank that succeeded in pursuing an inflation target were not enough to revert overall excess expenditure, exchange rate misalignment, or, more generally, external vulnerability. Our conviction is that the fundamentals behind these events are not idiosyncratic to the Chilean case, but are valid for a more general case of emerging economies open to international financial markets. This chapter concentrates on the policy dilemmas faced by successful emerging economies in the context of voluntary financial flows.

The main point stressed here is that when inflation is endogenous in an otherwise Mundell-Fleming context, the efficacy of alternative policy instruments changes substantially. We argue that conventional monetary and/or exchange rate policies handled by the central bank are effective to pursue nominal targets, but ineffective to alter real variables in the short run, including the real exchange rate. Fiscal policy, in turn, is always effective on real variables in the short run, irrespective of the exchange rate regime.

The author is a member of the Board of the Central Bank of Chile and was Director of the Division of Economic Development, Economic Commission for Latin America and the Caribbean, and Senior Adviser on Macroeconomic Policy to the Minister of Finance, Under-Secretary of Finance, and Minister of Finance of Chile during the 1990s.

There are relevant additional conclusions related to the previous point. First, inflation is an incomplete measure of economic overheating and macroeconomic inconsistency. Inflationary pressures coming from unsustainable growth may be totally or partially reverted by currency appreciation. Excess growth and currency appreciation, in turn, may co-exist as long as current account deterioration is feasible in the short run. A deteriorating current account may also be a symptom of overheating and macroeconomic inconsistency.

Second, exuberant private sector behavior arising from optimistic medium-term prospects may generate short-run overheating. Conventional central bank policies (monetary and/or exchange rate policies) are unable to restore a sustainable equilibrium. The government, however, can correct misalignment of real variables by generating a fiscal surplus that compensates for excess private expenditure. The greater the exuberance of the private sector, the greater the fiscal thrift needed.

Third, the public sector does not have the institutional role of compensating for excess private expenditure, imposing a policy dilemma that cannot be solved by conventional policy instruments. We explore some unconventional policy instruments, such as a cyclical tax and a simplified version of a tax on financial flows.

The chapter has five sections. The first one makes a basic algebraic approximation of the model. The second section constructs a theoretical argument applicable to the general case of a small economy open to voluntary financial flows. It concludes that fiscal policy is the unique conventional policy instrument that is effective on real variables and derives the optimal fiscal policy that ensures sustainable equilibrium. The third section argues that the optimal fiscal policy derived in the previous section is politically unfeasible. It presents broad data for nine economies that faced episodes of private exuberance throughout the 1990s. The fourth section analyzes the pros and cons of two heterodox policy instruments that can help attain overall consistency. The final section summarizes the main findings. The annex develops the underlying mathematical model.

A Basic Approximation

Our approach concentrates on the short run, where the time span is the relevant one for fiscal policy analysis (normally a year). The analysis considers that inflation is an endogenous variable, explained by cost-push pressures and demand inflation. Within the cost-push component, we concentrate on nominal exchange rate pressures. Nominal depreciation may be inflationary as long as it raises the price of traded goods and services, including the price of traded inputs used in nontraded goods production. In the very short run, lagged effects may induce overshooting and/or price oscillations. We simplify these effects by assuming that the pass-through of nominal depreciation to inflation is completed within the time span relevant for fiscal policy analysis, with no lags remaining. We also simplify wage inflation dynamics by assuming that wage contracts consider productivity growth and expected inflation.[1] Within demand inflation, the relevant component is the gap between actual and potential gross national product (GNP).

Equation (6.1) summarizes these components:

$$p = c_0 e + (1 - c_0)p* + c_1(y - y_d); \quad 0 < c_0 < 1; \quad c_1 > 0, \quad (6.1)$$

where p and $p*$ represent actual and expected inflation, e is the rate of nominal depreciation ($e > 0$ means a depreciation), and y and y_d are actual and potential GNP growth, respectively.[2] A straightforward dynamics for the real exchange rate ($e - p$) is derived from (6.1):

$$(e - p) = (c_1/c_0)(y_d - y) + ((1 - c_0)/c_0)(p - p*). \quad (6.2)$$

The real exchange rate is sensitive to inflation surprises ($p - p*$). However, under rational expectations there are no systematic deviations of p from $p*$, so the real exchange rate evolves according to the state of the cycle ($y_d - y$). In the absence of surprises, real appreciation would be associated with cyclical peaks ($y > y_d$), whereas real depreciation would need a depressed economy. This argument has nothing to do with whether depreciation is expansionary or contractionary; rather it concerns how a change in the nominal exchange rate is split between inflationary pressures and changes in the real exchange rate. A nominal devaluation would generate inflation if $y \geq y_d$, and the same nominal devaluation would generate a real depreciation if $y < y_d$. This outcome is irrespective of the exchange rate regime, which usually determines the evolution of the nominal exchange rate.

Our third equation considers the current account of the balance of payments. We take the standard view in which the current account improves with a real depreciation or with lower GNP growth:

$$C = a_1(d(e - p) - y); \quad a_1, d > 0, \quad (6.3)$$

where C represents the change in the current account surplus as a percentage of GNP.

From (6.2) we observed that excess growth and real appreciation go together. Thus, an overheated economy deteriorates the current account as a percentage of GNP because of both the direct effect of excess growth and the indirect effect of an appreciating currency. To consider the situation of a sustainable current account, we define $\hat{C}$ as the threshold for C consistent with long-run sustainability. If external financing is available, C may fall below $\hat{C}$ in the short run, at the expense of increasing external vulnerability. For algebraic simplicity we also define y_x as the GNP rate of growth consistent with a sustainable current account:

$$y_x \equiv -\hat{C}/a_1. \tag{6.4}$$

Combining the last two expressions, we derive the equation for the current account:

$$C = a_1(y_x + d(e - p) - y) + \hat{C}. \tag{6.5}$$

That is, the actual current account C would deviate from its sustainable path $\hat{C}$, depending on the gap between actual growth (y) and the one consistent with external equilibrium plus the slack provided by real exchange rate movements ($y_x + d(e - p)$).

Note that when expectations are fulfilled ($p = p*$ in equation [6.1]) and the current account is in its sustainable path ($C = \hat{C}$ in equation [6.5]), we can derive the sustainable equilibrium rate of GNP growth and the equilibrium rate of real depreciation:

$$y = \hat{y} = (c_0\, y_x + c_1 d\, y_d)/(c_0 + c_1 d) \tag{6.6}$$

$$(e - p) = \hat{e} = c_1(y_d - y_x)/(c_0 + c_1 d). \tag{6.7}$$

The sustainable rate of growth is a weighted average of the domestic constraint on growth (y_d) and the external sustainability growth (y_x). The equilibrium real exchange rate, in turn, depends on the gap between these two constraints on growth: It depreciates when the external constraint is more binding than the domestic constraint on growth ($y_x < y_d$) and appreciates when the domestic constraint is more binding ($y_d < y_x$), an intuitive outcome. Notice that excess growth is unambiguously linked to real exchange rate misalignment and an unsustainable current account:

$$y > \hat{y} \Leftrightarrow C < \hat{C} \Leftrightarrow (e - p) < \hat{e}. \tag{6.8}$$

Throughout the text we refer to $\hat{y}$, $\hat{e}$, and $\hat{C}$ as the optimal or sustainable rate of growth, real depreciation, and current account, respectively.

From a different perspective, the current account is also equal to excess domestic expenditure, which may be rooted either in private or public sector excess expenditure:

$$0 = C + S + H, \tag{6.9}$$

where S is the change in the fiscal deficit as a percentage of GNP (or fiscal stance), and H is the change in private sector excess expenditure (or private deficit pressure), also as a percentage of GNP. Excess expenditure is defined as the difference between savings and real investment.

So, on the one hand, the current account performance is linked to GNP cycles that, in turn, are linked to real exchange rate cycles. On the other hand, the current account performance is also linked to expenditure cycles, whether public or private.

For the sake of completeness, we list the rest of our assumptions:

1. A budget law known in advance by all economic actors sets government expenditures.

2. The central bank handles its policy instruments to optimize a loss function representing its policy targets. All agents know the central bank's loss function.

3. The private sector spends according to an (expected) intertemporal plan. In particular, changes in its deficit (H) depend positively on private sector confidence—or medium-term prospects—and depend negatively on the real interest rate. Private sector confidence, in turn, may be affected in the short run by macroeconomic inconsistency. Unexpected private income is completely saved in the short run.

4. The central bank and the underlying policy regime determine the (nominal) supply of money. The demand for real cash balances evolves, depending on the rate of GNP growth and the nominal interest rate, with the conventional signs.

5. The interest rate follows a conventional arbitrage rule, equal to the international interest rate plus the expected nominal depreciation and a country-specific risk premium (perfect financial mobility). The risk premium may be affected by macroeconomic inconsistency.

6. The central bank reacts instantaneously to surprises, a plausible assumption when the short run is a whole fiscal year. Private agents set their expectations rationally but are subject to surprises. The government also sets its expectations rationally and is the slowest agent (that is, private agents set their expectations knowing the fiscal policy in place). When pursuing a macroeconomic goal, the government optimizes the expected value of the target variable.

Fiscal Policy Efficacy Under an Open Capital Account

With perfect capital mobility the private sector faces no liquidity constraints. So the private sector deficit responds to an intertemporal optimization dominated by private sector confidence and an interest rate following an arbitrage rule. There is no a priori reason why the private deficit should be positive or negative in the short run. An exuberant private sector with a high degree of confidence in medium-term prospects may exhibit an expanding deficit in the short run. A depressed private sector would display a conservative attitude with a smaller deficit or even a surplus. An exuberant or depressive private sector does not imply irrational behavior. It is merely the outcome of the optimization of the net present value of the relevant variables.

Some of our results are dependent on the fact that whereas the private sector optimizes its behavior on an intertemporal basis, the evolution of the real exchange rate is determined by an equation such as (6.2), which only has short-run components. Conventional macroeconomic policy, especially when responding to reaction functions known by all agents, is less effective to dominate the arguments behind private sector behavior.

If inflation was exogenous—that is, if equation (6.1) was not valid—the model would reproduce the standard conclusion that fiscal policy is effective on short-run growth under a fixed exchange regime, whereas monetary policy would be the effective instrument under a floating regime. Under such a setting, however, a floating exchange rate regime means that the real exchange rate floats, and a fixed exchange rate regime means that the real exchange rate is fixed. But with endogenous inflation such as equation (6.1), the exchange rate regime is a rationale for the nominal exchange rate. The effects on the real exchange rate are dependent on the rate of inflation. In this new context, the conclusion on the efficacy of policy instruments changes.

We first analyze the situation where fiscal policy is designed to attain a sustainable current account. The central bank, in turn, pursues an inflation target (see annex, case 1). It can be shown that in the absence of surprises the government and the central bank achieve their respective goals: Short-run equilibrium displays a current account consistent with medium-term sustainability, with no inflation. As noted before, whenever the current account is in its sustainable medium-term path, equilibrium growth ($\hat{y}$) is a weighted average of y_d and y_x and the equilibrium real exchange rate ($\hat{e}$) evolves depending on the gap between y_d and y_x. We label the sustainable equilibrium with no inflation as the "optimal case," and that provides a benchmark against which we compare all other situations.

The current account deficit is the sum of public plus private deficits. To achieve a sustainable current account, the fiscal stance must accommodate for excess private expenditure. The more exuberant the private sector, the thriftier the concomitant optimal fiscal policy; the more depressed the private sector, the larger (that is, the more expansionary) the fiscal stance needed.[3] An optimal fiscal schedule thus derived implies that the private sector crowds out or crowds in the public sector in the short run, instead of the other way around.

If the government deviates from the optimal fiscal policy rule, equilibrium changes. For instance, consider a situation in which the central bank continues targeting inflation but the fiscal stance is larger than optimal (see annex, case 2). In that case the effects would be unambiguously predictable. GNP growth would be larger than optimal ($y > \hat{y}$), the real exchange rate would over-appreciate ($(e - p) < \hat{e}$), and the current account would deteriorate below its sustainable level ($C < \hat{C}$). Likewise, if the fiscal stance is smaller (that is, less expansionary or more contractionary) than optimal, the final outcome would be the opposite [$y < \hat{y}$, $(e - p) > \hat{e}$ and $C > \hat{C}$]. If private sector confidence and the country risk premium accommodate for deviations from the optimal equilibrium, misalignment of real variables would diminish but would not be eliminated.

The government may take advantage of the previous outcome and adjust fiscal policy to attain a short-run growth target. If the growth target is ambitious, the government will succeed and attain excess growth in the short run, but at the expense of an unsustainable current account path (external vulnerability) and exchange rate misalignment. The central bank, in turn, would continue succeeding in its inflation target. These results do not depend on whether the policy instrument of the central bank is the exchange rate or, alternatively, monetary policy with a floating currency. Fiscal policy would be effective on short-run growth, whatever the exchange rate regime.

Fiscal policy may also succeed when targeting other real variables. For instance, the government may target a neutral fiscal stance ($S = 0$) to signal fiscal discipline. The authority would also succeed in this alternative target. But in this case fiscal policy would resign to compensate for private sector exuberance. The final outcome would deviate from the optimal equilibrium depending on private sector behavior. Private sector exuberance would lead to excess growth, excess appreciation, and an unsustainable current account. Depressed private sector confidence would lead to the opposite results. Moreover, such a fiscal policy exacerbates the cycles provoked by private sector behavior, turning itself into a pro-cyclical policy scheme.

Alternatively, fiscal policy may follow a cycle-free rule. For instance, it may target a "structurally" neutral fiscal stance, setting its expenditures at the level of revenues consistent with sustainable growth. Again, cycles will be determined by private sector behavior, but these would not be amplified by fiscal policy.

Fiscal policy may also target a constant real exchange rate ($(e - p) = 0$), a special case to which we will refer later. The government will succeed again, but the side effects are less straightforward. In an economy that is rapidly increasing its competitiveness (that is, $y_x > y_d$), the optimal real exchange rate should appreciate, as we noted in the first section above. If the government targets a constant real exchange rate and succeeds, it would reduce short-run growth to below its optimal path ($y < \hat{y}$), and the current account would exhibit a larger than optimal surplus ($C > \hat{C}$). On the other hand, in an economy where potential output grows faster than international competitiveness ($y_d > y_x$), the optimal real exchange rate should depreciate. If fiscal policy forces a constant real exchange rate, the final equilibrium would be with excess growth and an unsustainable current account.

In our previous conclusions, the efficacy of fiscal policy on real variables is independent of the exchange rate regime. This outcome is the result of endogenous inflation. The standard Mundell-Fleming approach assumes that inflation is exogenous. As we noted earlier, exchange rate floating in that context means real exchange rate floating. Likewise, monetary policy with exogenous inflation means real money supply management. With endogenous inflation, the policy instruments of the central bank are nominal in nature: the nominal exchange rate or the nominal supply of money. Exchange rate floating is a rationale for the nominal and not for the real exchange rate. If the private sector responds exclusively to the stimulus of real variables—whether in actual or expected value—nominal policy management is ineffective if their changes are completely captured by inflation. Fiscal policy, on the other hand, is a real policy instrument and has real effects.

An alternative explanation for the efficacy of fiscal policy could be the particular reaction function assumed so far for the central bank. Perhaps fiscal policy may be ineffective *per se*, and real effects may be the outcome of the reaction of the central bank. Our model rejects this alternative hypothesis. However, we can consider alternative reactions of the central bank to the deviations provoked by a non-optimal fiscal policy. For instance, if the central bank follows a preannounced monetary rule and lets the exchange rate float, all real variables—including growth and the real exchange rate—would continue to be determined by fiscal policy. Inflation is the sole variable that would be affected by the monetary rule. Alternatively, consider a situation in which fiscal policy is more expansionary than the optimal rule, generating excess growth, exchange rate misalignment, and an unsustainable current account. The central bank may try to restore a sustainable equilibrium by simultaneously targeting an optimal real exchange rate path ($(e - p) = \hat{e}$) and inflation ($p = 0$). When such behavior on the part of the central bank is anticipated by the private sector, the new equilibrium will not affect real variables, but inflation would turn positive.

The straightforward conclusion is that a conventional central bank succeeds solely when targeting nominal variables, such as inflation or the nominal exchange rate, but fails when trying to target real variables when fiscal policy is set. Even if the central bank cares about misalignment of real variables, it is better off when monitoring inflation only. The central bank, however, would be the effective institution to tackle unexpected shocks.

Because central bank intervention can only make things worse, it may refrain from any intervention at all and "dollarize" the economy (or "euroize" or set a currency board), so that there is neither exchange rate policy nor monetary policy. Not surprising at this stage, fiscal policy would maintain its efficacy on real variables. The sole main difference is that inflation would replace the role of the exchange rate with the opposite sign.[4] Inflation would play the role of a real depreciation and deflation of a real appreciation. Because fiscal policy is effective on the real exchange rate, in this particular case it would be effective on inflation as well. Inflation targeting through fiscal policy for economies joining a currency area such as the Euro Area would be equivalent to real exchange rate targeting.

In fact, the sole situation in which the central bank may have a systematic influence on real variables is when inflation generates systematic real effects (for example, by affecting private sector confidence and/or the country risk premium). It can be shown that an active central bank may generate whatever inflation rate it pursues. So it can use this potential and use the rate of inflation as its policy instrument. This is a theoretical case that apparently has no practical significance and that we will not explore further.

Conventional central banks should pursue nominal targets only, even in cases of real variable misalignment. This conclusion has to do with how a central bank should use its "hard" policy instruments, such as monetary and exchange rate policy. But central banks may also try "soft" policy interventions, using the Lucas critique in their favor. For instance, a reputable central bank may publicize its assessment of whether private markets are in an exuberant or a depressed situation. The idea is to guide market confidence and the country risk premium to internalize the consequences of suboptimal short-run equilibria. Such types of soft interventions are difficult to measure and are strongly dependent on the reputation of the spokesperson. If reputable enough, private agents may internalize the risks and consequences of the overall situation and change their behavior accordingly, but no private agent has any incentive to internalize the aggregate consequences of his or her own behavior. As long as private agents do not have incentives to internalize externalities, private exuberance resembles traffic congestion. Following the guidance of a reputable spokesperson may enable such agents to diminish the degree of misalignment of real variables, but they can never completely eliminate misalignment.

In sum, in small economies open to free financial flows, conventional fiscal policy is always effective on real variables in the short run. Conventional central bank policies are effective to monitor nominal variables or to tackle unexpected shocks, but are ineffective in influencing real variables in a systematic way. Optimal fiscal policy should be designed to compensate for episodes of private exuberance or depressed confidence. Deviations from this rule may generate suboptimal short-run growth and exchange rate misalignment. Excess expenditure, excess growth, or, more generally, economic overheating is better measured by current account sustainability and real exchange rate misalignment than by inflation. Inflation measures central bank inconsistency but is a poor measure of economic overheating under an open capital account.

The larger role of fiscal policy under an open capital account compared with a closed capital account suggests that proper fiscal governance is a prerequisite for capital account opening.

Some Unpleasant Political Economy Arguments

We have argued that optimal fiscal policy should compensate for excess private expenditure. Exuberant private behavior requires a negative fiscal stance, and a depressed private sector needs a positive fiscal stance. Fiscal policy should be such that viable overall domestic expenditure—private plus fiscal—is targeted, with public expenditure being the residual variable.

If such a rule implies a reduction of an existing fiscal deficit, our arguments would end here. But increasing an already existing fiscal surplus (resulting from increased excess spending of the private sector) may be macroeconomically advisable but politically unfeasible. The public sector does not have the institutional role of compensating for excess private expenditure.

Before getting into the argument in depth, we provide some empirical evidence of private exuberance. Figure 6.1a presents the surplus accounting for Chile 1994–2001.[5] The nonfiscal surplus is a proxy of "private sector surplus." The subperiod 1994–7 is the epilogue of a lengthy cycle of accelerated growth. Years 1998–2001, in turn, depict a subperiod of adjustment and adverse external shocks. Figure 6.1b exhibits the concomitant dynamics of growth and the real exchange rate (RER).[6] The period of accelerated growth coincided with RER appreciation and current account deterioration, the symptoms we have identified for a case of overheating. Also, the source of excess domestic expenditure was private sector behavior rather than fiscal policy, which exhibited a surplus during the overheating phase. Adjustment was initiated in 1998, with a

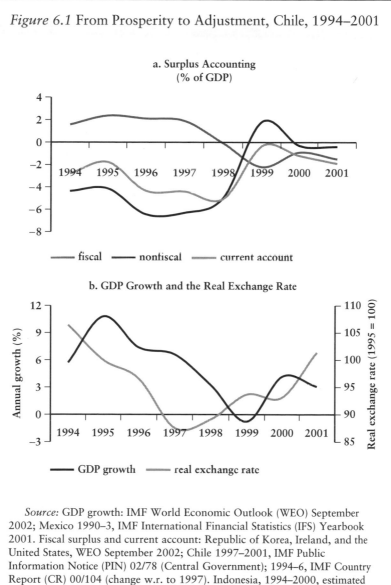

Figure 6.1 From Prosperity to Adjustment, Chile, 1994–2001

a. Surplus Accounting
(% of GDP)

— fiscal   — nonfiscal   — current account

b. GDP Growth and the Real Exchange Rate

— GDP growth   — real exchange rate

Source: GDP growth: IMF World Economic Outlook (WEO) September 2002; Mexico 1990–3, IMF International Financial Statistics (IFS) Yearbook 2001. Fiscal surplus and current account: Republic of Korea, Ireland, and the United States, WEO September 2002; Chile 1997–2001, IMF Public Information Notice (PIN) 02/78 (Central Government); 1994–6, IMF Country Report (CR) 00/104 (change w.r. to 1997). Indonesia, 1994–2000, estimated according to data published by IFS (various issues); 2001, CR 02/154 (change w.r. to 2000). Malaysia, 1996–2000, PIN 01/114; 1994–5, PIN 99/88 (change w.r. to 1996). Mexico, 1997–2001, PIN 02/109; 1996, PIN 00/24; 1990–5, estimated according to IFS. The Philippines, 1997–2001, PIN 02/41; 1994–6, estimated according to CR 99/93. Thailand 1997–2001, PIN 02/94; 1996,

(Source continues on the following page.)

(continued)

PIN 00/5; 1994–5, estimated with data published by IFS. Real exchange rates: Chile, Malaysia, and the Philippines, IFS (various issues). Ireland and the United States, Real Effective Exchange Rate Index (Consumer Price Index based) from IFS world tables. Indonesia, Republic of Korea, Mexico, and Thailand, according to the same common procedure: Bilateral RER with the United States were estimated using series of nominal exchange rates against the U.S. dollar and GDP deflators. REF with the non-U.S. world estimated by multiplying the previous bilateral RER with the United States' RER. The final RER is the simple average of the two previous measures.

Note: The nonfiscal surplus is the difference between the current account and the fiscal surplus. An increase in real exchange rates means depreciation.

steep deceleration of growth and a correction of private exuberance. The RER appreciated when gross domestic product (GDP) growth was high and depreciated when GDP growth decelerated, showing that fiscal management was not enough to compensate for cycles in private sector expenditure.

Figures 6.2 and 6.3 depict a similar pattern of excess private expenditure in eight economies chosen for being successful within the 1990s. We chose successful cases because, according to our arguments, the perception of success is closely linked to excess private expenditure.[7] With the exception of Ireland, all these economies also suffered economic downturns, with varying degrees of severity.

The perception of success in the five Southeast Asian economies considered was founded on a dynamic growth profile for a long period, the same as in Chile. Mexico did not display an impressive dynamism prior to the "Tequila crisis" (1994–5), but the perception was that joining the North American Free Trade Agreement (NAFTA) would radically improve prosperity. Ireland is the star case of the Euro Area. Finally, we also included the United States, which by no means is a small open economy to which our arguments may apply. However, it is also an interesting case of private exuberance while it was the staple case of the "new economy."

Figures 6.1, 6.2, and 6.3 show some similarities among these nine economies prior to the initiation of their adjustment processes:

1. With the exception of Ireland, they exhibited sizable current account deficits (excess domestic expenditure) ranging from 3.4 percent of GDP (Indonesia 1996) to 9.5 percent (Malaysia 1995).

2. Strong fiscal policies were in place, ranging from a fiscal balance (Republic of Korea 1996) to a surplus of 6.9 percent of GDP (Malaysia 1997).

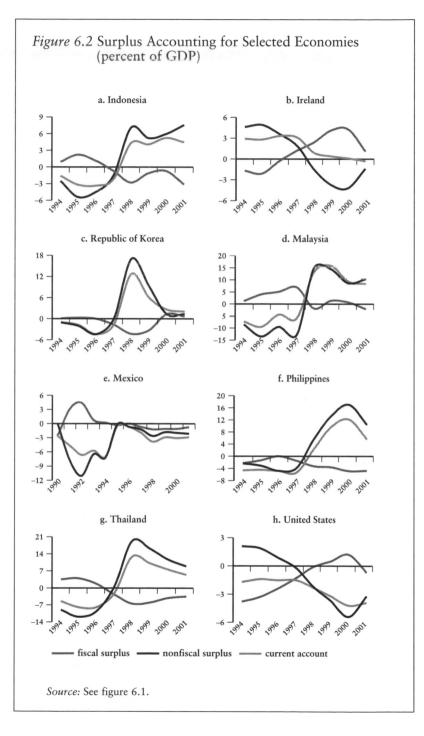

Figure 6.2 Surplus Accounting for Selected Economies
(percent of GDP)

a. Indonesia

b. Ireland

c. Republic of Korea

d. Malaysia

e. Mexico

f. Philippines

g. Thailand

h. United States

fiscal surplus ——— nonfiscal surplus ——— current account

Source: See figure 6.1.

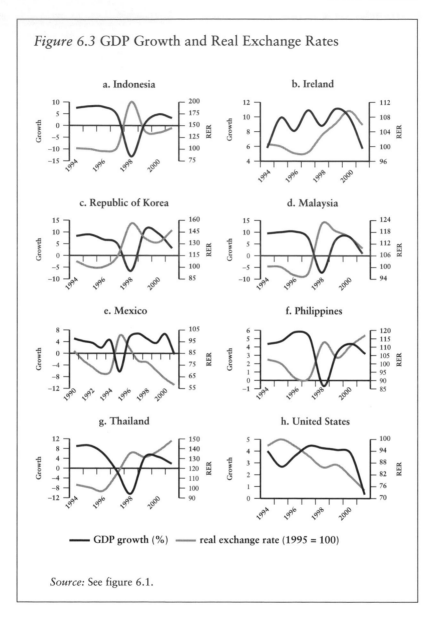

Figure 6.3 GDP Growth and Real Exchange Rates

Source: See figure 6.1.

3. As a natural counterpart, they all exhibited significant private deficits, which we approximate as the difference between the fiscal and the current account surpluses.[8] The orders of magnitude—ranging up to −12.8 percent of GDP (Malaysia 1997)—show that the driving force of excess domestic expenditure was private sector behavior.

4. With the exception of Ireland, all economies exhibited an over-heating phase characterized by the combination of large current account deficits and an appreciating currency.

5. Finally, and again with the exception of Ireland, inflation (not shown) was not a problem. On the contrary, some of these economies showed significant deceleration in their respective rates of inflation (Chile and Mexico).

In almost all other aspects these economies differed, with no homo-geneity in country size, per capita income, the exchange rate regime, export structure, quality of financial regulation, term structure of the foreign debt, and so forth. Obviously these elements also affected private sector behav-ior and, especially, the intensity of their subsequent loss of dynamism. We do not want to over-argue around the similarities stressed, nor say that all economies displaying these features may have acute recessions as in Mexico and Southeast Asia. However, with obvious caveats, we do infer that excess private expenditure does have a common root, proper of economies perceived as successful by the local and international commu-nity, and that such behavior explains vulnerability and the losses in dy-namism immediately after the respective booms. In particular, we want to stress that when private sector exuberance is not fully compensated for by increasing fiscal austerity, there are symptoms of overheating not captured by inflation.

We made an exception with Ireland on several occasions. This econ-omy was capable of applying an extremely disciplined fiscal policy throughout the 1990s, enough to compensate for excess private expen-diture. Fiscal rigor had more to do with controlling inflation—the only macroeconomic standard of the European Union not accomplished by Ireland—than with compensating for excess private expenditure. As ar-gued before, inflation is a measure of real appreciation in a small econ-omy belonging to a common currency union. With a pegged nominal exchange rate, inflation targeting is equivalent to real exchange rate tar-geting. It is interesting to note, however, that the Irish fiscal stance has turned more expansionary recently, in spite of a European Central Bank reprimand, a policy change that has coincided with real appreciation, and a mild deterioration of the current account.

In the eight remaining cases, fiscal discipline was not enough to com-pensate for private deficits. They all displayed a combination of current account deficits with real currency appreciation, a symptom of over-heating according to our model. The eight economies ended up with episodes of recession and complicated situations of excessive private debts (the natural counterpart of cumulative private deficits). When ac-companied by less than acceptable banking regulation (Southeast Asia and Mexico prior to their respective downturns), acute financial crises amplified the economic contraction. With sound prudential regulation (the United States and Chile), the accompanying recession was milder and the financial sector responded solidly, but still faced a problem of excess household and private business debt. In the aggregate, private deficits distorted relative prices—especially the real exchange rate—altering resource allocation in a sort of financial Dutch disease.

Our conclusion is that private deficits matter, and when they appear, policy makers should act promptly to reduce vulnerability. Our model suggests that the optimal conventional policy to face private exuberance is to generate a fiscal surplus. But, as already mentioned, the political economy of increasing a fiscal surplus is complicated. When a structural fiscal surplus is attained, it is not obvious that raising taxes and/or cutting public programs is optimal. A skilled fiscal authority is not only the one able to design a consistent technical solution to a macroeconomic problem. The fiscal authority must also construct appealing arguments for reasonable public opinion, the Congress, and its own government and constituency to convince them to perpetuate such a policy scheme. To garner support for the idea that economic success *reduces* the degrees of freedom of an already solvent public sector is difficult, to say the least. This would be tantamount to asking the political class to convince their constituencies that, notwithstanding a fiscal surplus, taxes should be raised and/or public programs should be reduced.

The sense of prudent citizens is that a disciplined public sector is one that adjusts its expenditures to its legislated revenues. Moreover, their sense is that increasing fiscal surpluses should be returned to society— where they belong—through lower taxes and/or improved supply of public goods and social programs.[9]

The main underlying problem is that the public sector does not have the institutional role of compensating for private exuberance. Each of the fiscal policy instruments, whether on the expenditure or on the revenue side, has a complicated political economy, which tends to be exacerbated when trying to increase a surplus. The problem is that, as shown by our model, there are no conventional policy alternatives.

Heterodox Policy Instruments

A possible solution could be to explore unconventional policy instruments. In this section we analyze the costs and benefits of two heterodox solutions to the policy dilemma introduced by private sector exuberance, which are valid for fiscal surplus cases only. The first one is a trivial solution to enhance fiscal policy flexibility. The second alternative is less trivial and consists of providing additional policy instruments to the central bank.

A Flexible Tax

Analytically, this proposal is straightforward. Fiscal policy flexibility was our major proposal in the third section of this chapter. Whether fiscal flexibility is on the revenue side or on the expenditure side does not make a major difference from a formal perspective. But the triviality of the proposal ends there because there are complex practical differences, especially political and institutional ones. The main political advantage of institutionalizing a flexible tax is that its implementation requires congressional approval. Such approval, in turn, requires the acceptance of an institutional reform in which the government should have the explicit role of compensating for excess private expenditure, an issue that is neither explicit nor implicit in any state's charter.

From a practical perspective, the design of a flexible tax should allow the authority to manage the rate with some discretion, while preventing moral hazard behavior. In particular, the flexible tax should be disconnected from the funding of permanent government expenditure. It should also prevent time inconsistency. For instance, if a sizable fund is accumulated, it may encourage the political class to be creative in deciding how to use it, regardless of macroeconomic considerations.

A possible starting point might include the following ingredients:

1. The flexible tax rate should operate exclusively in situations where there is a structural fiscal surplus in order to ensure that government expenditures are being financed with permanent government revenues. Changes in permanent government expenditures and/or revenues leading to a structural fiscal deficit should imply the immediate removal of the flexible tax.

2. The flexible revenue should have no other purpose or use than accumulation, and should not be recycled to finance further private deficits. This may require the creation of an autonomous institution with explicit property rights to the accumulated stabilization fund. The basic principle is that the government may manage the rate of the flexible tax with discretion, but that it cannot manage its revenues.

3. With this policy tool in place, the government should be accountable for structural fiscal deficits and for economic situations of overall excess expenditure. With an extra policy instrument, the fiscal authority can pursue two independent targets.

A possible arrangement could take the form of the revenue from the flexible tax being transferred—with full property rights—to the (autonomous) central bank (see annex, case 3).[10] From an accounting perspective, such an arrangement would leave the actual fiscal balance unchanged, but a quasi-fiscal surplus would register at the central bank. The accounting identity of equation (6.9) would be modified in this way:

$$0 \equiv C + S + H - Q, \qquad (6.10)$$

where Q represents the extra revenue of the flexible tax—and a measure of the change in the quasi-fiscal surplus—as a proportion of GNP.

By assumption, the government targets the structural fiscal surplus and overall excess expenditure (public and private). This means that the government should manage expenditures according to its structural revenues, and use the flexible tax rate to target a sustainable current account. The central bank, in turn, continues targeting inflation. The final outcome is relatively intuitive: an optimal equilibrium with zero inflation and no real variable misalignment.

A flexible tax would still display various shortcomings difficult to tackle. Among other outcomes, the flexible tax should imply income effects only, with no distorting effects on resource allocation, a mix not trivial to attain. Also, the solution still has severe political economy problems. With the true problem being excess aggregate expenditure, the payers of the flexible tax would have a point when protesting their being designated to subsidize the system. The argument would be symmetrical to the one stressed by the beneficiaries of public programs when fiscal flexibility is attained through the expenditure side. From a different perspective, the efficacy of the flexible tax may be lessened, given its transitory nature, by Ricardian equivalence effects or by intertemporal tax planning—issues that our formal model does not tackle. Finally, when the flexible tax is in place, time-inconsistent behavior cannot be ruled out (for example, the authority might reduce the flexible tax in an election year).

A Tax on Financial Flows

In cases where the main driving force of vulnerability is the presence of private deficits, a tax on the funding of those deficits would tackle the problem at its root.[11] In terms of our model, such a tax would interfere in the arbitrage equation, affecting the cost of external funding. Case 4 of the annex describes the algebra of this situation, where we assume that the tax on financial flows generates no revenue (or it is reimbursed as a lump sum transfer to the private sector), so it acts as an efficiency tax rather than as a means of generating revenue.

The case considers that the central bank manages the tax on financial flows, whereas the fiscal authority seeks a structurally neutral fiscal stance. With an extra degree of freedom given by its new independent policy instrument, the central bank can pursue two independent policy goals. In particular, we assume that the central bank becomes accountable for overheating episodes, in addition to inflation. So it targets inflation and a sustainable current account. The final outcome of this case is also optimal in that the resulting equilibrium is with no inflation, no excess growth, no exchange rate misalignment, and with a sustainable current account.

As stated here, the tax on financial flows would solve some of the problems displayed by the flexible tax. It has a nice political economy advantage in that it taxes the true problem (excess expenditure). It has no time-inconsistency problems either, to the extent that it is managed by an independent central bank. But it would display other shortcomings. First, there are administration problems that are not tackled here and are not simple to solve. Second, if there is no explicit mandate for the central bank to remove the tax in the event of structural fiscal deficits, then the government may use the new device to its advantage. In effect, an expansionary fiscal policy may induce the central bank to raise the tax rate in order to achieve zero inflation and external sustainability. The central bank will continue to achieve its own policy targets, but the private sector would be crowded out by fiscal activism.

Some of these problems may be overcome with a proper design. For instance, the rules of the game for which the central bank should be accountable may include the following items[12]:

1. The tax on financial flows should be removed in the event of a structural fiscal deficit.

2. It may operate as an ad valorem toll tax on financial flows, irrespective of their volume and maturity. This facilitates its management, prevents discriminatory practices, and ensures that there will be no time-inconsistent attitudes on the part of the authority.

3. The central bank should be subject to international surveillance to ensure that these criteria are met and that the tax is used exclusively for prudential macroeconomic purposes.

Final Remarks

Mundell-Fleming implications on policy efficacy in small economies with perfect capital mobility need an exogenous inflation to be valid. With endogenous inflation, fiscal policy affects short-run growth, the real exchange rate, and the current account regardless of the policy regime. Central bank policies—namely, monetary and/or exchange rate policies—are effective to face unexpected shocks. But they have systematic effects only when targeting nominal variables, such as inflation or the nominal exchange rate, and are ineffective on real variables.

The exchange rate regime is innocuous in terms of altering the efficacy of alternative policy instruments. Rather, the exchange rate regime is a form of organizing the signaling of macroeconomic policy. Any exchange rate regime would collapse with an unsustainable fiscal policy.

In the absence of liquidity constraints, the private sector optimizes the net present value of its future flows. In the short run it can display positive or negative excess expenditure. But overall excess expenditure in the short run—public plus private—generates exchange rate misalignment, excess growth, and an unsustainable current account. Sustainable short-run equilibria can be attained when fiscal policy compensates for excess private expenditure. Exuberant private behavior requires a contractionary fiscal stance, and depressed private behavior requires an expansionary fiscal stance.

Inflation is a poor measure of economic overheating, especially because inflation may be curbed in the short run by an appreciating currency. Unsustainable current account deficits along with an appreciating currency are clearer symptoms of overheating. Fiscal policy is the sole conventional policy instrument able to tackle this problem systematically.

Economic success generates exuberant private behavior that, in turn, requires a contractionary fiscal stance. Economic success and improved economic prospects require increasing taxes and/or removing public programs, even in cases where a fiscal surplus is already in place. The public sector does not have the institutional role of compensating for excess private expenditure, thus imposing a policy dilemma with no conventional solution.

An alternative policy instrument could be the introduction of a flexible tax, depending on the state of the economic cycle, which may restore a sustainable equilibrium path. Such a device would still display political economy shortcomings, could be subject to time-inconsistent attitudes, and could have a small potential if Ricardian equivalence effects or intertemporal tax planning were significant.

Finally, a tax on financial flows may also restore sustainable equilibrium in the event of private exuberance. This device has a nice political economy advantage because it taxes the true problem (the funding of excess expenditure). It may also avoid time inconsistency if correctly managed by an independent central bank. But it displays administration challenges that would be difficult to overcome.

Annex: The Formal Model

The main assumptions of the model are specified in the first section of the text. Also, the first three equations are the ones developed in the text, with the same notation:

$$p = c_0 e + (1 - c_0) p* + c_1(y - y_d); \quad 0 < c_0 < 1; \quad c_1 > 0 \quad (6.1)$$

$$C = a_1(y_x + d(e - p) - y) + \hat{C} \quad (6.5)$$

$$0 = C + S + H. \quad (6.9)$$

The fiscal stance S corresponds to the change in public expenditures (g) minus public revenues (ty), both as a percentage of GNP:

$$S - g - ty; \quad 0 < t < 1. \quad (6.11)$$

In the absence of liquidity constraints, the private sector spends according to an intertemporal plan. In particular, private expenditure evolves, depending on the gap between its medium-term prospects (w) and the real interest rate ($i - p*$). Unexpected income is saved. Thus, the private sector deficit as a percentage of GNP follows this rule:

$$H = (1 - t) (y* - y) + a_0(w - (i - p*)); \quad a_0 > 0. \quad (6.12)$$

Equilibrium in the money market has a conventional form:

$$m - p = b_0 y - b_1 i; \quad b_0, b_1 > 0, \quad (6.13)$$

where m is the rate of growth of the nominal supply of money and i is the nominal interest rate.

The interest rate follows a conventional arbitrage rule:

$$i = i_x + e* + u, \quad (6.14)$$

where i_x is the relevant international interest rate, $e*$ is expected nominal depreciation, and u is the country-specific risk premium.

To simplify the algebra, a number of helpful assumptions are introduced. First, financial flows are made in fixed interest rate bonds so that variations in i_x do not generate contemporaneous changes in interest payments. Second, to avoid strange outcomes we assume that a real depreciation expands aggregate demand. A sufficient condition for an expansionary devaluation is that the current account effect of a real depreciation is larger than the financial effect of an expected real depreciation: $a_1 d - a_0 > 0$.[13]

Third, throughout most of our analysis we also assume that the risk premium u and private confidence w are exogenous.[14]

With these equations and assumptions, we analyze various special cases. Unless otherwise stated, all cases consider the final equilibrium with no unanticipated shocks.

Case 1: Open Capital Account and External Sustainability

All equations hold, including the price equation (6.1) and the arbitrage equation (6.14). This case depicts the situation in which the central bank pursues an inflation target ($p = 0$), and fiscal policy targets a sustainable path of domestic expenditure or, what is the same, a sustainable current account ($C^* = \hat{C}$):

$$L_B = p^2 \quad \text{central bank loss function} \tag{6.15}$$

$$L_G = (C^* - \hat{C})^2 \quad \text{government loss function} \tag{6.16}$$

Case 1 is the basic situation around which the rest of our analysis pivots because all the relevant equilibria are met. We denote with "^" the outcome of the consistent equilibrium:

$$y = \hat{y} = (c_0\, y_x + c_1 d\, y_d)/(c_0 + c_1 d) \quad \text{growth} \tag{6.17}$$

$$(e - p) = \hat{e} = c_1\, (y_d - y_x)/(c_0 + c_1 d) \quad \text{real exchange rate} \tag{6.18}$$

$$C = \hat{C} \quad \text{current account} \tag{6.19}$$

$$p = p* = 0 \quad \text{inflation} \tag{6.20}$$

$$H = \hat{H} = a_0(w - i_x - \hat{e} - u) \quad \text{private deficit} \tag{6.21}$$

$$(i - p) = \hat{\imath} = i_x + \hat{e} + u \quad \text{real interest rate} \tag{6.22}$$

$$S = \hat{S} = -(\hat{C} + \hat{H}) \quad \text{fiscal stance} \tag{6.23}$$

$$g = \hat{g} = t\hat{y} - (\hat{C} + \hat{H}) \quad \text{fiscal expenditure} \tag{6.24}$$

$$m = \hat{m} = b_0\hat{y} - b_1(i_x + \hat{e} + u) \quad \text{nominal money supply} \tag{6.25}$$

The solution to this case does not depend on whether the central bank optimizes L_B with respect to e or to m. That is to say, the results would be the same whether the central bank's policy instrument were the nominal exchange rate or nominal monetary policy. The government and the central bank achieve their respective policy targets (equations [6.19] and [6.20]). Equilibrium growth (6.17) is a weighted average of the external and internal constraints on growth (y_x and y_d), whereas the real exchange rate (6.18) depends exclusively on the gap ($y_d - y_x$). The private sector deficit is not constrained by fiscal policy (6.21). The international interest rate (i_x), the equilibrium real depreciation ($\hat{e}$), private sector confidence (w), and the country risk premium (u) become the driving forces of the private deficit.

The main point to be stressed is related to fiscal policy: The fiscal stance $\hat{S}$ consistent with current account sustainability is the one that compensates for excess private expenditure. In effect, the optimal fiscal stance (6.22) is the one that compensates for any private deficit in excess of the slack provided by a sustainable current account. Exuberant private behavior ($\hat{H} > -\hat{C}$) would require a negative fiscal stance ($\hat{S} < 0$), whereas a depressed private sector ($\hat{H} < -\hat{C}$) would require an active fiscal policy ($\hat{S} > 0$). Perfect capital mobility implies that private behavior crowds out optimal fiscal policy, instead of the other way around. Optimal fiscal policy is clearly countercyclical.[15]

Case 2: Open Capital Account and Fiscal Efficacy

Case 2 explores the situation in which fiscal policy departs from the rule derived in (6.24) ($g \neq \hat{g}$). To analyze this case, consider a positive fiscal expenditure bias θ where

$$g = \hat{g} + \theta; \quad \theta > 0.^{[16]} \tag{6.26}$$

The central bank continues to minimize inflation:

$$L_B = p^2 \quad \text{central bank loss function.} \tag{6.27}$$

In the absence of surprises, the final outcome would be

$$y = \hat{y} + c_0\theta/h > \hat{y} \quad \text{growth,} \tag{6.28}$$

where $h = c_0t + a_1(c_0 + c_1d) - a_0c_1 > 0.^{[17]}$

$$(e - p) = \hat{e} - c_1\theta/h < \hat{e} \quad \text{real exchange rate} \tag{6.29}$$

$$C = \hat{C} - a_1(c_0 + c_1d)\theta/h < \hat{C} \quad \text{current account} \tag{6.30}$$

$$p = p* = 0 \quad \text{inflation} \tag{6.31}$$

$$H = \hat{H} + a_0 c_1 \, \theta/h > \hat{H} \quad \text{private deficit} \tag{6.32}$$

$$i - p = \hat{\imath} - c_1 \, \theta/h < \hat{\imath} \quad \text{real interest rate} \tag{6.33}$$

$$S = \hat{S} + (h - c_0 t)\theta/h > \hat{S} \quad \text{fiscal stance}^{18} \tag{6.34}$$

$$g = \hat{g} + \theta > \hat{g} \quad \text{fiscal expenditure} \tag{6.35}$$

So, larger-than-optimal fiscal expenditure expands GNP growth (6.28), over-appreciates the real exchange rate (6.29), and deteriorates the current account below its sustainable path (6.30). Likewise, smaller-than-optimal government expenditure ($\theta < 0$) generates the opposite results. An expansionary fiscal policy would also crowd in additional private deficit (6.32) through a lower real interest rate (6.33) that, in turn, is the result of an over-appreciating currency. The central bank achieves its price stability target (6.31).

Active fiscal policy has an unambiguous short-run impact on growth, the real exchange rate, and the current account.[19] The fiscal authority may take advantage of this result in the short run. For instance, the government might seek a growth target $y_{target} > \hat{y}$. Then, according to (6.28), it should set

$$\theta = \theta_y = (y_{target} - \hat{y})h/c_0 > 0. \tag{6.36}$$

In the absence of surprises, such a fiscal policy would succeed in the short run ($y = y_{target} > \hat{y}$) at the expense of an appreciating currency ($e < \hat{e}$) and an unsustainable current account ($C < \hat{C}$). The short-run efficacy of fiscal policy is independent of the exchange rate regime. Whether the central bank handles e or handles m with a floating e, the outcome remains: Fiscal policy is always effective.

This result contrasts with the Mundell-Fleming intuition, an outcome that critically depends on the validity of the price equation (6.1). The intuition has to do with the fact that the central bank handles nominal policy instruments, whereas the fiscal instrument is real government expenditure. Rational private agents care only about real variables, whether in actual or expected value, and are not sensitive to nominal stimulus, except when unexpected.

Fiscal policy is effective and authorities may use this feature for good or for bad. To avoid noisy outcomes, the government may stick to different fiscal rules, of which we analyze two possibilities. First, the authority seeks a neutral fiscal stance ($S = 0$) and, second, the authority seeks a neutral fiscal stance in structural terms ($g = t\hat{y}$). From expressions (6.34) and (6.35) we can derive the value for θ of each case:

Rule 1: $g = ty \Rightarrow \theta = \theta_1 = (\hat{C} + \hat{H}) \, [h/(h - c_0 t)].$

Rule 2: $g = t\hat{y} \Rightarrow \theta = \theta_2 = (\hat{C} + \hat{H}).$

In neither of these two cases does the government accommodate excess private expenditure. So the term $(\hat{C} + \hat{H})$, which we use as an indicator of private exuberance, appears. $(\hat{C} + \hat{H}) > 0$ implies that both rules would lead to overall excess expenditure. Because $[h/(h - c_0 t)]$, rule 1 amplifies private sector exuberance by more than rule 2 and, thus, is more pro-cyclical.

Case 3: Flexible Tax

Analytically this case is trivial because tax flexibility is similar to public expenditure flexibility. To formulate this case, we consider that the revenue of the flexible tax is accumulated in a stabilization fund that is separated from central government. We also assume that the flexible tax has income effects only, with no effects on resource allocation. With these assumptions we accommodate equations (6.9) and (6.12) of the initial model:

$$0 = C + S + H + Q \tag{6.37}$$

$$H = (Q^* - Q) + (1 - t)(y^* - y) + a_0[w - (i - p^*)], \tag{6.38}$$

where Q denotes the change in the revenue of the flexible tax as a percentage of GNP. We also assume that the fiscal authority handles two independent policy instruments (g and Q) seeking two targets: a balanced budget ($S = g - ty = 0$) and a sustainable current account ($C = \hat{C}$):

$$L_G = S^{*2} + (C^* - \hat{C})^2 \quad \text{government loss function.} \tag{6.39}$$

The central bank continues pursuing price stability ($L_B = p^2$). In the absence of surprises, this setting ensures an optimal macroeconomic equilibrium. All variables would coincide with optimal case 1 above, except for the following:

$$S = 0 \quad \text{fiscal stance} \tag{6.40}$$

$$g = t\hat{y} \quad \text{fiscal expenditure} \tag{6.41}$$

$$Q = -(\hat{C} + \hat{H}) \quad \text{flexible tax} \tag{6.42}$$

Note that Q compensates the effect of our measure of private sector exuberance $(\hat{C} + \hat{H})$.

Case 4: Tax on Financial Flows

Case 4 considers a tax on financial flows (τ) affecting the arbitrage equation (6.7). It also assumes that the revenue of the tax is returned to the private sector, with no income effects:

$$i = i_x + e* + u + \tau. \tag{6.43}$$

We consider the case where the tax rate τ is handled by the central bank, which thus manages two independent policy instruments and pursues two targets: price stability $(p = 0)$ and current account sustainability $(C = \hat{C})$. The government seeks a neutral fiscal stance $(L_G = S^{*2})$.

$$L_B = p^2 + (C - \hat{C})^2 \quad \text{central bank loss function} \tag{6.44}$$

Again, the final outcome ensures an optimal macroeconomic equilibrium. All variables would coincide with optimal case 1, except for the following:

$$H = -\hat{C} \quad \text{private deficit} \tag{6.45}$$

$$i - p = w + \hat{C}/a_0 \quad \text{real interest rate} \tag{6.46}$$

$$S = 0 \quad \text{fiscal stance} \tag{6.47}$$

$$g = t\hat{y} \quad \text{fiscal expenditure} \tag{6.48}$$

$$\tau = (\hat{C} + \hat{H})/a_0 \quad \text{financial tax rate} \tag{6.49}$$

The role of τ is to tax any excess private expenditure. We have used $(\hat{C} + \hat{H})$ as a measure of private exuberance. A positive τ is consistent with a positive value of $(\hat{C} + \hat{H})$.

In the four cases developed here, the algebra was simplified by assuming that the country risk premium (u) and private sector prospects (w) are exogenous. Alternatively, it could be assumed that the risk premium and economic prospects deteriorate along with macroeconomic misalignment[20]:

$$w = \hat{w} + w_0(C - \hat{C}) \quad w_0 > 0 \tag{6.50}$$

$$u = \hat{u} - u_0(C - \hat{C}) \quad u_0 > 0. \tag{6.51}$$

In such a case, all the main conclusions remain, although orders of magnitude would vary. Only changes in the interest rate and the private deficit may have ambiguous signs under certain circumstances.

Also, parameters a_0, w_0, and u_0 may be subject to the Lucas critique. That is to say, because they are behavioral parameters, rational agents may change their behavior (and thus the value of the parameters) if the authority tries to take advantage. In such a case, the orders of magnitude of the solutions may change, but not the signs or the main conclusions, except in the extreme case where $[a_0(w_0 + u_0)] \to \infty$.

Endnotes

1. Thus, the wage-push inflation would be given by expected inflation.

2. Notice that, in the special case of a closed economy, $c_0 = 0$ and, thus, $p = p* + c_1(y - y_d)$. In this special case and under rational expectations, it is straightforward that expected growth and potential growth coincide ($y* = y_d*$). Actual inflation would deviate from expected inflation only to the extent that there are surprises.

3. The government successfully targets $C = \hat{C}$. Then, from equation (6.9) it is straightforward that the optimal fiscal stance is $S = -(\hat{H} + \hat{C})$, where $\hat{H}$ is the private deficit when all the relevant equilibria are met. The larger the value of $\hat{H}$, the smaller the value of S.

4. In the optimal equilibrium case, $p = -\hat{e}$.

5. We used International Monetary Fund data, which do not necessarily coincide with the official Chilean figures.

6. A higher RER represents a depreciation.

7. We omitted cases of dynamic growth in economies closed to voluntary financial flows, such as China and the Dominican Republic. We also omitted Singapore because we do not know how to interpret the combination of high fiscal surplus with a growing public debt. The peculiarities of the Singaporean pension system may be an explanation for this mix.

8. There are no data available to construct a precise measure for the private deficit. Our proxy is not strictly consistent from an accounting standpoint.

9. There are numerous practical examples in this respect. In the United States, before the economic downturn was initiated, the two main presidential candidates in the 2000 election proposed to use the fiscal surplus they were to inherit (either to reduce taxes or to tackle structural problems of the pension and health systems). In Chile in 1997, also with a fiscal surplus, Congress had to decide about a drop in the value added tax rate. The government coalition proposed an educational reform instead, whereas the opposition backed the tax cut (and a few wanted both). Nobody was in favor of maintaining the fiscal situation. Ireland, after reaching a sizable surplus, entered into "austerity fatigue" in fiscal year 2000/01 and moved to a more expansionary stance.

10. Alternatively, economies with fully funded pension schemes may consider introducing a flexible rate of contributions to the system. Singapore has had some episodes in which the contribution rate has been moved according to macroeconomic considerations.

11. Under voluntary financial flows, excess expenditure is not necessarily punished by increased cost of funding. Even if the country risk premium rises with an

unsustainable equilibrium, an over-appreciating exchange rate reduces the cost of external funding in the short run.

12. Most of these elements were present in the Chilean reserve requirements on capital inflows that were put in place in 1991.

13. From equation (6.5) a real depreciation improves the current account balance by a_1d. Also, from equations (6.12) and (6.14) an expected real depreciation $(e* - p*)$ reduces the private sector deficit by a_0. This assumption implies that wealth effects of changes in the real exchange rate are not dominant.

14. The consequences of this assumption are discussed at the end of the annex.

15. None of these conclusions depends on whether private confidence (w) and/or the risk premium (u) are endogenous.

16. For $\theta < 0$, the conclusions are inversely symmetrical.

17. Parameter h is unambiguously positive when $a_1d - a_0 > 0$, the condition that ensures that a real depreciation is expansionary.

18. Notice that $(h - c_0t) > 0$ and that $(h - c_0t)/h < 1$.

19. If private confidence and the country risk premium $(w$ and u, respectively) deteriorate with an unsustainable current account, our main conclusions would still hold. The sole difference would be that the private deficit (H) and the interest rate (i) become ambiguous for $\theta \neq 0$. Also, the "multiplier" h would be affected in terms of its size but not its sign.

20. $(C - \hat{C})$ is sufficient as a measure of macroeconomic disequilibrium because $(C - \hat{C}) \Leftrightarrow (e - \hat{e}) \Leftrightarrow (y - \hat{y})$.

7

External Debt, Growth, and Sustainability

Roberto Frenkel

IN A PREVIOUS ESSAY (FRENKEL 2001) we analyzed the situation of the Latin American countries in the context of financial globalization in the late 1990s. This chapter sets out a more formal analytical approach to this subject. In particular, we examine the dynamics of external debt from a balance of payments perspective, using the concept of sustainability.[1]

External debt may be described as sustainable when there are no foreseeable major difficulties in meeting contracts in a timely and proper manner. Obviously, this does not actually guarantee that those contracts will be met. Sustainability is a judgment with respect to uncertain future events, based on present information and probable conjectures. The conditions of sustainability examined in this chapter are reasonable *a priori*.

The country's interest rate, which is determined by the international rate and the country risk premium, plays an important role in our analysis. The model we set forth reflects certain features of the "emerging market" economies; that is to say, developing economies that were involved in three aspects of the financial globalization process: the opening of the local financial market and its integration with the international market, the absorption of net capital flows, and the resulting accumulation of a significant stock of external obligations. Let us assume that the

The author is Senior Researcher, Centro de Estudios de Estado y Sociedad (CEDES), Buenos Aires, Argentina, and Professor at the University of Buenos Aires. I thank José Antonio Ocampo, Lance Taylor, and Sebastián Katz for their comments on a preliminary version. Martín Rapetti assisted with the model simulations. Although few of those exercises are reflected in the present version, his collaboration was important for the final result.

189

countries we are examining have issued a certain amount of sovereign debt denominated in foreign currency (dollars) that has been placed on the international financial market and the local market. Information about the prices of bonds is freely available and any local or foreign agent can acquire sovereign bonds at market prices.

Based on the above-mentioned hypotheses, the chapter presents a model intended to define and discuss the sustainability of external debt in emerging markets. The first sustainability condition is the existence of a maximum in the debt-output ratio. Using some simple behavior hypotheses, we show that sustainability depends on the initial debt-export ratio, the rate of export growth, and the country risk premium. An endogenous country risk premium leaves room for multiple equilibria. The model allows for the discussion of vulnerability relative to financial shocks and the propensity of the economy to jump to unsustainable paths. The first sustainability condition is not a stringent one. We thus add two additional and more restrictive sustainability conditions: a positive rate of growth and a minimum in the domestic absorption-output (or absorption-income) ratio.

Segmented Integration, the Real Interest Rate, and the Country Risk Premium

Interest rates display significant differences between developed and emerging economies, despite the integration[2] that exists among financial markets. Here we will consider how interest rates are determined in an emerging market.

We have said that the country issued dollar-denominated sovereign bonds, which were traded on the secondary markets. The price of those bonds determines their yield, which we will call i. Yield is conventionally broken down into two terms:

$$i = r^* + k, \qquad (7.1)$$

where r^* is the yield on a U.S. sovereign bond with the same maturity and identical characteristics, and k is the country risk premium.

First, i represents the opportunity cost of any foreign investment in the country, to the extent that the asset in question, real or financial, is subject to country risk. So, the cost of international credit to local banks or to other private agents will generally have to be equal to or greater than i.

To facilitate a discussion of how the real interest rate is determined without losing generality, let us assume that the national financial system is partially dollarized. This means that assets and liabilities denominated in dollars are issued by the financial system together with assets and liabilities in local currency.

Because local banks can acquire sovereign bonds yielding i, this rate is the opportunity cost of local bank lending in dollars. Consequently, i is the floor price of dollar bank loans, even if the credit has not been funded in the international market. The interest rate on dollar loans must be equal to or greater than i. Let us assume that it is equal to i.

To determine the rate in local currency, we need to take into account the expected evolution of the exchange rate:

$$j = i + E(e) + \pi, \text{ where } \pi > 0, \tag{7.2}$$

where j is the nominal rate of interest in local currency, $E(e)$ is the expected rate of nominal devaluation, and π represents the exchange risk premium.

Let p and p^* be the rates of local and international inflation, respectively. We can subtract p from both sides of equation (7.2) and add and subtract p^* on the right-hand side:

$$j - p = (i - p^*) + [E(e) - p + p^*] + \pi. \tag{7.3}$$

This gives an expression in which $j - p$ is the real interest rate in local currency and $E(e) - p + p^*$ is the expected rate of real devaluation. It is easy to see that the real interest rate in local currency must be greater than or equal to $i - p^*$, except in the case of an expected real appreciation trend strong enough to offset the exchange risk premium π. We will disregard this case, however. We will therefore assume that

$$j - p \geq i - p^*. \tag{7.4}$$

For the sake of simplicity, let us assume that $p^* = 0$ (which is equivalent to considering p as the difference between local and international inflation) and that (7.4) holds as an equality

$$r = j - p = i = r^* + k. \tag{7.5}$$

External Financing

The country has received capital income that generates an amount $D(t)$ of external debt. The capital inflows result from a bond issue with a maturity L, which yields an international interest rate r^* and whose capital must be redeemed in full at maturity.

The current account balance (CC) is

$$CC = X - M - r^*D, \qquad (7.6)$$

where X represents exports, M imports, and r^*D is the interest accrued on external debt.

We will assume a zero variation in reserves and we will assume (for the time being and for the sake of the presentation) that the current account is in deficit. Financing needs (NF) are

$$NF = -CC + \lambda D = -X + M + r^*D + \lambda D, \qquad (7.7)$$

where $\lambda = 1/L$ is the portion of the debt that matures at t.

Because the bonds are issued at a rate under par ($k \geq 0$), to obtain NF amount of financing, a volume Z of new debt must be issued, so that $Ze^{r^*L} = NF\, e^{(r^*+k)L}$ and therefore

$$Z = NF\, e^{kL}. \qquad (7.8)$$

The variation in debt is therefore $dD = \frac{\partial D}{\partial t} = Z - \lambda D$.

If we replace with (7.7) and (7.8) and regroup, we obtain:

$$dD = [e^{kL}r^* + \lambda(e^{kL} - 1)]\, D - e^{kL}\, X + e^{kL}M. \qquad (7.9)$$

We calculate

$$\delta = e^{kL}, \quad \delta \geq 1 \text{ because } k \geq 0, \qquad (7.10)$$

$$\gamma = \delta r^* + \lambda(\delta - 1), \quad \gamma \geq r^* > 0 \text{ because } \delta \geq 1, \qquad (7.11)$$

and equation (7.8) is expressed as

$$dD = \gamma D - \delta(X - M). \qquad (7.12)$$

The variation in debt can be broken down into a purely financial term, which depends on the amount of debt and a term that depends on the trade balance. The first term represents the cost of financing the sum of the interest accrued on existing debt plus refinancing of capital maturities. If there is a trade deficit ($X < M$), the second term represents the cost of financing it. In both terms, the factor δ appears as a multiplier. The higher the country risk premium and—consequently—the higher the interest rate the country must commit to paying in order to secure financing, the higher this factor. Notice that equation (7.12) is also valid in the case of a trade surplus $(X > M)$. In this case the proceeds of the trade balance are used to finance the interest and maturing capital of existing debt, which is equivalent to assuming that the trade balance is used to buy debt bonds at market prices. If the trade surplus is large enough, the absolute value of the second term may be larger than the first and the debt contracts. It can therefore be seen that the current account deficit we assumed above for the purposes of the presentation is not necessary, because equation (7.12) is valid in either case. If the risk premium is nil, equation (7.12) is reduced to

$$dD = r^*D - X + M; \qquad (7.13)$$

that is, the variation in debt is the same as the current account balance with the opposing sign.

Division of equation (7.12) by D gives the growth rate of the debt:

$$\frac{dD}{D} = \hat{D} = \gamma - \delta \frac{X - M}{D}. \qquad (7.14)$$

Let Y be output and y its rate of growth. The rate of variation of the debt-output ratio is

$$\frac{d(D/Y)}{D/Y} = \hat{D} - y = \gamma - y - \delta \frac{X - M}{D}, \qquad (7.15)$$

which, multiplied and divided by Y in the final term, can be expressed as

$$\frac{d(D/Y)}{D/Y} = \hat{D} - y = \gamma - y - \delta \left(\frac{X - M}{Y} \right) \Big/ \frac{D}{Y}. \qquad (7.16)$$

The rate of variation of the debt-output ratio in equation (7.16) is expressed as a function of commonly used macroeconomic ratios. For example, if $L = 10$ years, $r^* = 5$ percent, and the country risk premium $k = 0.03$ (300 basis points), then $\gamma = 0.1025$. With trade in balance, the growth rate of the debt-output ratio is zero only if output grows at an annual rate of 10.25 percent. If the economy is growing at a rate of 7 percent and the debt-output ratio is 50 percent $(D/Y = 0.5)$, a trade surplus of 1.2 percent of output is needed to stabilize the debt-output ratio.

Growth Rates of Output and Imports

We shall complete the model by making endogenous the growth rates of output and imports. We will assume that the rate of growth of exports is exogenous. The influence of the country risk premium on the real economy is incorporated into the model by means of the real interest rate. We will opt for the simplest form, assuming that the economy's growth rate is a function of the interest rate:

$$y = y(r) = \bar{y} + \rho r = \bar{y} + \rho r^* + \rho k, \text{ with } \rho < 0, \qquad (7.17)$$

where ρ is the interest rate elasticity of output.

We shall also make endogenous the growth rate of imports, assuming that this rate is a function of the output growth rate:

$$m = m(y) = \mu y, \text{ with } \mu > 0, \qquad (7.18)$$

where μ is the import elasticity of output.

The Dynamics of Debt

To resolve differential equation (7.12) and obtain debt trajectory $D(t)$, we must specify the trajectories of exports and imports:

$$X = X_0 \, e^{xt} \qquad (7.19)$$

$$M = M_0 \, e^{mt}, \qquad (7.20)$$

where x and m are the growth rates of exports and imports, respectively. With this specification, equation (7.12) becomes

$$dD = \gamma D - \delta(X_0 \, e^{xt} - M_0 \, e^{mt}). \qquad (7.21)$$

In the general case that $x \neq \gamma$ and $m \neq \gamma$, the solution to the differential equation is

$$D(t) = \left[D_0 + \delta\left(\frac{X_0}{x - \gamma} - \frac{M_0}{m - \gamma} \right) \right] e^{\gamma t}$$

$$- \delta\left(\frac{X_0}{x - \gamma} e^{xt} - \frac{M_0}{m - \gamma} e^{mt} \right). \qquad (7.22)$$

Obviously, the way the debt behaves depends on the financial parameters mentioned earlier, on the growth rates of exports and imports, and on the conditions of trade deficit or surplus at $t = 0$.

We will focus our analysis of the problem of debt sustainability on the debt-output ratio. The trajectory of output is

$$Y = Y_0 \, e^{yt}. \tag{7.23}$$

Consequently, using (7.22), the debt-output ratio follows the trajectory

$$\frac{D}{Y} = \frac{D_0}{Y_0} e^{(\gamma - y)t} - \frac{X_0}{Y_0} \frac{\delta}{x - \gamma} [e^{(x - y)t} - e^{(\gamma - y)t}]$$

$$+ \frac{M_0}{Y_0} \frac{\delta}{m - \gamma} [e^{(m - y)t} - e^{(\gamma - y)t}]. \tag{7.24}$$

The evolution of the debt-output ratio, like debt itself, depends on the initial position of the trade balance. We want to remove this element to focus the analysis on the parameters. In order to do this, we will assume henceforth that the starting point is a trade balance. We will therefore make $M_0 = X_0$ and substitute $\frac{D_0}{Y_0} = \frac{D_0}{X_0} \frac{X_0}{Y_0}$ in (7.24), which gives the following expression of the debt-output ratio trajectory:

$$\frac{D}{Y} = \frac{X_0}{Y_0} \left[e^{(\gamma - y)t} \left(\frac{D_0}{X_0} + \frac{\delta}{x - \gamma} - \frac{\delta}{m - \gamma} \right) \right.$$

$$\left. - \left(\frac{\delta}{x - \gamma} e^{(x - y)t} - \frac{\delta}{m - \gamma} e^{(m - y)t} \right) \right]. \tag{7.25}$$

This expression clearly shows the initial conditions that influence the evolution of the debt-output ratio: the degree of openness of the economy (X_0/Y_0) and the debt-export ratio (D_0/X_0). The first of these is a scale factor that does not alter the characteristics of the debt-output trajectory. This trajectory depends essentially on the initial debt-export ratio. A devaluation, for example, brings about an increase in the relative price of tradable goods, which increases the degree of openness of the economy and therefore multiplies the whole curve of the debt-output ratio by this factor. This same devaluation does not affect the debt-export ratio, however, which therefore does not alter the form and characteristics of the debt-output ratio trajectory. The devaluation affects the shape of this curve only through its real effects; that is, through its influence on the rates of exports and imports.

The introduction of the hypotheses for the real economy (7.17) and (7.18) defines a model whose operation can be explained by observation of equation (7.25). An increase in the country risk premium tends to raise the debt-output ratio on the financial side because parameters δ and γ increase. The incorporation of the recessionary effect of a rise in the interest rate adds another element on the real side: An increase in the country risk premium tends to lower the output growth rate and, as a result, tends to raise the debt-output ratio. But a downturn in the growth rate of the economy causes a dip in the growth rate of imports. With an export growth rate unaltered, the trade surplus expands (or the deficit contracts) and this effect tends to lower the debt-output ratio.

Financial Deficit and Trade Surplus

In order to analyze the evolution of the debt-output ratio, we will establish a number of restrictions on the model parameters. The best way to do this is to start with equation (7.15) and rewrite it, assuming initial conditions of trade in balance ($M_0 = X_0$).

$$\hat{D} - y = \gamma(k) - y(k) - \delta(k)\, X_0 \, \frac{e^{xt} - e^{m(k)t}}{D}. \qquad (7.26)$$

Equation (7.26) expresses the growth rate of the debt-output ratio. In this equation we have specified the parameters that depend on the country risk premium. Let us imagine that in $t < 0$ the economy experiences a country risk premium (which we will call k_0) such that the rate of growth (y_0) is equal to the cost of refinancing interest and capital maturities on external debt (γ_0). With this growth rate, the rate of expansion in imports (m_0) is equal to the rate of expansion of exports (x_0), so that the economy grows with trade in balance. In $t < 0$, equation (7.26) would give

$$\hat{D} - y = \gamma_0 - y_0 = 0. \qquad (7.27)$$

The rate of growth of the debt-output ratio is nil and the economy is on a sustainable debt trajectory with a constant debt-output ratio.

Let us now imagine that a contagion effect pushes up the country risk premium in $t \geq 0$ ($k > k_0$). In consequence, γ rises, and at the same time the rate of growth y declines ($\gamma > \gamma_0, y < y_0$) so that $\gamma > y$. The growth rate of the debt-output ratio will turn positive through this effect. But the downturn in the rate of economic growth brings about a fall in the growth rate of imports ($m < m_0$), and therefore $x > m$ when $t \geq 0$. In addition, note with equation (7.26) that in $t = 0$ the growth rate of the debt-output ratio is positive:

$$\hat{D} - y = \gamma - y. \tag{7.28}$$

The effect of the increase in the country risk premium is an upward trend in the debt-output ratio. But from a zero value when $t = 0$, the surplus begins to expand when $t > 0$. In what circumstances can a growing trade surplus offset the financial effect of a rise in the country risk premium and make external debt sustainable?

In general terms, this problem implies the following restrictions on the parameters:

$$\gamma > y; \; x > m. \tag{7.29}$$

Let us analyze the dynamics of the debt-output ratio with these assumptions. Independent of the problem that justifies them, the restrictions we are assuming appear to be the only ones of interest for analysing debt sustainability. If $\gamma > y$ and the economy is not generating a trade surplus, the debt-output ratio is explosive and the debt is unquestionably unsustainable. If $y \geq \gamma$, we could discuss, for example, how much of a trade deficit the debt trend can tolerate without becoming explosive, but this avenue of enquiry does not appear to be particularly interesting.

First Condition of Sustainability

The first condition of sustainability is that the debt-output ratio must not become explosive. The curve expressed by equation (7.22) must have a maximum. The first order condition is

$$\frac{\partial (D/Y)}{\partial t} = \frac{X_0}{Y_0} \left\{ (\gamma - y)e^{(\gamma - y)t} \left(\frac{D_0}{X_0} + \frac{\delta}{x - \gamma} - \frac{\delta}{m - \gamma} \right) \right.$$
$$\left. - \left[\frac{\delta}{x - \gamma}(x - y)e^{(x - y)t} - \frac{\delta}{m - \gamma}(m - y)e^{(m - y)t} \right] \right\} = 0. \tag{7.30}$$

The second order condition is

$$\frac{\partial^2 (D/Y)}{\partial t^2} = \frac{X_0}{Y_0} \left\{ (\gamma - y)^2 \, e^{(\gamma - y)t} \left(\frac{D_0}{X_0} + \frac{\delta}{x - \gamma} - \frac{\delta}{m - \gamma} \right) \right.$$
$$\left. - \left[\frac{\delta}{x - \gamma}(x - y)^2 e^{(x - y)t} - \frac{\delta}{m - \gamma}(m - y)^2 e^{(m - y)t} \right] \right\} < 0. \tag{7.31}[3]$$

From (7.30) it is clear that the debt-export ratio is the only initial condition relevant for the existence of a maximum. Because $X_0/Y_0 > 0$, the expression within the square brackets must cancel itself out to verify (7.30), and this depends exclusively on the initial condition D_0/X_0.

The existence of a maximum (of a value $t > 0$, which satisfies [7.30]) depends, first of all, on the growth rate of exports. If $x > \gamma$, there will always be a maximum and the debt will be sustainable whatever the values of the growth rates of output and imports (with the restrictions we have already mentioned, $\gamma > y$; $x > m$). The annex to this chapter contains a demonstration of this. In terms of the problem set out above, an economy would experience an increase in its risk premium such that $\gamma > y > y_0$, but the value of γ would still be lower than the growth rate of exports ($\gamma < x_0$). In this case the debt-output ratio would tend to grow because of the rise, but would reach a maximum point.

If $x < \gamma$, the condition to verify (7.30) and (7.31) when $t > 0$ is

$$\frac{\delta(x - m)}{(x - \gamma)(m - \gamma)} > \frac{D_0}{X_0}. \tag{7.32}$$

This is demonstrated in the annex. In terms of our problem, a rise in the risk premium makes the new value of γ higher than the growth rate of exports. In this case, the debt would be sustainable only if (7.32) were verified. Otherwise, the debt-output ratio would grow explosively.

Given L and r^*, an export growth rate x, and elasticities ρ and μ, the left-hand member of (7.22) is a decreasing function of the country risk premium:

$$H(k) = \frac{\delta(k)\,[x - m(k)]}{[x - \gamma(k)][m(k) - \gamma(k)]}. \tag{7.33}$$

Curve H is illustrated on the left panel of figure 7.1. The debt-output ratio has a maximum only if the value of H corresponding to a given k is greater than D_0/X_0. The intersection of curve H with straight line D_0/X_0 determines the critical risk premium k_c, such that the debt-output ratio becomes explosive for any $k \geq k_c$.

The two panels of figure 7.1 illustrate the above problem in the case that the rise in the risk premium determines a value $\gamma > x_0$. When $t < 0$, the country risk premium was k_0 and the growth of the economy was equal to the growth rate of the debt. If the country risk premium were to rise by $k_1 - k_0$, such that $H(k_1) > D_0/X_0$, the debt-output ratio would tend to grow, but it would reach a maximum, as shown in the right-hand panel of figure 7.1. By contrast, if the rise in the country risk premium is $k_2 - k_0$, it would be large enough for $H(k_2) < D_0/X_0$, and

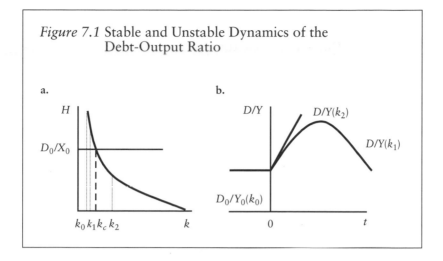

Figure 7.1 Stable and Unstable Dynamics of the
Debt-Output Ratio

the debt-output ratio would tend to grow explosively, as is also shown in the right-hand panel.

We are now in a position to sum up the conclusions we have drawn and express them in terms of the problem set out above. In the event of an increase in the country risk premium, debt sustainability depends first of all on the growth rate of exports. If the economy is growing with balanced trade, but increasing trade openness, the debt is sustainable, provided that γ is still lower than the growth rate of exports after the rise in the risk premium. In a different scenario (for example, if the economy is growing with constant external trade/output coefficients), debt sustainability depends on the debt-export ratio. The lower the debt-export ratio, the larger a rise in the risk premium the debt-output ratio can bear without becoming explosive.

Let us now consider two countries that have the same initial conditions and behavior parameters, except for their degree of trade openness and, consequently, their debt-export ratios. Both have the same initial debt-output ratio, but the first economy has a significantly lower export-output ratio (and therefore import-output ratio) than the second. We will call the first economy Chilmex and the second Brasarg. Both have the same curve $H(k)$, as shown in figure 7.2. Let us assume that both experience an identical variation in country risk premium $k_1 - k_0$ (such that the new value of γ is higher than the growth rate of exports) caused, say, by an across-the-board drop in the prices of emerging market bonds. With the new country risk premium, the debt-output ratio grows explosively in Brasarg, while in Chilmex the debt remains sustainable.[4]

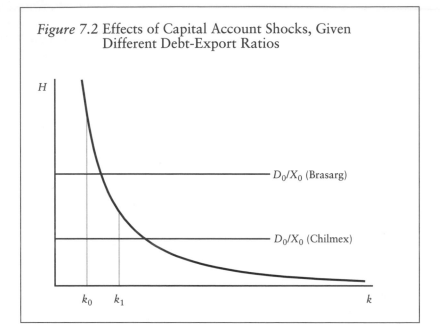

Figure 7.2 Effects of Capital Account Shocks, Given Different Debt-Export Ratios

Multiple Equilibria and Self-Fulfilling Prophecies

Let us imagine that international investors include the debt-export ratio in their country risk assessment. *Ceteris paribus*, the higher the debt-export ratio, the higher the country risk premium, because a higher debt-export ratio makes the country more likely to enter into an explosive debt trajectory in the event of a slump in the price of its bonds. The reasoning behind this assessment of risk is capable of allowing for economic policy reactions. In the event of a change in international financial conditions that threatens the sustainability of external debt, the country's government can implement measures to increase the growth rate of exports and thus ensure sustainability. As can be seen in equation (7.32), however, the higher the debt-export ratio, the larger the needed increase in exports.

The model consisting of the condition of sustainability and the function of the risk premium,

$$k = k[H(k) - D_0/X_0] \, k' < 0, \qquad (7.34)$$

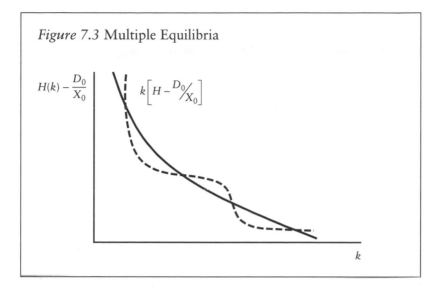

Figure 7.3 Multiple Equilibria

can have multiple equilibria, as shown in figure 7.3. Curves $H(k)$ and $k(H, D_0/X_0)$ intersect at several points. In other words, the function is satisfied by different risk premiums, which determine certain debt-output ratio trajectories. *Ceteris paribus*, the debt is sustainable with a small country risk premium. By contrast, the debt is unsustainable for country risk premiums in which $H(k) \leq D_0/X_0$.

Figure 7.4 uses Chilmex and Brasarg to show the model in which countries that are similar but have different external debt-export ratios perform with different country risk premiums. In the figure, Chilmex's premium k_{Ch} is lower than Brasarg's premium k_B because Brasarg has a significantly higher debt-export ratio than Chilmex. However, this assessment by the international financial market has pushed Brasarg's country risk premium close to the critical value that would make its debt unsustainable. As a result, Brasarg is more vulnerable to alterations in international financial conditions than Chilmex, because an increase of equal magnitude in the two countries' risk premiums makes Brasarg's debt unsustainable, while that of Chilmex continues to be sustainable.

For the same reason, Brasarg's sustainability is more prone to self-fulfilling prophecies. When the risk premium is such that the value of $H(k)$ comes close to the debt-export ratio (as is the case of Brasarg in figure 7.4), we may reasonably assume that international investors will become more prone to sudden changes of opinion in response to

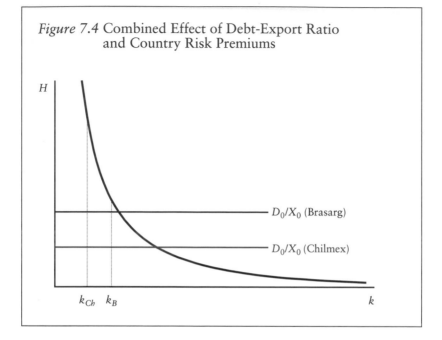

Figure 7.4 Combined Effect of Debt-Export Ratio and Country Risk Premiums

domestic or international signals, which can easily lead to increases in the risk premium that make the country's debt unsustainable.

Complementary Conditions of Sustainability

The existence of a maximum in the debt-output ratio is not a particularly demanding condition. As well as nonexplosiveness, debt sustainability ought to satisfy other conditions, such as those set forth below.

Positive Growth Rate

The first additional condition we will consider is the requirement for the economy to maintain a positive growth rate.

In the event of an increase in the country risk premium, the debt may be sustainable in the sense that it is not explosive; even so, this condition may be verified in the context of a downturn in output. If the nonexplosive trajectory is based on a prolonged contraction in output and imports, sooner or later it will become impossible for the country to meet its contractual obligations.

In consequence, this condition of sustainability is $y > 0$, which in terms of our problem can be expressed as

$$y = y_0 + \rho(k - k_0) > 0, \tag{7.35}$$

where $\rho < 0$ is the interest rate elasticity of output and $(k - k_0)$ is the increase in the country risk premium. From (7.35) it follows that

$$k - k_0 < -\frac{y_0}{\rho} \quad \text{or} \quad k < k_0 - \frac{y_0}{\rho}. \tag{7.36}$$

Restriction (7.36) is binding for a country risk premium that is lower than that which would make the debt unsustainable from the point of view of nonexplosiveness. Figure 7.5 illustrates this possibility. The lower panel of the figure shows two curves $y(r^* + k)$, which express the growth rates as a function of the interest rate. Curve Y_2 cuts straight line $y = 0$ at $k = k_2$, a higher risk premium than that which makes the debt-output ratio explosive. In this case, condition (7.36) is not relevant: When the risk premium rises, the debt becomes explosive, even when economic growth rates are positive. On the other hand, if the economy demonstrates curve Y_1, which cuts straight line $y = 0$ at $k = k_1$, a lower risk premium than would make the debt-output ratio explosive, the binding sustainability condition is the one that requires a positive growth rate. In this case, the growth rate turns negative for country risk premiums with which the debt would still be sustainable from the point of view of nonexplosiveness.

Lower Limit to the Absorption-Output Ratio

Another condition of sustainability can be derived from the existence of an upper limit on the proportion of output that must be transferred out of the country to meet debt commitments.

Let us assume that there is an increase in the country risk premium, which is sustainable from the perspective of nonexplosiveness. In the process that generates the rise in the risk premium, the trade surplus trends steadily upward as a proportion of output. As a result, the absorption-output ratio declines continuously. At the same time, the debt-output ratio increases until it reaches a maximum at a given point in time. From then on, providing there is no alteration in the parameters, the surplus will continue to increase as a proportion of output and the debt-output ratio will trend downward.

It may be assumed that, once the debt-output ratio has reached its maximum level, economic policy will be directed at increasing the economy's

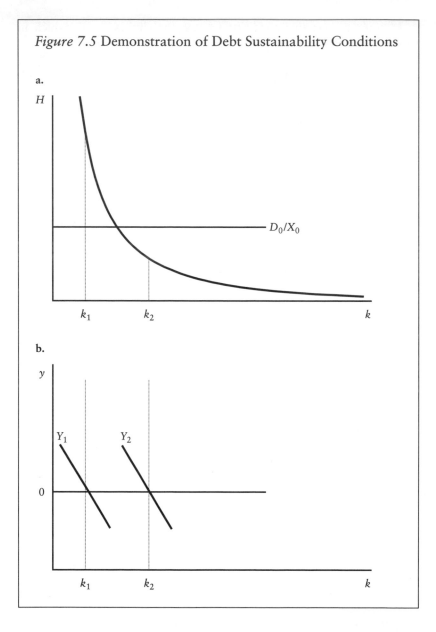

Figure 7.5 Demonstration of Debt Sustainability Conditions

growth rate (and hence the rate of growth of imports), preserving sustainability, stabilizing or reducing the downward trend in the debt-output ratio, and balancing or mitigating the contraction in the absorption-output ratio.

This process could not come about if the absorption-output ratio were to bottom out before the debt-output ratio reached its maximum point. This would make the debt unsustainable.

The limit on the contraction of absorption is determined essentially by the existence of an admissible level in the economy's consumption rate, because the investment rate cannot drop below a certain floor level without affecting the output growth rate and imports.[5]

We can approach this condition of sustainability in a formal manner using expression (7.16):

$$\frac{d(D/Y)}{D/Y} = \hat{D} - y = \gamma - y - \delta \left(\frac{X - M}{Y} \right) \Big/ \frac{D}{Y}.$$

This rate turns nil when the debt-output ratio reaches its maximum level,

$$0 = \gamma - y - \delta \left(\frac{X - M}{Y} \right) \Big/ \left(\frac{D}{Y} \right)_{max}, \qquad (7.37)$$

and therefore

$$\left(\frac{D}{Y} \right)_{max} = \delta \left(\frac{X - M}{Y} \right) \Big/ (\gamma - y). \qquad (7.38)$$

Let s be the maximum admissible value of the trade surplus-output ratio (the absorption-output ratio is therefore $1 - s$). Substituting in (7.38), the condition of sustainability may be expressed as

$$\left(\frac{D}{Y} \right)_{max} \leq \frac{\delta s}{\gamma - y}. \qquad (7.39)$$

Condition (7.39) specifies the ceiling that the economy's debt-output ratio may reach without exceeding the maximum admissible outward transfer. For a given country risk premium, which determines a nonexplosive debt trajectory, the debt becomes unsustainable if the debt-output ratio violates condition (7.39).[6]

Let us note that by defining a maximum flow of admissible external transfer, we arrive at a determination of a ceiling on the debt-output ratio. The condition is formally analogous to the condition that arises from directly assuming that the country is facing an external financing squeeze (in proportion to its level of gross domestic product).[7] Clearly, in (7.39) the restriction is not a mechanical one, but depends on the

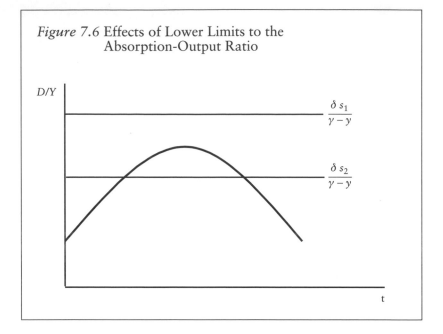

Figure 7.6 Effects of Lower Limits to the
Absorption-Output Ratio

international interest rate and the country risk premium. The higher the country risk premium, the lower the ceiling on the debt-output ratio.

Figure 7.6 illustrates this condition of sustainability. The figure shows the trajectory of the debt-output ratio for a determined risk premium k. The trajectory satisfies the nonexplosiveness condition. If the maximum admissible proportion of outward transfer is s_1, the condition is not binding and the debt is sustainable. With a lower maximum admissible external transfer, s_2, the straight line of the restriction cuts the trajectory of the debt-output ratio before it reaches its maximum point. In this case, the debt is unsustainable.

Multiple Equilibria (II)

Each of the conditions of sustainability we have considered raises the possibility of multiple equilibria when we take into account the risk assessment conducted by international investors. Such a possibility arises if we assume, for example, that the closer to each of the restrictions imposed by the conditions, the higher the risk premium. This can be formally expressed by assuming that the risk premium is determined by the following function:

$$k = K\left[H(k) - D_0/X_0; y; \frac{\delta s}{\gamma - y} - \left(\frac{D}{Y}\right)_{max}\right]$$

$$K_1 < 0; \ K_2 < 0; \ K_3 < 0. \tag{7.40}$$

This means of determining risk premium can be used to extrapolate each of the conditions of sustainability from the arguments set out in the earlier section on multiple equilibria and self-fulfilling prophecies.

Annex

The first order condition is the equation (7.30):

$$\frac{\partial(D/Y)}{\partial t} = \frac{X_0}{Y_0}\left\{(\gamma - y)e^{(\gamma - y)t}\left(\frac{D_0}{X_0} + \frac{\delta}{x - \gamma} - \frac{\delta}{m - \gamma}\right)\right.$$
$$\left. - \left[\frac{\delta}{x - \gamma}(x - y)e^{(x - y)t} - \frac{\delta}{m - \gamma}(m - y)e^{(m - y)t}\right]\right\} = 0.$$

Because $\frac{X_0}{Y_0} > 0$, the expression in square brackets must be cancelled out. Division of the expression between square brackets by $\delta(\gamma + y)e^{(\gamma - y)t}$ gives

$$\frac{1}{\delta}\frac{D_0}{X_0} + \frac{1}{x - \gamma} - \frac{1}{m - \gamma}$$
$$- \left[\frac{1}{x - \gamma}\frac{x - y}{\gamma - y}e^{(x - \gamma)t} - \frac{1}{m - \gamma}\frac{m - y}{\gamma - y}e^{(m - \gamma)t}\right] = 0. \tag{7.41}$$

The problem is how to show that there exists a $t > 0$ that satisfies equation (7.28) with the parameters $x > m$ and $\gamma > y$.
Let us take

$$A = \frac{1}{x - \gamma}\frac{x - y}{\gamma - y} \quad \text{and} \quad B = \frac{1}{m - \gamma}\frac{m - y}{\gamma - y}. \tag{7.42}$$

Expression (7.41) may thus be written as

$$F(t) = Ae^{(x-\gamma)t} + Be^{(m-\gamma)t} - (A - B) = \frac{1}{\delta}\frac{D_0}{X_0}, \qquad (7.43)$$

where $A - B = \dfrac{m - x}{(x - \gamma)(m - \gamma)}$. Note that $F(0) = 0$ and $F'(t) > 0$.

Let us consider three cases:

1. $x > \gamma \wedge m > \gamma$

2. $x > \gamma \wedge m < \gamma$

3. $x > \gamma\ (\Rightarrow m < \gamma)$.

In cases 1 and 2, $F(t) \to \infty$. There is always a value of $t > 0$, such that $F(t) = \frac{1}{\delta}\frac{D_0}{X_0}$.

In case 3, $F(t) \to -(A - B)$. Thus, there is only one value of $t > 0$, such that $F(t) = \frac{1}{\delta}\frac{D_0}{X_0}$, if $\frac{1}{\delta}\frac{D_0}{X_0} < -(A - B) = \frac{x - m}{(x - \gamma)(m - \gamma)}$. In consequence, the condition is

$$\frac{D_0}{X_0} < \frac{\delta(x - m)}{(x - \gamma)(m - \gamma)}. \qquad (7.44)$$

Endnotes

1. See Simonsen (1985) and Bhaduri (2001).

2. On "segmented integration," see Frenkel (2001).

3. In fact, verification of the second order condition is redundant because we know that $\frac{\partial(\tilde{D}/\gamma)}{\partial t}(0) > 0$, so that if (7.30) has a point of inflexion, it must be a maximum.

4. Let us consider a numerical example. We will assume that Chilmex and Brasarg have the same debt-output ratio, $D_0/Y_0 = 50$ percent. Let us also assume that Chilmex has an export-output ratio of 33 percent, and Brasarg has an export-output ratio of 10 percent. The debt-export ratio is thus $D_0/X_0 = 1.5$ in Chilmex, and $D_0/X_0 = 5$ in Brasarg. Let us assume that in both economies $r^* = 5$ percent, $k_0 = 200$ hundredths of a percentage point, $y_0 = 8$ percent, $x_0 = 10$ percent, $m_0 = 10$ percent, $\rho = -1$, and $\mu = 1.25$. It can be seen that these conditions represent an exceptionally good performance. With these parameters, Brasarg's debt becomes unsustainable for risk premiums above 800 hundredths of a percentage point, whereas Chilmex's debt is sustainable with risk premiums of up to 2,000 hundredths of a percentage point.

5. This argument was commonly used in the second half of the 1980s, when the adjustment of the Latin American economies to postcrisis conditions was on the agenda.

6. With $L = 10$ years, $r^* = 5$ percent, $k = 500$ hundredths of a percentage point, and a maximum outward transfer rate $s = 3$ percent of output, the debt-output ratio could not rise above 51 percent.

7. The restriction is analogous to the existence of a limit on the debt-net worth ratio in the case of corporate financing. Bacha (1986) used this argument as a basis for an "external financing restriction" that limits the growth of an economy.

Bibliography

Bacha, Edmar. 1986. "Crecimiento con oferta limitada de divisas: Una revaluación del modelo de dos brechas." In *El milagro y la crisis. Economía Brasileña y Latinoamericana*, ed. Edmar Bacha. Mexico City: Fondo de Cultura Económica.

Bhaduri, Amit. 2001. "On the Viability of External Debt." In *External Constraints on Sustainable Growth in Transition Countries*, ed. Kazimierz Laski. Working Paper 19, Institute for International Economic Studies, Vienna, Austria.

Frenkel, Roberto. 2001. "Reflections on Development Financing." *CEPAL Review* 74: LC/G.2135-P.

Simonsen, Mario Henrique. 1985. "The Developing-Country Debt Problem." In *International Debt and the Developing Countries*, eds. Gordon W. Smith and John T. Cuddington, 101–26. Washington, DC: World Bank.

8

Divergence and Growth Collapses: Theory and Empirical Evidence

Jaime Ros

OVER THE PAST 15 YEARS, THE inability of traditional growth theory to account for the stylized facts of post-World War II (WWII) economic growth has prompted modern growth economics to take approaches that range from extending the traditional neoclassical model to moving radically away from it. The present chapter evaluates these recent attempts and considers the alternative offered by the classical development approach.[1] More precisely, the chapter focuses on two stylized facts that do not fit neatly into modern growth economics: the processes of divergence in income levels between rich and poor countries and within the group of developing countries, and the growth collapses observed in low- and middle-income countries.

The three-part argument presented here can be described schematically as follows. The first section shows that the processes of divergence observed in the data are inconsistent with the neoclassical model and its different extensions and variants. The second section argues that classical development theory seems to offer a better explanation of divergence processes than do the new endogenous growth theories. The main reason is that according to the classical model, when an economy reaches the middle-income level its growth speeds up, exceeding the long-run

The author is currently Professor of Economics at the University of Notre Dame and Faculty Fellow at the Helen Kellogg Institute of International Studies. I am grateful to José Antonio Ocampo and two anonymous referees for their comments on an earlier version of this chapter. The responsibility for any error is, of course, exclusively my own.

equilibrium growth rate, and is therefore compatible with convergence processes at high- and middle-income levels. However, classical theory is consistent with the growth collapses observed in low- and middle-income countries only if the poverty traps predicted by the model are attributable to vicious circles of low profitability generated by the interaction between increasing returns to scale and an elastic labor supply. The last section looks at empirical evidence suggesting that many more factors come into play in the processes that cause growth to stall or collapse. The factors that appear to affect the propensity to growth collapses include the potentially negative influence of inequality on growth, the role of the pattern of trade specialization, and the interaction between those two factors. In the work of Prebisch, these issues play a significant role in explaining economic development processes in Latin America.

The Evidence for Divergence and the Neoclassical Growth Models

Table 8.1 shows the observed levels of output per worker in 1965 and 1997 and the growth rate of that variable between those two years in a group of 73 countries divided into five income groups.[2] The table illustrates the processes of divergence in per capita income levels that occurred over that period between rich and poor countries and among developing countries. The income gaps between rich and poor countries are not only huge—on the order of 23 to 1 between groups 1 and 5—but also increasing: In 1965 the difference in income between groups 1 and 5 was on the order of 12 to 1. The gaps between middle- and low-income countries have also been widening, from a difference of 3.7 to 1 in 1965 to a difference of about 6 to 1 in 1997 between groups 3 and 5. These divergence processes clearly reflect the fact that the economies of the high- and middle-income countries grew faster (by 2.1 percent and 1.5 percent a year in groups 1 and 3, respectively) than those of the lower-income countries (the rate for group 5 was 0.2 percent).

Similar divergence processes have been well documented for other periods and samples of countries and regions. Pritchett (1997) showed that the ratio of the richest country's per capita GDP to that of the poorest country increased from 8.7 in 1870 to 51.6 in 1985, whereas the standard deviation of the logarithm of per capita income, which had been between 0.513 and 0.636 in 1870, rose to 1.025 in 1985 (see also DeLong 1997; Jones 1997; and Maddison 1995). A study by the United Nations Conference on Trade and Development (UNCTAD 1997) estimated that the ratio of the income of the richest developing countries to that of the poorest has almost doubled over the past four decades. A

Table 8.1 International Differences in Income Levels and
Growth Rates

(Average for groups of countries)

Factor	Group 1	Group 2	Group 3	Group 4	Group 5
GDP per worker (1997)[a]	46,693	26,488	11,775	4,995	1,988
GDP per worker (1965)[a]	23,358	17,471	7,378	4,358	1,973
Annual growth rates (1965–97)					
GDP	3.5	3.4	4.5	3.1	2.6
GDP per worker	2.1	1.3	1.5	0.5	0.2
Number of countries	18	14	13	15	13

Source: Ros, 2000, tables 7 and 8.

Note: Group 1: Australia, Austria, Belgium, Canada, Denmark, Finland, France, Hong Kong (China), Ireland, Israel, Italy, Japan, the Netherlands, Norway, Singapore, Switzerland, United Kingdom, United States. Group 2: Argentina, Chile, Costa Rica, Greece, Malaysia, Mexico, New Zealand, Portugal, South Africa, Republic of Korea, Spain, Sweden, Uruguay, República Bolivariana de Venezuela. Group 3: Algeria, Brazil, Colombia, Dominican Republic, Ecuador, Arab Republic of Egypt, Guatemala, Morocco, Paraguay, Peru, the Philippines, Thailand, Tunisia. Group 4: Cameroon, El Salvador, Ghana, Honduras, India, Indonesia, Côte d'Ivoire, Jamaica, Mauritania, Nicaragua, Pakistan, Senegal, Sri Lanka, Togo, Zimbabwe. Group 5: Bangladesh, Benin, Burkina Faso, Burundi, Haiti, Kenya, Madagascar, Malawi, Mali, Niger, Nigeria, Rwanda, Zambia. GDP = gross domestic product.

a. Figures in 1997 international dollars.

number of studies have verified the growth spurt at middle-income levels that causes the divergence between middle- and low-income countries.[3] Ades and Glaeser (1999) found that growth rates were positively correlated with initial development levels among developing countries in the 20th century and among states of the United States in the 19th century.

Can neoclassical growth models account for these trends? The evidence for divergence in absolute income levels is not conclusive in this respect, because neoclassical theory predicts only conditional convergence, or convergence at each country's long-term income level. Table 8.2 presents the long-term income levels and growth rates predicted by three variants of neoclassical theory: the traditional Solow (1956) model, with physical capital and labor; the Mankiw, Romer, and Weil (1992) model, which includes human capital in the production function; and the model estimated by Islam (1995), which takes into account the existence of technology gaps between countries.[4]

None of the three models manages to reproduce the divergence processes observed in the data. The growth rates predicted for the low-income countries (groups 4 and 5) are systematically higher than the

Table 8.2 Long-Term Income and Growth Rates Predicted by Three Neoclassical Models

(Average for groups of countries)

Factors and Models	Group 1	Group 2	Group 3	Group 4	Group 5
Investment rate (%)[a]	23.2	21.4	24.9	21.4	19.4
Growth of the labor force[b]	1.4	2.2	3.0	2.7	2.4
Rate of investment in education[c]	9.5	7.2	6.7	5.0	2.2
Technological level[d]	1.0	0.58	0.35	0.18[e]	0.10[f]
Model with physical capital and labor					
Income as percentage of group 1 (1997)	100	56.7	25.2	10.7	4.3
Long-term income as percentage of group 1 (predicted)	100	90.5	92.7	87.6	85.0
Annual GDP growth (1965–97)					
Observed	3.5	3.4	4.5	3.1	2.6
Predicted	3.5	4.7	7.9	9.1	10.2
Number of countries	18	14	13	15	13
Model with human capital					
Income as percentage of group 1 (1985)	100	49.5	27.9	15.6	7.1
Long-term income as percentage of group 1 (predicted)	100	63.9	37.9	26.4	18.1
Annual GDP growth (1960–85)					
Observed	4.2	4.3	5.5	4.6	3.3
Predicted	4.2	5.2	6.6	6.5	6.5
Number of countries	18	16	14	14	13

Model with technology gaps

Income as percentage of group 1 (1997)	100	56.7	25.2	10.7	4.3
Long-term income as percentage of group 1 (predicted)	100	52.5	32.8	16.1	8.4
Annual GDP growth (1965–97)					
Observed	3.5	3.4	4.5	3.1	2.6
Predicted	3.5	3.4	5.2	4.4	4.5
Number of countries	18	14	13	15	13

Source: Ros 2000, chapter 2, tables 7, 8, 9, and 10.

a. Gross investment as a fraction of GDP (average 1965–97).
b. Trend growth rate of the labor force (1965–97) (annual percentage).
c. Percentage of working-age population attending secondary school. Average 1960–85. See Mankiw, Romer, and Weil (1992).
d. Estimates from Islam (1995).
e. Average excludes Indonesia.
f. Average excludes Burkina Faso.

rates actually observed, and higher than the growth rates of high- and middle-income countries (groups 1 and 2, although they are not higher than those of group 3 in the models that include human capital and technology gaps).[5] In other words, the models predict not only conditional convergence but also absolute convergence. The reasons for this are different in each model. The Solow model predicts very small differences in long-term income (15 percent between groups 1 and 5). The gaps between initial income and predicted long-term income are thus very wide for the low-income countries and as a result their predicted growth rates are very high (the highest of all the groups). In the other two models, the consideration of investment in education (Mankiw, Romer, and Weil 1992) or of differences in technology (Islam 1995) tends to widen the predicted gaps in long-term income.[6] This is because each of these models assumes that there are huge differences between countries in terms of their supply of human capital or level of technology. Accordingly, the gap between the low-income countries' initial and long-term income is much smaller than in the traditional neoclassical model, and thus the growth rates predicted for these countries are lower than in that model. Even so, these rates are higher than the ones actually observed and the ones posted by the high-income groups, implying the existence of absolute convergence. The trend toward conditional convergence implied by the assumption of diminishing returns to capital counteracts the effect of these smaller gaps between initial and long-term income.[7]

Divergence, Endogenous Growth, and Classical Development Theory

If the limitations of neoclassical models stem from the assumption of diminishing returns to capital, the presence of divergence would seem to imply the existence of increasing or constant returns to capital in the aggregate production function. This is precisely the assumption made in a number of endogenous growth theories, including the original Romer (1986) and Lucas (1988) models, as well as the AK model with constant returns to capital (Barro 1990; Rebelo 1991). Adopting a very-long-term perspective, Romer (1986, 1991) found attractive the assumption that the external effects of capital accumulation are so great that they generate increasing returns to capital, as this premise is consistent with the increase in the productivity growth rates of technology leaders through the centuries. However, when an attempt is made to use this analytical framework to explain the differences in growth rates between countries, a number of problems arise.

The major problem is that these models seem to imply an excessive degree of divergence. In the first place, the models imply growing gaps in per capita income at all income levels, not only between poor and rich countries or between low- and middle-income countries.[8] Thus, they fail to explain the tendency toward convergence between high- and middle-income countries or among regions within a country. These convergence processes have been extensively documented in the case of the Organisation for Economic Co-operation and Development (OECD) countries in the post-WWII period, the states of the United States between 1880 and 1980, and the prefectures of Japan between 1955 and 1990 (see Barro and Sala-i-Martin 1995; Baumol and Wolff 1988; Maddison 1991; and Ros 2000).

Second, these models imply that not only gaps in per capita income, but also differences in growth rates themselves should increase over time. No one, to my knowledge, has suggested that this is happening. Although this particular difficulty does not arise in endogenous growth models that limit the capital coefficient to 1 in the aggregate production function (AK model), thus generating steady growth at a constant rather than a rising rate, the properties of those models also fail to explain the convergence processes that have occurred at middle- and high-income levels. In addition, these models' distinctive properties are critically dependent on the assumption that returns to capital are exactly constant, thus limiting still further the assumptions made on technology, even though there is no clear empirical support for this.[9]

What is needed is a model in which increasing returns to capital prevail at low- and middle-income levels, while at high-income levels the aggregate production function exhibits diminishing returns to capital. This is precisely what happens in models of classical development theory in which increasing returns to capital at low-income levels result not from technology but from the interaction between increasing returns to scale and an elastic labor supply. This point can be illustrated by a simple example in which increasing returns to scale are generated by technological externalities.

Consider an economy with two sectors (S and M) that produce the same good (or basket of goods). Sector S uses traditional production techniques that are labor-intensive (or, more generally, with low-productivity owing to the limited use of capital). The other sector (M) uses a mass production technology subject to increasing returns to scale. The corresponding production functions are

$$S = L_S \qquad\qquad (8.1)$$

$$M = (K^{\mu})K^a L_M^{1-a} \qquad \mu > 0,\, a + \mu < 1, \qquad (8.2)$$

where S and M are the levels of production in the two sectors, L_S and L_M are the labor inputs in each sector, K is the capital stock, and K^μ reflects the existence of technological externalities associated with the capital stock accumulated in the past. A positive value of parameter μ guarantees that the capitalist technology exhibits increasing returns to scale. The restriction $a + \mu < 1$ implies the assumption of diminishing returns to capital in the production function of the capital-intensive sector.

Let us also assume that both sectors operate in competitive conditions. The assumption that the capitalist sector is profit maximizing generates the following labor demand function:

$$L_M = [(1 - a)K^\mu/w_M]^{1/a} K. \qquad (8.3)$$

In addition, assuming that workers who do not find employment in the capitalist sector are employed in the traditional sector and that wages in the two sectors are equal owing to labor market competition, we have

$$L = L_S + L_M \qquad (8.4)$$

$$w_M = 1, \qquad (8.5)$$

where L is the total labor force and w_M is the wage in sector M. We have chosen units so that $w_S = 1$, and because $w_S = w_M$, we have $w_M = 1$.

Using the production functions of the two sectors—(8.1) and (8.2)—total output $(Y = S + M)$ can be written as $Y = L_S + K^{a+\mu} L_M^{1-a}$. Using (8.4) to eliminate L_S from this expression and (8.3) to eliminate L_M (and using equation [8.5]) gives the following equation:

$$Y = L + a(1 - a)^{(1-a)/a} K^{1+\mu/a}. \qquad (8.6)$$

Equation (8.6) shows that even though the capitalist sector's technology is subject to diminishing returns to capital $(a + \mu < 1)$, the aggregate production function shows increasing returns to capital $(1 + \mu/a > 1)$. This is so, of course, provided that the two sectors coexist (because [8.6] is derived from the assumption $w_S = w_M = 1$). Otherwise, if the traditional sector disappears, the aggregate production function is the same as that of the capital-intensive sector.

Increasing returns to capital during the phase in which the two sectors coexist are the result of interactions between an elastic labor supply for the capital-intensive sector $(w_M = 1)$ and increasing returns to scale $(\mu > 0)$. Increasing returns to scale strengthen the effects of capital accumulation on productivity, whereas the elastic labor supply weakens the effects of capital accumulation on real wages. The rates of profit and capital accumulation may thus be increasing functions of the capital stock. This has two implications. The first is that at very low income levels, the profit rate may be so low that the rate of accumulation falls below the depreciation rate and the capital stock contracts instead of expanding. The economy is then in a profitability trap in which the elastic labor supply and increasing returns interact negatively to block the expansion of the modern sector: The elastic labor supply sets a floor on the real wages that the modern sector has to pay and this, combined with the initial conditions of low productivity, prevents the profitable use of capital-intensive technologies with increasing returns.

The second implication is that the dynamics of growth are very different from the transition to long-term equilibrium in neoclassical models and from accumulation processes in endogenous growth models. In contrast to what happens in neoclassical models (and in line with what happens in endogenous growth models with increasing returns) at low income levels, but beyond the profitability trap, the interactions between increasing returns to scale and an elastic labor supply are positive and counteract the influence of diminishing returns to capital in the technology of the capital-intensive sector. As a result, the growth rate may increase over a long period, generating a trend toward divergence in income levels. In contrast to what happens in endogenous growth models (and in line with what happens in neoclassical models), a reduction in the elasticity of the labor supply at higher income levels, as the ratio of capital to labor increases and the traditional sector disappears, tends to reduce the rates of profit and growth and, therefore, to generate convergence. Thus, the model implies transitional dynamics characterized by a pattern of conditional divergence followed by convergence, in which the highest rates of accumulation are found in the intermediate rather than the initial stages of the transition, as occurs in the neoclassical model, or in more advanced stages, as in models with increasing returns to capital.

This pattern of divergence/convergence may be summed up in a schematic and approximate way as a quadratic equation in which the rate of income growth (g_y) is related to the initial income level and the square of initial income $(y_0$ and $y_0^2)$:

$$g_y = a_0 + a_1 y_0 + a_2 y_0^2 \qquad a_1 > 0, a_2 < 0. \qquad (8.7)$$

The growth rate then reaches a maximum at an income level equal to

$$y^M = -a_1/2a_2, \qquad (8.8)$$

provided that a_2 is negative (the condition for a maximum) and a_1 is positive (so that y is positive). The corresponding maximum growth rate is $g_M = a_0 - a_1^2/4a_2$. The equation also implies a convergence threshold, or the income level at which the growth rate equals that of higher-income countries (g^*), at

$$y_C = y^M + [a_1^2 - 4a_2(a_0 - g^*)]^{1/2}/2a_2, \qquad (8.9)$$

which is less than y^M, because a_2 is negative.

The results of estimates from quadratic equations generally support the pattern of divergence/convergence (see Ros 2000, ch. 4). The signs of the coefficients are systematically favorable to the hypothesis and survive the inclusion of human capital variables and other possible determinants of long-term equilibrium. The results of the estimates tend to confirm that, after taking into account differences in investment rates, education, and political risk factors, the economies of poorer countries have tended to grow more slowly than those of middle- and high-income countries, and only after a threshold was passed did a process of convergence begin. Needless to say, these results call into question the conclusion that, "given the human-capital variables, subsequent growth is substantially negatively related to the initial level of per capita GDP" (Barro 1991, p. 409). The positive coefficient of initial income implies the presence of significant forces for divergence that are countered only at middle- and high-income levels.[10] With respect to the positive rate of convergence estimated in neoclassical models in the manner of Barro and Sala-i-Martin (1992), a comment made by Lucas (2002) is relevant and consistent with the quadratic equations: "The annual income convergence rate of about .02 that Barro and Sala-i-Martin (1992) estimated from postwar data is an average of a few much higher rates with a lot of zeros" (p. 9) and, it might be added, quite a few negative rates. It is interesting to note that in his most recent research, Barro himself included a quadratic term for initial income, together with other growth determinants, with results that support the pattern of divergence/convergence (see Barro 1999).

Growth Collapses, Inequality, and Trade Specialization

The classical approach can be used to explain the pattern of initial divergence followed by convergence at middle- and high-income levels. A careful reading of the post-WWII experience, however, reveals that the acceleration of growth at middle-income levels has been accompanied by cases in which growth slows down or even becomes negative. These growth collapses have affected many middle-income countries and low-income countries that, after having apparently taken off, slipped back to

Table 8.3 Incidence of Growth Collapse at Different Income Levels

(Percentage)

| | Growth Collapse | | Total | Sustained |
Initial Income Level	Catastrophic	Severe	Collapses	Growth
High	0	0	0	100
Middle				
High	13.6	22.7	36.4	63.6
Low	27.3	31.8	59.1	40.9
Low	35.3	23.5	58.8	41.2

Source: Based on Perala 2002, table 3.4.
Note: High income = more than US$890. Upper middle income = between US$340 and US$890. Lower middle income = between US$170 and US$300. Low income = US$170 or less. All amounts figured in 1960 dollars.

income levels they had reached years or even decades earlier. Table 8.3, based on Perala (2002), shows the incidence of growth collapses—defined as the experience of economies that achieved their current levels of real per capita income in or before the 1960s (catastrophic collapses) or in the 1970s or 1980s (severe collapses)—in different categories of countries grouped according to their per capita gross domestic product (GDP) in 1960. The table confirms that the incidence of collapse is highest in lower-middle- and low-income countries and falls quickly in higher-income groups, dropping to zero among the high-income countries. Cases of sustained growth, defined as the remaining subset,[11] are thus more numerous among the upper-middle- and high-income countries.

The transition matrices estimated by Quah (1993) for the period 1962–84 illustrate the same phenomenon. These matrices divide the world economy into five groups, based on per capita income level in relation to the world average, and show the likelihood that a country in a particular group will still be in the same group the following year or will move from that group to a higher- or lower-income group. The countries most likely to stay in the same group are those with the highest and lowest incomes. The countries least likely to stay in the same group, and thus most likely to move to a higher- or lower-income group, are those in the middle- and low-middle-income groups. It is noteworthy that in these groups downward mobility is as common as upward mobility, which suggests that collapses are as frequent as growth spurts in those countries. (On the greater mobility of relative income at the middle levels of the international income distribution, see Chari, Kehoe, and McGrattan 1996.)

Table 8.4 Cases of Growth Collapse

Catastrophic Collapse		Severe Collapse	
Burundi	Somalia	Cameroon	Paraguay
Central African	South Africa	Congo, Dem.	Peru
Republic	Togo	Rep. of	Trinidad and
Chad	Zambia	Kenya	Tobago
Congo, Dem.	Bolivia	Malawi	Iran, Islamic
Rep. of	Haiti	Mali	Rep. of
Côte d'Ivoire	Jamaica	Mauritania	Jordan
Ghana	Nicaragua	Nigeria	Saudi Arabia
Liberia	Venezuela,	Zimbabwe	Philippines
Madagascar	R. B. de	Ecuador	
Niger		El Salvador	
Rwanda		Guatemala	
Senegal		Guyana	
Sierra Leone		Honduras	

Source: Based on Perala 2002, table 3.5.

The cases of collapse are shown in table 8.4. Catastrophic collapses are concentrated in Sub-Saharan Africa (16 cases) and Latin America (5 cases). Sub-Saharan Africa, Central America and the Caribbean, and South America have the highest incidence of severe collapses (8 cases in each region), followed by the Middle East (3 cases) and East Asia (1 case). It is possible that in some cases these processes of stagnation or decline are attributable to classic underdevelopment traps, characteristic of economies that have not yet managed to create the conditions for sustained growth. But in many other cases the classical approach seems insufficient or even irrelevant for explaining these processes. According to that approach, a growth spurt—that is, the opposite of a collapse— would be expected at middle- and low-middle-income levels.

The question, then, is whether there are other factors that can explain these processes of stagnation or collapse. The recent literature on the comparative analysis of growth has emphasized the role of the following factors:

1. *Size of the economy.* Auty (2001) and Perala (2002) presented empirical evidence supporting the hypothesis that the highest incidence of collapse occurs in small economies. Auty attributed this to the fact that small economies' export structures are more concentrated in a few products and their domestic economic activity is less diversified, whereas their greater openness to external trade makes them more vulnerable to external shocks.

2. *Abundance of natural resources.* Ranis (1991, cited by Auty 1997) sums up the mechanisms whereby an abundance of natural resources may be inimical to growth:

a. Income from natural resources causes the State and society to neglect the development of human resources and the process of wealth creation, allows import-substitution processes to continue even after they no longer contribute to development, and generates conditions that encourage rent-seeking on the part of interest groups. This last hypothesis was recently formalized and investigated by Tornell and Lane (1999).

b. Natural resource booms may give rise to "Dutch disease," meaning they may have destructive effects that persist even after the boom is over, on tradable (non-natural-resource-intensive) goods sectors (see Corden and Neary 1982; Rodríguez and Sachs 1999; and Sachs and Warner 1997, 2001).

c. International trade in natural-resource-intensive goods may worsen income distribution and lead society to identify trade with the interests of the rich.

d. Commodity prices are more volatile than manufactures prices, paving the way for growth collapses in the absence of export diversification.

Most of these mechanisms concern the adverse effects that an abundance of natural resources may have on the growth rate (that is, the explanation of why some economies grow more slowly than others), but if we add to this the downward trend in relative commodity prices (the famous Prebisch-Singer thesis, which is timely and relevant to developments in the past two decades), we come closer to an explanation of these collapses.[12]

3. *Type of natural resources.* The distinction between the performance of mineral- and oil-exporting economies and that of economies rich in agricultural resources dates back to the Economic Commission for Latin America and the Caribbean literature of the 1950s and 1960s and to Hirschman (1981). Economies in the first category seem to be particularly prone to growth collapses, to the extent that they are usually "enclave economies" with weak internal linkages that hinder the economy's diversification and significant fiscal linkages that lead governments to carry out tasks that are intrinsically more difficult than those taken on by the private sector (Hirschman 1981). Auty (2001) added that capital-intensiveness and the concentration of ownership in mineral resource sectors generate a high degree of inequality that has adverse effects on growth. Gelb (1988, ch. 2), in turn, pointed out that mineral prices and export earnings are more volatile than those of agricultural products. The resulting economic instability acts as a drag on growth, given the consequent asymmetries in the economy's adjustment to fluctuations in

demand (which reduce the average level of use of productive capacity) and volatility in government revenues and public investment.

4. *Unequal income distribution.* The recent literature on this subject identifies two types of mechanisms whereby higher levels of inequality may hinder growth. Economic mechanisms include the adverse effects of inequality on market size for industries with increasing returns to scale (present in the structuralist literature of the 1960s; see also the more recent formalization by Murphy, Shleifer, and Vishny [1989]) or on aggregate demand and the use of productive capacity (with negative effects on investment [Dutt 1984]), as well as the links between income distribution and investment in education (in the presence of imperfect credit markets, lower levels of inequality ease the budgetary constraints of the poor and allow more investment in education [Birdsall, Ross, and Sabot 1995; Galor and Zeira 1993]) and the lower fertility and population growth rates that result from less inequality (Perotti 1996). Sociopolitical mechanisms include the fiscal effects (such as taxes on capital) of the redistributive pressures that result from income concentration (Alesina and Rodrik 1994) and the effects of inequality on political instability and social conflict (Alesina and Perotti 1994) and on the polarization that undermines consensus on economic policies (Keefer and Knack 1999) and makes external shocks harder to manage (Rodrik 1998).

Tables 8.5 to 8.7 present empirical evidence for each of these hypotheses using three samples of countries.[13] Table 8.5 shows the incidence of collapses in different types of economies grouped by size, abundance of natural resources, and type of natural resources. The table illustrates three stylized facts concerning growth collapses. First, the incidence of collapses is higher in small economies than in large ones (67 percent opposed to 25 percent). The influence of size is even more apparent in the fact that small economies in all three categories (poor, rich in agricultural resources, and rich in minerals and oil) are more prone to collapses. The significance of size, which is confirmed by the findings of Auty and of Perala, probably reflects the vulnerability to external shocks that arises from a high degree of openness and specialization in foreign trade, and suggests that poverty traps related to increasing returns to scale play a role in explaining the collapses. Second, consistent with the recent literature on the relationship between natural resource abundance and growth, collapses are more frequent in economies rich in natural resources than in resource-poor economies (30 percent compared with 17 percent among large economies and 70 percent compared with 55 percent among small ones). Third, economies rich in mineral resources and oil seem more prone to collapses than economies rich in agricultural resources (67 percent compared with 14 percent among large economies and 78 percent compared with 64 percent among small

Table 8.5 Incidence of Collapse in Different Types of Economy

(Developing countries)

Type of Economy	Number of Countries	Number of Collapses	Incidence of Collapse (%)
Large	16	4	25
Resource-poor[a]	6	1	17
Resource-rich	10	3	30
Agricultural[b]	7	1	14
Minerals and oil[c]	3	2	67
Small	54	36	67
Resource-poor[d]	11	6	55
Resource-rich	43	30	70
Agricultural[e]	25	16	64
Minerals and oil[f]	18	14	78
Total	70	40	57

Source: Author's calculations, based on Auty (1997) and Perala (2002).

Note: Type of economy: size, abundance of natural resources and type of natural resources. Large economies: 1970 GDP higher than US$6.99 billion. Resource-poor economies: less than 0.3 hectares of arable land per inhabitant. In the notes below, growth collapses are indicated by*.

a. Bangladesh, Colombia, Arab Republic of Egypt, Indonesia, the Philippines*, and Republic of Korea.

b. Argentina, Brazil, India, Mexico, Pakistan, South Africa*, and Turkey.

c. Chile, Nigeria*, and República Bolivariana de Venezuela*.

d. El Salvador*, Haiti*, Hong Kong (China), Jordan*, Kenya*, Mauritania*, Mauritius, Nepal, Singapore, Somalia*, and Sri Lanka.

e. Burundi*, Cameroon*, Chad*, Costa Rica, Côte d'Ivoire*, Ghana*, Guatemala*, Guyana*, Honduras*, Lesotho, Madagascar*, Malawi*, Malaysia, Mali*, Morocco, Nicaragua*, Panama, Paraguay*, Rwanda*, Senegal*, Sudan, Thailand, Tunisia, Uruguay, and Zimbabwe*.

f. Bolivia*, Botswana, Burkina Faso, Central African Republic*, the Democratic Republic of Congo*, the Republic of Congo*, Dominican Republic, Ecuador*, Jamaica*, Liberia*, Niger*, Peru*, Saudi Arabia*, Sierra Leone*, Syrian Arab Republic, Togo*, Trinidad and Tobago*, and Zambia*.

ones), supporting the hypotheses of Hirschman, Auty, and Gelb on the role played by the type of natural resources. It is worthwhile noting the significance of the interaction between size, abundance of natural resources, and trade specialization in minerals and oil: The highest incidence of collapses occurs in economies that are small and rich in natural resources (70 percent), particularly those that specialize in mineral and oil exports (78 percent).

Table 8.6 illustrates the influence of inequality on the incidence of collapses. There have been no collapses in the group of countries with a low

Table 8.6 Inequality and Incidence of Collapse

(Developed and developing countries)

Degree of Inequality	Number of Countries	Number of Collapses	Incidence of Collapse (%)
High[a]	21	11	52
Moderate[b]	20	11	55
Low[c]	21	0	0
Total	62	22	35

Source: Author's calculations, based on Perala (2002) and Ros (2000).
Note: In the following groups of countries, growth collapses are indicated by*.
  a. Gini higher than 0.45. Includes Brazil, Central African Republic*, Chile, Colombia, Costa Rica, Dominican Republic, Guatemala*, Honduras*, Kenya*, Lesotho, Malawi*, Malaysia, Mexico, Nicaragua*, Panama, the Philippines*, Senegal*, South Africa*, Thailand, República Bolivariana de Venezuela*, and Zimbabwe *.
  b. Gini lower than or equal to 0.45 and higher than or equal to 0.36. Includes Australia, Bolivia*, Côte d'Ivoire*, Ghana*, Guyana*, Hong Kong (China), Jamaica*, Jordan*, Madagascar*, Mauritania*, Mauritius, Morocco, New Zealand, Niger*, Nigeria*, Portugal, Singapore, Tunisia, Turkey, and Zambia*.
  c. Gini lower than 0.36. Includes Bangladesh, Belgium, Canada, Denmark, Arab Republic of Egypt, Finland, Greece, India, Indonesia, Ireland, Italy, Japan, the Netherlands, Norway, Pakistan, Republic of Korea, Spain, Sri Lanka, Sweden, United Kingdom, and United States.

level of inequality, whereas the incidence of collapses is over 50 percent in the groups with moderate and high levels of inequality. Table 8.7 shows the incidence of collapses in different types of economy classified by degree of inequality and abundance and type of natural resources. The evidence presented in the table is consistent with the influence of the pattern of trade specialization on the incidence of collapses: Economies rich in natural resources, especially those that export minerals and oil, are clearly the most prone to growth collapses. The data are also consistent with the influence of inequality: The incidence of collapse is higher in resource-poor economies with a high level of inequality than in resource-poor economies with a low level of inequality, and also higher in economies with abundant agricultural resources and a high level of inequality than in economies of the same type with a low level of inequality. Because economies rich in natural resources have a higher level of inequality than poor economies, the evidence seems to agree with the two main hypotheses in the recent literature: Growth collapses seem to be produced by a combination of highly unequal income distribution and a pattern of trade specialization determined by an abundance of natural resources.

On the other hand, Auty's (2001) conjecture that mineral- and oil-exporting countries have a higher level of inequality than economies with abundant agricultural resources is not supported by our sample of

Table 8.7 Type of Economy, Inequality, and Growth Collapse

(Developing countries)

Type of Economy and Inequality	Number of Countries	Number of Collapses	Incidence of Collapse (%)	Average Gini Coefficient
Resource-poor	13	4	31	0.40
Low inequality[a]	7	0	0	
High inequality[b]	6	4	67	
Economies rich in agricultural resources	23	11	48	0.48
Low inequality[c]	12	4	33	
High inequality[d]	11	7	64	
Economies rich in minerals and oil	9	7	78	0.47
Low inequality[e]	5	5	100	
High inequality[f]	4	2	50	
Total	45	22	49	

Source: Author's calculations, based on Auty (1997), Perala (2002), and Ros (2000).

Note: In the following groups of countries, growth collapses are indicated by*.

a. Bangladesh, Arab Republic of Egypt, Indonesia, Mauritius, Republic of Korea, Singapore, and Sri Lanka.

b. Colombia, Hong Kong (China), Jordan*, Kenya*, Mauritania*, and the Philippines*.

c. Costa Rica, Côte d'Ivoire*, Ghana*, Guyana*, India, Madagascar*, Malaysia, Morocco, Pakistan, Thailand, Tunisia, and Turkey.

d. Brazil, Guatemala*, Honduras*, Lesotho, Malawi*, Mexico, Nicaragua*, Panama, Senegal*, South Africa*, and Zimbabwe*.

e. Bolivia*, Jamaica*, Niger*, Nigeria*, and Zambia*.

f. Central African Republic*, Chile, Dominican Republic, and República Bolivariana de Venezuela*.

countries (the average Gini coefficient for mineral- and oil-exporting countries is indistinguishable from that of economies with abundant agricultural resources). In addition, the interaction between abundance of minerals and oil and a high level of inequality does not increase the number of collapses. Within the group of economies rich in minerals and oil, it is those with a lower level of inequality (although their degree of inequality is high by the standards of poor economies) that have the highest incidence of collapses.[14] These last two observations suggest that although economies rich in mineral resources and oil are more prone to collapses than economies rich in agricultural resources, this is not because they have more unequal income distribution. The higher incidence of collapse must result from factors other than the pattern of income distribution in this type of economy. Mention has already been made of these economies' low level of diversification (associated with a lack of forward and backward links), the high volatility of international mineral prices, and the importance of the fiscal linkage, all of which may accentuate the destabilizing effects of external shocks on the country's macroeconomic performance.

Conclusions

This chapter has discussed the processes of divergence in income levels between rich and poor countries and the ability of growth economics to explain these processes. Behind these processes of divergence we find growth collapses in low- and middle-income countries, especially in Sub-Saharan Africa and Latin America. Neither neoclassical growth models, which predict convergence, nor classical development theory, which predicts an acceleration of growth at middle-income levels, can adequately explain these economic setbacks. The chapter has argued that these processes of growth collapse reflect the combined influence of unequal income distribution and the pattern of specialization, as determined by the abundance of natural resources and the size of the economy.

Endnotes

1. Here I refer to the approach taken by the pioneers of development economics, especially Rosenstein-Rodan, Nurkse, Prebisch, and Hirschman.

2. The information used is presented in detail in Ros (2000). The five income categories were selected in order to minimize the dispersion of income around the mean and to have approximately 15 countries in each group. For example, group 1 comprises 18 high-income countries (most of them OECD members) and group 5 comprises 13 low-income countries, mainly in Sub-Saharan Africa and South Asia.

3. See Abramovitz (1986), Baumol (1986), Baumol and Wolff (1988), Chenery and Syrquin (1975), Kristensen (1974), Lucas (1988), and Syrquin (1986).

4. The exercise consists of estimating the long-run equilibrium level of income of country groups 2 to 5 as percentages of group 1, using the information available for each model's parameters, such as rates of investment and growth of the labor force in the case of the Solow model. The model estimated by Islam (1995), based on panel data and country-specific fixed effects, is used for the variant that adjusts the neoclassical model to allow for technology gaps between countries. Once the long-term steady-state level of income has been estimated, the growth rates predicted by each model can be obtained from the gap between initial income and long-term income. The existence of diminishing returns to capital implies that the growth rate predicted is an increasing function of this gap. See Ros (2000, ch. 2) for a detailed presentation of the methodology used.

5. The differences in rates of growth of the labor force are not large enough to have a qualitative effect on the comparisons in terms of growth of GDP per worker.

6. Other studies accounting for differences among countries in GDP per worker show results similar to those of Islam. Klenow and Rodríguez-Clare (1997b) found that differences in total factor productivity account for more than

half of the differences in GDP per worker for a sample of 98 countries, using 1985 figures. Hall and Jones (1999) estimated that in developing countries, differences in the residual (the contribution of productivity) are the most important factor in explaining the gaps in GDP per worker with respect to developed countries. Easterly and Levine (2001) found that total factor productivity accounts for most of the differences among countries in levels of per capita income. An exception to these findings is Kumar and Russell (2002), which will be discussed later.

7. It may be argued that the growth rates observed in poor countries would be better reproduced by a blend of the models that include human capital and technology gaps (such as the one in Jones 1998). Ros (2000) presented an analysis on the subject. The main difficulty with this "solution" is that once technology gaps are introduced (especially gaps of the size required to bring the model in line with the data), it is impossible to maintain the assumption of uniform technical progress among countries. The natural hypothesis, which goes back to Gerschenkron (1962), is that the bigger the technology gap, the faster the rate of technical progress, because profit opportunities and potential technological leaps are greater. Depending on the function relating the rate of technical progress to the technology gap, the resulting model may agree with the data more or less closely than the traditional neoclassical model. However, to the extent that technology gaps are proportional to income gaps (as they are in the estimates of Islam and others; see note 6), this model, like Solow's model, will show that, for countries with similar characteristics (similar long-term income levels), growth rates should increase as we consider lower income levels.

8. See Klenow and Rodríguez-Clare (1997a) and Ros (2000) for a more extensive analysis. These models are not easy to evaluate. One reason is that most recent empirical research has concentrated on testing the neoclassical growth model and its revisions and extensions rather than on examining the empirical implications of endogenous growth models. Also, as Klenow and Rodríguez-Clare (1997a) observed, the literature has not included methods for distinguishing empirically between different models of endogenous growth, so that the latter have not proved very useful for understanding the differences in growth rates between countries.

9. The evidence for increasing returns and Verdoorn's law, and research on the external effects of capital accumulation, suggest the presence of increasing returns to scale and diminishing returns to capital, especially in the case of the aggregate production function (see Ros 2000).

10. Other studies support this conclusion. Jones (1997) showed that in the period 1960–88, convergence took place in the upper half of the international income distribution and divergence took place in the lower half. The sensitivity analysis of cross-country growth regressions carried out by Levine and Renelt (1992) shows that the finding of conditional convergence (a negative coefficient at the starting level of per capita income) is not robust for the period 1974–89, or when the OECD countries are excluded (see Levine and Renelt 1992, p. 958). The exclusion of the group of OECD countries—which largely coincides with the group of high-income countries—leaves the sample with (for the most part) middle- and low-income countries. The result is thus consistent with classical theory, according to which conditional convergence would not be expected in such a sample.

11. Perala identified an intermediate category of recent collapses, defined as those economies whose per capita income levels were lower in 1999 than in 1990. I include the countries in this category as cases of sustained growth. The incidence of recent collapse is less than 20 percent in all the groups except the low-income group (35.3 percent).

12. It is worth noting that these hypotheses are challenged by the literature on the so-called "staples thesis," which considers the positive effects that an abundance of natural resources may have on growth. (See Ros 2000, for a review of this literature.)

13. Table 8.5 refers to developing countries grouped by type of economy. The sample of countries is the intersection between the samples considered by Auty (1997, 2001) and Perala (2002); that is, it includes, out of the countries considered by Perala in her analysis of growth collapses, those countries for which Auty provided information on the type of economy (size, abundance of natural resources, and type of natural resources). Table 8.6 refers to a sample of developed and developing countries considered by Perala (2002) for which Ros (2000) provided information on income concentration. Table 8.7 refers to a sample of developing countries for which Auty (1997, 2001) provided information on the abundance and type of natural resources and Ros (2000) presented information on income distribution.

14. In apparent contradiction with this finding, Perala (2002) showed that the interaction between abundance of minerals and oil and a lack of social cohesiveness has an adverse effect on growth. Her indicator of the lack of social cohesiveness is not, however, the degree of inequality of income distribution, but an index of ethnolinguistic fragmentation.

Bibliography

Abramovitz, M. 1986. "Catching Up, Forging Ahead, and Falling Behind." *Journal of Economic History* 46 (2): 385–406.

Ades, A., and E. Glaeser. 1999. "Evidence on Growth, Increasing Returns and the Extent of the Market." *Quarterly Journal of Economics* 114 (3): 1025–46.

Alesina, A., and R. Perotti. 1994. "The Political Economy of Growth: A Critical Survey of the Recent Literature." *World Bank Economic Review* 8 (2): 151–69.

Alesina, A., and D. Rodrik. 1994. "Distributive Politics and Economic Growth." *Quarterly Journal of Economics* 109 (2): 465–90.

Auty, R. 2001. *Resource Abundance and Economic Development* Oxford, UK: Oxford University Press.

———. 1997. "Natural Resource Endowment, the State and Development Strategy." *Journal of International Development* 9 (4): 651–53.

Barro, R. J. 1999. "Inequality, Growth and Investment." Working Paper 7038, NBER, Cambridge, MA.

———. 1991. "Economic Growth in a Cross-Section of Countries." *Quarterly Journal of Economics* 106 (2): 407–43.

———. 1990. "Government Spending in a Simple Model of Endogenous Growth." *Journal of Political Economy* 98 (5): S103–S126.

Barro, R. J., and X. Sala-i-Martin. 1997. "Technological Diffusion, Convergence, and Growth." *Journal of Economic Growth* 2 (1): 1–26.

———. 1995. *Economic Growth*. New York: McGraw-Hill.

———. 1992. "Convergence." *Journal of Political Economy* 100 (2): 223–51.

Baumol, W. J. 1986. "Productivity Growth, Convergence and Welfare: What the Long Run Data Show." *American Economic Review* 76 (5): 1072–85.

Baumol, W. J., and E. W. Wolff. 1988. "Productivity, Convergence and Welfare: Reply." *American Economic Review* 78 (5): 1155–59.

Birdsall, N., D. Ross, and R. Sabot. 1995. "Inequality and Growth Reconsidered: Lessons from East Asia." *World Bank Economic Review* 9 (3): 477–508.

Corden, W. M., and J. P. Neary. 1982. "Booming Sector and De-Industrialisation in a Small Open Economy." *Economic Journal* 92 (127): 825–48.

Chari, V., P. Kehoe, and E. McGrattan. 1996. "The Poverty of Nations: A Quantitative Exploration." Working Paper 5414, NBER, Cambridge, MA.

Chenery, H. B., and M. Syrquin. 1975. *Patterns of Development, 1950–1970.* London: Oxford University Press.

DeLong, J. B. 1997. "Cross-Country Variations in National Economic Growth Rates: The Role of Technology." In *Technology and Growth*, eds. J. Fuhrer and J. Sneddon Little, 127–49. Boston: Federal Reserve Bank of Boston.

Dutt, A. K. 1984. "Stagnation, Income Distribution, and Monopoly Power." *Cambridge Journal of Economics* 8 (1): 25–40.

Easterly, W., and R. Levine. 2001. "It's Not Factor Accumulation: Stylized Facts and Growth Models." *World Bank Economic Review* 15 (2): 177–219.

Galor, O., and J. Zeira. 1993. "Income Distribution and Macroeconomics." *Review of Economic Studies* 60 (1): 35–52.

Gelb, A., ed. 1988. *Oil Windfalls. Blessing or Curse?* Oxford, UK: Oxford University Press.

Gerschenkron, A. 1962. *Economic Backwardness in Historical Perspective.* Cambridge, MA: Harvard University Press.

Hall, R., and C. Jones. 1999. "Why Do Some Countries Produce So Much More Output Per Worker Than Others?" *Quarterly Journal of Economics* 114 (1): 83–116.

Hirschman, A. 1981. "A Generalized Linkage Approach to Development, with Special Reference to Staples." *Essays in Trespassing.* Cambridge, UK: Cambridge University Press.

Islam, N. 1995. "Growth Empirics: A Panel Data Approach." *Quarterly Journal of Economics* 110 (4): 1127–70.

Jones, C. 1998. *Introduction to Economic Growth.* New York: W. W. Norton.

———. 1997. "On the Evolution of the World Distribution of Income." *Journal of Economic Perspectives* 11 (3): 19–36.

Keefer, P., and S. Knack. 1999. "Polarization, Politics, and Property Rights: Links Between Inequality and Growth." Policy Research Working Paper 2418, World Bank, Washington, DC.

Klenow, P., and A. Rodríguez-Clare. 1997a. "Economic Growth: A Review Essay." *Journal of Monetary Economics* 40 (2): 597–617.

———. 1997b. "The Neoclassical Revival in Growth Economics: Has It Gone Too Far?" *NBER Macroeconomics Annual 1997.* Cambridge, MA: NBER.

Kristensen, T. 1974. *Development in Rich and Poor Countries.* New York: Praeger.

Kumar, S., and R. Russell. 2002. "Technological Change, Technological Catch-Up, and Capital Deepening: Relative Contributions to Growth and Convergence." *American Economic Review* 92 (3): 527–48.

Levine, R., and D. Renelt. 1992. "A Sensitivity Analysis of Cross-Country Growth Regressions." *American Economic Review* 82 (4): 942–63.

Lucas, R. E., Jr. 2002. *Lectures on Economic Growth.* Cambridge, MA: Harvard University Press.

———. 1988. "On the Mechanics of Economic Development." *Journal of Monetary Economics* 22: 3–42.

Maddison, A. 1995. *Monitoring the World Economy, 1820–1992*. Paris: OECD.

———. 1991. *Dynamic Forces in Capitalist Development*. Oxford, UK: Oxford University Press.

Mankiw, G., D. Romer, and D. Weil. 1992. "A Contribution to the Empirics of Economic Growth." *Quarterly Journal of Economics* 107 (2): 407–37.

Murphy, K., A. Shleifer, and R. Vishny. 1989. "Income Distribution, Market Size and Industrialization." *Quarterly Journal of Economics* 104 (3): 537–64.

Perala, M. 2002. "Essays on Development and Growth." Unpublished paper. Notre Dame, IN: University of Notre Dame.

Perotti, R. 1996. "Growth, Income Distribution, and Democracy: What the Data Say." *Journal of Economic Growth* 1 (2): 149–87.

Pritchett, L. 1997. "Divergence, Big Time." *Journal of Economic Perspectives* 11 (3): 3–17.

Quah, D. T. 1993. "Galton's Fallacy and Tests of the Convergence Hypothesis." *Scandinavian Journal of Economics* 95 (4): 427–43.

Ranis, G. 1991. "Towards a Model of Development." In *Liberalization in the Process of Economic Development*, eds. L. Krause and K. Kim, 59–101. Berkeley: University of California Press.

Rebelo, S. 1991. "Long Run Policy Analysis and Long Run Growth." *Journal of Political Economy* 99 (3): 500–21.

Rodríguez, F., and J. Sachs. 1999) "Why Do Resource Abundant Economies Grow More Slowly? A New Explanation and an Application to Venezuela." *Journal of Economic Growth* 4 (3): 277–303.

Rodrik, D. 1998. "Where Did All the Growth Go? External Shocks, Social Conflict, and Growth Collapses." Working Paper 6350, NBER, Cambridge, MA.

Romer, P. M. 1991. "Increasing Returns and New Developments in the Theory of Growth." In *Equilibrium Theory and Applications: Proceedings of the 6th International Symposium in Economic Theory and Econometrics*, eds. W. Barnett, Bernard Cornet, Claude d'Aspermont, Jean J. Gabszewicz, and Andreu Mas-Colell, 83–110. Cambridge, UK: Cambridge University Press.

———. 1986. "Increasing Returns and Long-Run Growth." *Journal of Political Economy* 94 (5): 1002–37.

Ros, J. 2000. *Development Theory and the Economics of Growth*. Ann Arbor, MI: University of Michigan Press.

Sachs, J., and A. Warner. 2001. "The Curse of Natural Resources." *European Economic Review* 45 (4–6): 827–38.

———. 1997. "Fundamental Sources of Long-Run Growth." *American Economic Review* 87 (2): 184–88.

Solow, R. M. 1956. "A Contribution to the Theory of Economic Growth." *Quarterly Journal of Economics* 70 (1): 65–94.

Syrquin, M. 1986. "Productivity Growth and Factor Reallocation." In *Industrialization and Growth: A Comparative Study*, eds. H. Chenery, S. Robinson, and M. Syrquin, 228–62. New York: Oxford University Press.

Tornell, A., and P. Lane. 1999. "The Voracity Effect." *American Economic Review* 89 (1): 22–46.

UNCTAD (United Nations Conference on Trade and Development). 1997. *Trade and Development Report, 1997*. Geneva: UNCTAD.

Index